KEIR HARDIE

J. KEIR HARDIE *in* 1906.

Keir Hardie

BY

EMRYS HUGHES

GEORGE ALLEN & UNWIN LTD
RUSKIN HOUSE · MUSEUM STREET · LONDON

First published in 1956

Printed in Great Britain in 10 point Times Roman type by The Blackfriars Press Limited Smith-Dorrien Road, Leicester

PREFACE

WHEN Mr. Gaitskell was elected to be the leader of the Labour Party, the *Economist* said in its leading article that the main function that must fall to any Labour leader in the next twenty years is 'to turn his back on the age of Keir Hardie'. It went on to say 'The struggle of the people is now an inspiring struggle for more wealth, better leisure and more equal opportunity; it is no longer a bitter struggle against hard-faced capitalists, grinding poverty and grime.' The concluding part of the sentence is clearly an admission that Keir Hardie, after all, had achieved something. For if we have arrived at a 'mainly middle-class society' from which grinding poverty and grime in Britain have largely disappeared it is due mainly to the influence that the Labour Party, which Hardie fought so doggedly to bring into being, has exerted on British politics.

Even the Conservative Party of to-day accepts ideas which were regarded as dangerously revolutionary when Hardie first fought his way into the House of Commons. To-day the Conservative Head Office issues posters boasting of what a Conservative Government has done for the old age pensioners and the unemployed. They not only accept the principles of work or maintenance which Hardie advocated in his Right to Work bills, they increase the scale of unemployment pay and declare that they have the welfare of the unemployed more at heart than the Socialists. When Keir Hardie first brought the plight of the unemployed to the attention of the House of Commons, Mr. Gladstone thought that this was not a subject with which Parliament should concern itself. Indeed, if Mr. Gladstone could come back to survey the political scene to-day he would have to come to the conclusion that Keir Hardie had been extraordinarily successful. Not only does the House of Commons spend a large proportion of its time discussing matters arising out of the recognition by all parties of the fact that the Welfare State has come to stay but a Conservative Government does not go back on the nationalisation of the mines, railways and other transport, gas, electricity, and proudly boasts of its achievement of

7

building 300,000 houses by Socialist enterprise, declaring jubilantly that it can do these things better than the Labour Party. Indeed, election speeches of Conservative Party leaders extolling action by the State are enough to make the old leaders of the Anti-Socialist Union, who regarded Keir Hardie as the very devil incarnate of politics, turn in their graves. The only way the Conservatives can win an election these days is to prove that in such matters as social welfare and housing they are more Socialist than the Socialists.

Such has been the result of the arrival of the Labour Party in British politics. Nobody regarded Keir Hardie as a successful politician during his lifetime. He roused intense antagonism as the champion of what were regarded as revolutionary and utopian ideas. Now, many of the things he advocated have become accepted parts of our national life. Yet they would not have come without the growth of the Labour Party and the spread of the ideas of Socialism which he pioneered. If to-day the miners have become the middle classes, with television sets and even motor cars bought on the instalment system, living in municipal houses with bathrooms and coming home clean from the pits, it is due to a large extent to the bloodless revolution which has come as the result of the work of a Labour Government.

'The Parliamentary Labour Party,' said the *Manchester Guardian* on the occasion of its fiftieth anniversary, 'has had its times of trial and of disaster, and learned from them, and risen again to put its stamp on the world as no other party of its kind has ever done . . . It has been the major agent, directly or indirectly, of a social revolution that very few in this country would seriously wish to reverse, and has righted wrongs which, unrelieved, might have led to a revolution of a very different kind.'

If in Great Britain to-day no child is cast on the streets to earn his living as an errand boy at the age of eight or is sent down to work long hours in the darkness of the mine at the age of twelve, if the lives of the working people, especially those living in the mining areas, are infinitely brighter than they were a hundred years ago, it is largely due to the advent of the Labour Party which Keir Hardie did so much to bring into being.

But if better social conditions have come in Britain as a result of a bloodless revolution that does not mean that the change has come without struggle and self-sacrifice. The road of the pioneers of the Labour Party was a hard one, and on the way there were many temptations. To stand alone as Keir Hardie did in the House of Commons, scoffed at, sneered at, shouted down, and to continue on undaunted and uncorrupted, demanded great strength of character and supreme courage. These were the qualities that marked Keir Hardie out from the other politicians of his day. Indeed, Hardie could hardly be described as a politician at all. He was a mixture of working-class leader, idealist and visionary, fifty if not a hundred years in front of his time.

Although so many of the reforms advocated in his early election addresses and speeches have been achieved, yet when one reads them one wonders sometimes whether the Labour Party to-day has caught up with Keir Hardie.

The Liberal Party has practically disappeared from Parliament. Less than a decade after Hardie had died the Labour Party had taken its place and Britain had its first short-lived Labour Government. The fortunes of Labour ebbed and flowed, there was another Labour Government five years later and in the aftermath of the Second World War, Labour was swept into power for the first time with a big majority which enabled it to put on the statute book many of the things that Hardie had advocated. Undoubtedly we will have a Labour Government again and, if we are not destroyed in a Third World War, a Socialist Britain of which Keir Hardie dreamed.

To-day the Labour Party has become a powerful political machine, with a huge membership. It has made many mistakes but it is the only party that can capture political power and advance on the Socialist road to which Hardie pointed.

But although the Labour Party has grown so much since the pioneering days of Keir Hardie, it lost something when the I.L.P. (contrary to Hardie's teaching) left it and went out into the political wilderness.

True there remains among the rank and file of many of the local parties in the country the same spirit of service and self-sacrifice which prevailed in the early days. But in the very process of becoming a big political machine, the Labour Party has shed much of its youthful enthusiasm and idealism.

There is the danger that a rank and file, seeing how the block vote of the big unions is used to influence decisions and determine party policy, may become cynical, frustrated and indifferent, leading to the Labour Party failing to inspire the masses. Indeed, the defeat of the Labour Party at the General Election of 1955 has been attributed to the fact that so many people stayed away from the poll because they saw so little difference between the parties. A party, like an individual, may gain the whole world and lose its own soul.

It was not because of its Socialism that the Labour Government was defeated after it had been swept into power at the end of the Second World War. The Conservatives were returned because of the rise in the cost of living that followed the Korean War and the big rearmament programme. In its foreign policy it had acted very much as the Liberal Government had done between 1906 and 1914.

By 1951 the Labour Party had travelled a long way from the ideas of the man who had urged a General Strike to stop war, who had declared that conscription was 'the badge of the slave', and had been the uncompromising critic of the theory that if you want peace you must prepare for war.

Asked in 1900 what was the greatest danger that threatened the world in the twentieth century, Hardie answered 'Militarism'. Two world wars have come to prove that Hardie was right. Hardie was an internationalist as well as a Socialist. One wonders, sometimes, what he would have thought of a Labour Party that approved of conscription and the Hydrogen Bomb!

Religious organisations have had a habit of making the prophets who had been stoned in their lifetime into saints. Then they put them into stained glass windows and forgot their message and lost their inspiration. Let us hope the Labour Party of to-day will not do that with Keir Hardie.

EMRYS HUGHES — *Cumnock*, 30/8/56.

I wish to express my thanks to Francis Johnson and E. G. Willis for their suggestions and help in reading the proofs.

E.H.

CONTENTS

CONTENTS

ILLUSTRATIONS

CHAPTER 1

THE UNWANTED CHILD

IN THE one room of the tumbledown thatched cottage with the mud floor, which was little more than a shelter from the cold and the rain, the widow's daughter gave birth to her unwanted child. The widow had lived a hard life and had seen much poverty and sorrow. She had come to live in the little village of Legbrannock in Lanarkshire, about twelve miles from Glasgow on the Edinburgh road when her husband died from fever, bringing with her, three children. She went out to work on the farms as a domestic servant and so did her eldest daughter Mary.

To the widow, the arrival of Mary's child was yet another calamity, another mouth to feed, a baby added to the overcrowded room. And she knew how hard and cruel the world could be to the young woman with the illegitimate child.

Mary Keir's boy was born on August 15th, 1856. She called him James, after her own father and registered the birth at Holytown, giving the father's name as William Aitken, miner.

Nothing more is known about the father except that he refused to acknowledge the child.

The mother returned to her work in the fields, for the widow and her family depended upon her wage and the boy was looked after by the grandmother. She remained in the little village regarded as a sinner and an outcast until the boy was three. Then another lover came and she married David Hardie, a ship's carpenter from Glasgow, and was glad to go away with him to the city where nobody knew her story and where it would be thought that her child was David Hardie's own. They went to live in one room at Govan near the shipyards.

There was no compulsory education and the boy did not go to school. The mother had two more children. Wages were low, and the family lived in poverty and near starvation.

David Hardie was, normally, a quiet, kindly man but when he took drink he became quarrelsome, reproached his wife about 'the bastard' and there were angry recriminations and bitter scenes which the sensitive young boy remembered. His aversion to drink in later life had its origins in these early memories.

At the age of eight, young James was sent out to work as a message boy with the Anchor Line company and stayed there for eighteen months. He was bright and observant and learned much from the shop windows and the Glasgow streets. From the Anchor Line office he went to work as message boy in a printer's shop in the Trongate but his parents could not afford to apprentice him to learn his trade. His next job was in a brass foundry and then he worked as errand boy in a baker's shop. At the age of ten he had his first experience of 'the sack'. It was one of the incidents of his boyhood life that he remembered vividly in later years. Fifty years after he remembered every detail of his humiliation:

'The year 1866 was nearing its close. Owing to a lock-out in the ship-building yards on the Clyde, my father had been out of employment for nearly six months. The funds of the Union were so exhausted that the benefits were reduced to 1s. 6d. and 2s. a week. I was the only breadwinner, being employed by a high-class baker in Lancefield Street, Glasgow, for 3s. 6d. a week. My hours were from 7 a.m. to 7.30 p.m., 12½ hours each day. I was the eldest of a family of three, and the brother next to me was down with fever, from which he never recovered, though his life dragged on for two years thereafter. As most of the neighbourhood had children, they feared coming into the house because of the danger of contagion, and my mother, who was very near her confinement, was in delicate health.

'It was the last week in the year. Father had been away for two or three days in search of work. Towards the end of the week, having been up most of the night, I got to the shop fifteen minutes late, and was told by the young lady in charge that if that occurred again I would be punished. I made no reply. I couldn't. I felt like crying. Next morning the same thing happened. I could tell why, but that was neither here nor there. It was a very wet morning, and when I reached the shop I was drenched to the skin, barefooted and hungry. There had not been a crust of bread in the house that morning.

'But that was pay-day, and I was filled with hope. "You are wanted upstairs by the master," said the girl behind the counter, and my heart almost stopped beating. Outside the dining-room door a servant bade me wait till "master had finished prayers". (He was noted for his piety.) At length the girl opened the door, and the sight of that room is fresh in my memory even as I write, nearly fifty years after. Round the great mahogany table sat the members of the family, with the father at the top. In front of

16

him was a very wonderful-looking coffee boiler, in the great glass bowl of which the coffee was bubbling. The table was loaded with dainties. My master looked at me over his glasses and said in quite a pleasant tone of voice : "Boy, this is the second morning you have been late, and my customers leave me if they are kept waiting for their hot breakfast rolls. I therefore dismiss you, and, to make you more careful in the future, I have decided to fine you a week's wages. And now you may go !"

'I wanted to speak and explain about my home, and muttered out something to explain why I was late, but the servant took me by the arm and led me downstairs. As I passed through the shop the girl in charge gave me a roll and said a kind word. I knew my mother was waiting for my wages. As the afternoon was drawing to a close I ventured home and told her what had happened. It seemed to be the last blow. The roll was still under my vest, but soaked with rain. That night the baby was born, and the sun rose on the first of January, 1867, over a home in which there was neither fire nor food, though, fortunately, relief came before the day had reached its noon. But the memory of these early days abides with me, and makes me doubt the sincerity of those who make pretence in their prayers.'

His next job was heating rivets in Thompson's Shipyard at a wage of half a crown a week. He worked on a scaffold with another boy who fell off and was killed, and James's frightened mother refused to let him return.

Life in Glasgow had become dreary and miserable and they decided to return to Lanarkshire and settled down in the mining village of Newarthill.

The boy was now ten and it was decided to send him to work in the pit. His father went back to sea, consoling his wife with the parting remark, 'You hae this consolation at least—sailors and colliers are the two classes that ministers pray maist for—if that does ony guid.'

Young Hardie's job in the coal pit was that of a trapper, to open and shut the doors which regulated the supply of air to the men working at the coal face.

He had to be down the pit by six o'clock in the morning and did not leave until half-past five in the evening. In the winter months he rarely saw sunshine. Even on Sunday he had to work four hours in the pit.

At twelve he was in charge of a pit pony that drew the wagons from the coal face to the bottom of the pit and working nights. It was dreary work; the pit was very old and very wet and there was a bond of sympathy between the young lad and the shaggy little Highland pony. They were brothers in misfortune and great friends and they drank

17

cold tea from the same tin flask, sip about while they listened to the monotonous drip, drip of the water from the roof.

He had his first experience of the dangers of the mine:

'One night, just after midnight hour, when the weird noises of the pit are always at their height, Donald and I were jogging along, when the voice of Rab Mair, the big, genial fireman, came reverberating out of the gloom, his little lamp shining like a star in the blackness. "Run into the dock and warn the men to come at once; the shank's closin". I did not stay on the order of my going. The shank was closing—it was our only outlet. Should it close in, we were entombed, and what that might mean I did not care to think. In a very short time all the men were at the pit bottom, only to find that already they were too late. We were seventy fathoms from the daisies, and the weary rocks, tired of hanging in mid air, seemed bent on settling down into some semblance of solidarity. For once in a way the drip of water could not be heard. The timber props were creaking and bursting all around us; whilst the strong rocks were groaning and cracking and roaring as they were settling down. As man after man rushed to the bottom, breathless and alarmed, they were met with the news that already the cage by which men and material are taken to the surface, was "stuck in the shank". The sides of the shaft had come together so far that the cage had no longer a free passage and was held fast some fathoms above us. We were prisoners.

'I can recall every detail of the scene. The men gathered in groups, each with his little lamp on his bonnet, their blackened faces serious, discussing what should be done. The roaring and crackling, as if of artillery, went on overhead, and gloom began to settle on every countenance. Some of the most susceptible were crying, and I remember two by themselves who were praying and crossing themselves. Rab Mair remained cool and strong, and did his best to keep up the spirits of his fellow prisoners. By and by I began to feel sleepy, and made my way to the stables whither Donald, my pony, had already gone. By this time it was evident the worst of the crises was over; the noise overhead was subsiding and the drip of water was again to be heard. But the shaft was closed. We were prisoners indeed. After cleaning Donald down I gave him a feed of corn, put some hay in his manger and, rolling myself in this, kissed him, as was our wont, and then went off to sleep. A boy of twelve will sleep when there is nothing to do, even cooped in a trap. How long I slept I have no means now of knowing. It was Rab Mair's voice—swearing, if the truth must be told—and some vigorous punches from his fist which brought me back to consciousness.

'The engineman, on finding the cages stuck fast in the shaft, and hearing the signals below, knew there was something wrong, and raised the alarm. In a short time the news spread, and soon the bulk of the people were at the pit, my mother among the rest. Volunteers were plentiful, and soon some fellows had been lowered by an improvised kettle into the shaft, where they soon discovered what was amiss. Coal chisels, picks and saws were requisitioned and the imprisoned cage cut free, allowed to drop in pieces to the bottom, after which the kettle—a bucket used by pit sinkers, and narrower than the cage—was used to bring the imprisoned men to the surface. But where was the trapper? Everyone had seen him in the bottom, and perhaps in the excitement of the moment no one would have missed him had there not been a mother there waiting for him. And so Rab Mair and two companions had to descend into the depths again and search. For a time their searching was in vain until Rab had bethought him of Donald's crib, and there, sure enough, I was, sound asleep. Rab pretended to be angry—but he wasn't. I think the reception on the top was the most trying part of the affair. At least it was the only part where I cried.'

Hardie worked in the pits of Lanarkshire until he was twenty-three. From pony driving he went to the coal face, working hard with pick and shovel. The toil made him strong and tough and his chest became broader. At twenty he had the stocky, sturdy build of the typical collier. He was lucky to escape serious accident. His mother now had six children, four boys and two girls. The boys too went into the pit. The family finally settled down in the miners' row known as 'The Quarter', near Hamilton. It was a typical miners' row of the time, a bleak, grim street of brick houses that the colliery company had built near the pit, no water, no sanitation, a pump in the street. Nearly every house was grossly overcrowded, all ages and sexes crammed together with little chance of comfort or decency. Here they were born—here they died. The men came home grimy with coal dust and washed in tubs in front of the fire. When death came the corpse was put in the coffin on the built-in bed. The miner became prematurely old with ceaseless toil. They had large families. They lived in constant dread of accident in the mine. Life was hard, primitive, brutish. Few of them could read or write. There were no cinemas, only here and there a library or a mission hall. Drunkenness, when there was money to spend, was common. For the men who worked in the darkness most of the week, it was one way they could escape from the sordidness and squalor of their lives.

CHAPTER 2

THE READER IN THE ATTIC

SLOWLY, laboriously, patiently, the young miner had learned to read and to write. He had first learned to spell by looking at the opened-out picture books in the stationers' shops in Glasgow. His mother had taught him how to read but he was fifteen before he could write.

He went to Fraser's night school in Holytown and shortly afterwards began to learn shorthand, practising writing the characters at spare moments in the pit on a slate smoked from his miner's lamp. He spent his spare money on books and was desperately anxious to learn. He had picked up a lot of fairy stories and folklore from his grandmother who believed in ghosts and witches. The first book he remembered reading was Wilson's *Tales of the Borders*, and a *Life of William Wallace* which made him a staunch Scots patriot.

There was a very ancient library connected with the village church and from this he borrowed *The Voyages of Captain Cook* and books on the trials and persecution of the Scots Covenanters. They were not exactly boys' books but he was seriously-minded and they suited his temperament. As soon as he could read he turned to the poems of Robert Burns. There was a melancholy strain in young Hardie and he had a lot in common with the inspired ploughman who had written bitterly that his early life had combined 'the loneliness of the hermit with the toil of the galley slave'.

Burns had known the drudgery of the peasant on the land, Hardie knew the slavery of the miner in the darkness of the pit. There was a melancholy strain in the young miner too, as there was in Burns.

He could understand to the full the theme of 'Man Was Made to Mourn':

> *See yonder poor o'erlaboured wight*
> *So abject mean and vile*
> *Who begs a brother of the earth*
> *To give him leave to toil,*

And see his lordly fellow-worm
The poor petition spurn
Unmindful tho' a weeping wife
And helpless offspring mourn.

*   *   *

If I'm designed yon lordling's slave—
By nature's law designed,
Why was an independent wish
E'er planted in my mind?
If not, why am I subject to,
His cruelty, or scorn
Or why has man the will and power
To make his fellow mourn?

Nearly a century later the young Scots miner in the pit was asking these questions too. He did not just read Burns's poetry, he absorbed it; it entered into his very being.

'I owe more to Burns,' he wrote in later life, 'than to any man living or dead. Long ere Carlyle, or Emerson, or Whitman, or Morris had come into my ken, and ere their message would have any meaning to me even had I access to their writings, I had imbibed the liberty loving spirit and humanitarianism of Burns.

'He expressed for me as a boy my better self and gave form and substance to my half-formed thoughts and vague feelings.'

He read Burns over and over again until he knew many of the poems by heart.

When he was a little over sixteen a friend sent him a copy of *Sartor Resartus,* by Thomas Carlyle. He read it by the light of his pit lamp in the attic. It was stiff reading and he found difficulty in understanding what it was all about. Why had his friend sent it to him?

He turned the pages over and over and then came to a passage which gripped him:

'Two men I honour, and no third. First the toilworn Craftsman that with earth made implement laboriously conquers the Earth and makes her man's Venerable to me is the hard Hand: crooked, coarse: wherein notwithstanding lies a cunning virtue, indefeasibly royal as of the sceptre of this Planet. Venerable too is the rugged face all weather tanned, besoiled with its rude intelligence for it is the face of a Man living manlike. O, but the more venerable for thy rudeness, and even because we must pity as well as love thee! Hardly entreated Brother! For us thy back so bent, for us were thy straight limbs and fingers so deformed; thou wert our conscript on whom the lot fell and fighting our battles wert so marred. For in thee too lay a god created form, but it was not to be unfolded, encrusted must it stand with the thick adhesions and defacements of Labour; and thy body, like thy soul, was not to know freedom. Yet toil on toil on: thou art in thy duty, be out of it who may; thou toilest for the altogether, indispensable for daily bread.'

Why, this was all about him! He read on:

'A second man I honour, and still more highly. Him who is seen toiling for the spiritually indispensable; not daily bread but the bread of Life. Is not he too in his duty; endeavouring towards inward Harmony, revealing this by act or by word, through all his outward endeavours, be they high or low. Highest of all when his outward and his inward endeavour are one when we can name him Artist; not earthly craftsman only, but inspired Thinker, who with heaven-made implement conquers Heaven for us! If the poor and humble toil that we have Food, must not the high and glorious toil for him in return, that he have Light, have Guidance, Freedom, Immortality?

'These two in all their degrees I honour; all else is chaff and dust which let the wind blow whither it listeth.'

He marked the passages in pencil, as was his wont, and re-read the book three times.

There was the story of the men from the little village of Dumdrudge:

'Dumdrudge at her own expense has suckled them and nursed them, she has not without difficulty and sorrow fed them up to manhood, and even trained them to crafts, so that one can weave, another build, another hammer. Nevertheless, amid much weeping and swearing, they are selected; all dressed in red; and shipped away, at the public charges, some two thousand miles, or say only to the South of Spain; and fed till wanted: And now to that same spot in the South of Spain, are thirty similar French artisans, from a French Dumdrudge, in like manner unending, until at length after infinite effort, the two parties come into actual juxtaposition: and thirty stands fronting thirty each with a gun in his hand. Straightway the word, "FIRE" is given and they blow the souls out of one another; and in place of sixty brisk useful craftsmen, the world has sixty dead carcases, which it must bury and anew shed tears for. Had these men any quarrel? Busy as the devil is, not the smallest! they lived far enough apart; were the entirest strangers; nay in so wide a Universe, there was, even by Commerce, some mutual helpfulness between them. How then? Simpleton! Their Governors had fallen out and instead of shooting one another, had the cunning to make these poor blockheads shoot.'

Dumdrudge could be Holytown or Blantyre or Larkhall or any of the scores of such villages in Lanarkshire. It could all have been written about the young recruits who joined up at Hamilton and donned the red coats because they did not want to go down the pits or be out of work. He became a worshipper of Carlyle.

'I mark the reading of *Sartor*,' he wrote in later life, 'as a real turning point and read through the book three times in succession until the spirit of it somewhat entered into me.

'He was indeed to me in those days a hero more particularly when *Past and Present* and *The French Revolution* followed in the wake of *Sartor*. About this period also I read Boswell's *Johnson* and made the acquaintance through its pages with the literary and social life of his times. Some years later Henry George came to Scotland and I read *Progress and Poverty*, which unlocked many of the industrial and economic difficulties which beset the mind of the worker trying to take an intelligent interest in his own affairs, and led me much to George's horror in later life when we met personally into Communism.'

He did not read Marx, who was still living and writing in London, but his works were known at that time to only a comparatively few people in Scotland. Marx died when Hardie was twenty-five. He was to meet Engels later and to read Marx much later in life. But it was Burns and Carlyle and Henry George who started Hardie thinking about Socialism.

The Hardie family did not go to church. Indeed they were not only indifferent to organised religion, they were actively hostile, called themselves atheists and no clergyman or minister entered their door. There was no Bible in the house and the young Hardies were not sent to the Sunday School. He had, however, when he started working at the pit, started attending the Band of Hope which was run for the young people by the Temperance enthusiasts of the local Church. He probably started going there because he had nowhere else to go and there was warmth and light and company in the little hall. He had his own reasons for disliking drunken men and the drunkenness of the miners now revolted him too. He became one of the regular attenders at the Band of Hope and then graduated into the Good Templars Lodge, another form of the temperance organisation which had just been introduced into Scotland. There he met some of the local ministers. One of them was the Reverend Dan Craig, a Hamilton minister. He took a great interest in young Hardie and persuaded him to go to his Church.

'He studied the New Testament from the human much more than from the doctrinal standpoint,' Hardie wrote of him in later years. 'I am certain now that he must have been a Socialist although I cannot recall that he ever mentioned the word. He took a great interest in me, and completely changed the current of my religious thought which

23

up till then, about my nineteenth year, had been of a very negative character.'

To the surprise of the Hardie household Jamie began to go to the kirk and regularly listened to the exposition of the New Testament by the Rev. Dan Craig. He had become a Socialist when he was twenty-one. It was not until 1879, when he was twenty-three, that he wrote in a diary that he had become converted to Christianity. He had read Renan's *Life of Jesus* and there was something in the New Testament (it was always the New Testament, not the Bible, which he mentioned) that appealed to him. He did not join the Established Church of Scotland but the Evangelical Church, which was at that time very similar to the Congregational or one of the other Nonconformist Churches in England. It was not the theology or the doctrine of the Church that had attracted him but the compassion of the Sermon on the Mount.

The parents remained sceptical and unconverted. They could not understand what had happened to Jamie. He had always been a little strange. He would get over it. Neither the New Testament nor the Old made any appeal to them. They remained atheists until the end of their days.

CHAPTER 3

THE MINER IN REVOLT

YOUNG Hardie was a regular attender at the miners' trade union meetings. He could express himself better than most of them and there was something about his earnestness and sincerity which won him the confidence and respect of the older men. And he could read and write. So they put him in the chair. Normally there were not many attending these meetings, for the organisation of the union was weak and it was difficult to get the men to take an interest in their own affairs except during a strike. Hardie had ideas about the union and how to improve its organisation. First of all they should get all the groups centred round the different pits into the County Union and then strive to build up a union which would unite all the miners in Scotland. Then they could all come out together and the coalowners would be forced to yield to their demands.

The best-known personality in the miners' movement in Lanarkshire at the time was the elderly Alexander Macdonald, who had entered the mines at the age of eight, had studied and become a schoolteacher and then had become Liberal M.P. for Staffordshire. After one of his meetings at Hamilton, Hardie was called upon to move a vote of thanks. His head was full of Carlyle's *Heroes and Hero Worship,* and one of the heroes was Martin Luther. Hardie, referring to Macdonald, declared that he 'was an unparalleled benefactor of the mining community', and compared his work for the miners to that of Luther at the rise of Protestarianism.

It was exactly the wrong thing to say to an audience where there were a large number of Irish Roman Catholics and there was a rumble of dissent and then a row. It was the first lesson he was to receive on the danger of mixing up religion with trade union and political questions, especially in Lanarkshire, where sectarian feeling ran high.

The danger of a reduction in wages grew and the miners' meetings grew bigger. They held them at the Old Quarry at Hamilton. This was Hardie's first attempt to address a big crowd. He spoke from a large boulder and looked down on the sea of faces. It was difficult at first. Many of them were his comrades with whom he had worked at the coalface. There were old miners smoking their clay pipes, with the blue marks of old scars on their faces where the coal dust had got under the skin; tough, hard old veterans of the mine, the fittest who had survived. They all looked pale after their long days of toil in the darkness. They were all badly dressed and shabby, some of them wore their heavy pit boots because they had nothing else, some of them limped along on sticks, for they had been crushed under falls of the roof and had lain for months with broken limbs and backs, others were coughing their lungs out with miner's chest, not yet known as pneumoconiosis. All had come to hear what could be done to stop their miserable wages becoming lower still.

Hardie spoke hesitatingly, quietly and earnestly, with few gestures. The theme of his speech was that they must stand together and become organised. There were a series of meetings and at one of them they decided by an overwhelming majority to make young Hardie their secretary. He was then twenty-three.

The next day the blow fell. The news had reached the colliery manager. Half-way down the pit the cage was stopped and brought to the surface again. Curtly the manager told him to clear out. 'We'll hae nae damned Hardies in this pit,' he said, and his two young brothers were sent home too. Hardie's name went on the 'black list'. There was no more work for him at any of the Lanarkshire pits..

Luckily he was not quite down-and-out at the time. They had to leave the Company's house at the Quarter and move a few miles away to Low Waters. He had saved enough money to start a small shop in the front room and the miners rallied round him. He remained their secretary. Almost immediately the trouble in the mines came to a head. In August 1879 the coalowners announced another reduction in wages. Many men were still outside the union and Hardie doubted whether a strike could be successful. Another big meeting at the Quarry decided on a strike.

Once the decision was taken Hardie did everything he could to help the men, picketing day after day at the pits, addressing and encouraging the men, going into Ayrshire to raise funds and urging the Ayrshire men to keep away. There were practically no funds in the union and the officials pledged themselves to the shopkeepers to buy potatoes for the soup kitchens. The strike became known as the 'Tattie Strike', because the potatoes helped the men to hold out for twelve weeks. Then the employers withdrew their attempt to reduce wages by 1s. 6d. a day and the men returned to the pits. But it ended Hardie's career as a miners' leader in Lanarkshire. The union funds had gone in paying the shopkeepers for the potatoes and the ageing Alexander Macdonald, who had been against the strike, blamed Hardie and the other younger spirits. There were angry letters in which the younger man defended himself vigorously. Hardie prided himself as having had the better of the argument. But Macdonald had influence and could raise money to pay the debts to the shopkeepers if Hardie ceased to be secretary. Hardie felt a deep sense of injustice. He had, however, received an invitation from the Ayrshire miners to be their secretary and he accepted it.

He was now a married man.

His young wife was eighteen, tall, dark and handsome, and still wearing her hair hanging down her back. She was Lily Wilson, and her father owned a small public house, but she attended the temperance meetings. There was no honeymoon. Immediately after the marriage ceremony he went away to address a miners' meeting. She could read and write and had a little education. They went to live in one room in Hamilton and shortly afterwards, Hardie, leaving his young wife behind him, went on ahead to take up his new work at Cumnock, the little Ayrshire town about twenty miles away across the moors.

The Ayrshire miners lived in isolated little villages many miles apart. They were not well organised and the union membership was confined to a few rebellious spirits in every pit. It was Hardie's job to build up the union until it was in a position to present a demand for higher wages.

He was only twenty-four but his experience in Lanarkshire had given him confidence and he had all the energy and enthusiasm of youth. He needed it all. His reputation as a rebel had come before him. The men gathered to hear him speak at the pithead and the owners sent their hirelings to break up the meetings. He became accustomed to the shout of 'Throw him into the burn' and threats of physical violence, but he did not lack coolness and courage and he soon won the confidence and respect of the men. It took quite a lot of courage on their part, too, to stand by him and join the union committee because they risked being victimised and this meant not only losing their jobs at the pit but their houses as well, for the masters owned the colliers' rows.

It was dangerous in some places even to risk asking Hardie in to have a meal. One evening he had been addressing a meeting and one of the miners had arranged that he should sleep in his house in the row. Just before they were going to bed a gaffer came round to say that if Keir Hardie stayed there the night there would be no job for the man of the house in the morning. Hardie understood. He would not stay; and he tramped the twelve miles across the moors home.

It was a year of hard, ceaseless, persistent effort before the Ayrshire men were anything like organised.

They put in their claim for a ten per cent increase at the beginning of August 1881 and when the masters turned it down called a strike. This was the first time the Ayrshire men had come out together. The masters thought it would collapse after the first week when there were no wages; they thought that some of the pits at least could ke kept going. But Hardie's organisation worked better than they had thought. Many of the little villages had their bands. They paraded through the miners' rows. They brought out some bedraggled pipers with their kilts and their bagpipes and picketed the pits. There were a few clashes with the police but at last all the men were out.

Hardie again organised the soup kitchens as he had done in Lanarkshire, and tramped the countryside raising money. The weather favoured the strikers. Old miners saw more of the sun than they had done for many years. The pale faces grew tanned. They were having their first long holiday. Even if the food was scarce it was worth while. It lasted ten weeks. Cold and hunger drove them back to the pits at the end of October. A month after, the owners decided that after all they could afford to give them a rise.

The union's meagre funds were exhausted, and after the excitement of the strike, apathy set in.

They could no longer pay Hardie. He had broken his links with Lanarkshire and had brought his young wife and her child to live in a room and kitchen in Cumnock. Another child was expected and he had no hope of getting work in the pits. They were right up against it. Lily Hardie did not grumble or complain. They had decided to face life together and she would stand by and give encouragement to her man. She did not grumble or reproach him. The bonds of sympathy and understanding between them grew. Day by day they saw their little stock of savings dwindle. They dare not ask each other what was to happen next.

Then came a stroke of luck.

Hardie had joined the local Evangelical Church and had become friendly with the minister, who acted as correspondent for the local paper, *The Cumnock News,* the district edition of one of the country papers, *The Ardrossan and Saltcoats Herald.* The minister sent for Hardie and told him that his doctor had advised him to go away for a long holiday.

The minister knew that Hardie could write shorthand and invited him to take over the job in his absence at the sum of £1 a week. It solved the problem for the Hardies; he took on the job as the local reporter.

The minister did not return. The proprietor of the paper found Hardie capable and diligent; he knew the kind of news to send in.

Every week he sent in his news of the little town and the surrounding countryside and collected advertisements. The miners read the paper and its circulation went up. Hardie wrote a column on mining matters called 'Black Diamonds' and signed it 'The Trapper'. It was good experience for him and he became accustomed to writing simple, short, clear paragraphs that the miners and their families understood. It was invaluable to him in later years. He kept in touch with the miners, writing their letters for them and acting as their unpaid lawyer. He founded a Good Templar's Lodge and was an active member of the Evangelical Church. There were a few kindred spirits in the little town who wrote poems and letters to the local papers. Alexander Barrowman and James Neil were rebels like himself. They read the papers carefully and discussed books together. They still called themselves Liberals and spoke at Liberal meetings. But they were following closely what was happening in London. They read William Morris and pamphlets published by the S.D.F. (the Social Democratic Federation), for they were Socialists, impatient with the Liberal party; the time had come for more radical politics; they were more and more critical of the attitude of the miners' M.P.s in Parliament, who had entered as Liberals and then had become respectable and had forgotten what they had been sent to Parliament for.

29

For four years Hardie continued to be the reporter of the local paper. But he kept his membership of the miners' union and went to the meetings. Early in 1886 the miners sent a deputation to ask him to become their secretary again. He resigned from his reporter's job to give all his time once more to building up the Ayrshire Miners' Union. Later in the year there was a meeting of representatives of the miners from the different Scottish coalfields in Edinburgh. They decided to form the Scottish Miners' Federation and Hardie became its secretary also. His salary from the Ayrshire miners was £75 a year and from the Scottish Miners' Federation he was paid £5.

The miners were lucky in having Hardie as their secretary. He was conscientious and reliable, and his whole heart was in the miners' cause. To work for the men with whom he had toiled in the pit was something more than a mere job. He knew them, felt with them, understood them, these rough, tough, kindly, primitive men whose lives were one long, grim struggle. He felt a deep, fierce pride in having their confidence and being their spokesman and their leader.

CHAPTER 4

STRUGGLE WITH THE OLD SCHOOL

HARDIE thought that a monthly miners' journal would serve a useful purpose. It would deal with union topics, state the case for the miners and deal with topical industrial questions from the miners' point of view. With his experience as a reporter and journalist he would produce it himself.

The first issue of *The Miner*, 'A Journal for Underground Workers', appeared in January 1887 and was printed by the Ayrshire paper for which he had worked. It was a modest little magazine of sixteen pages with an introductory column by Hardie explaining its purpose.

While dealing primarily with mining affairs, the magazine would 'advocate reform in every direction which promises to bring relief to the toiling millions'. He added, 'The agitations for the suppression of the liquor traffic and the nationalisation of the land will have our utmost support. Free education, the abolition of the House of Lords as an irresponsible and hereditary body, the payment of Members of Parliament; these and kindred reforms may always reckon on our support.'

He had asked Thomas Burt, the veteran miners' leader and M.P. from Northumberland, to write the first article. Burt wished the venture every success, expressed satisfaction that a Scottish Miners' Federation had been formed, and referred to the fact that in 1887 the Government had promised to introduce a Mines Regulation Bill and Employers' Liability Bill, and that they would be fought every inch of the way by the mine-owners and other capitalists.

But he declared himself against Parliamentary legislation in favour of an Eight Hours Day, which the newly-formed Scottish Miners' Federation was advocating. He thought that hours should be fixed by union negotiation and not by Parliament. One of his arguments was that Parliament had limited the hours of labour both below ground and above for women and children; it had never done so 'for adult

31

males'. 'To do so now,' he added, 'would be a new departure, and there are no signs that Parliament is likely to depart soon from the lines on which its past legislation has been based.'

He appealed for caution. 'Newly-formed unions everywhere have shown a tendency to travel at too quick a pace and to expect impossibilities.' His advice was 'Learn to labour and to wait.'

This was hardly an inspiring clarion call for a new paper that in the same issue published a copy of an Eight-Hour Mines (Scotland) Bill— 'which will be introduced to the House of Commons during the coming session' (they were relying upon one of the Scots Liberal M.P.s to move it)—and a leading article in which Hardie outlined the case for it in flat contradiction to what Burt had said.

If Parliament had interfered to save the Irish and Highland tenant farmers from landlord oppression, why should it not interfere on behalf of the miner who worked in the darkness of the mine ten or eleven hours a day 'shut up in a dark, foul cave amidst surroundings of the most depressing kind? What wonder that they became stunted and dwarfed in mind and body . . . we have every claim to the support of our Members of Parliament on purely humanitarian grounds.'

In the very first number of *The Miner*, Hardie's struggle with the old school of leaders had begun.

The next month he started a series of character studies of well-known miners' leaders and M.P.s who he regarded as the miners' friends.

He began with Burt, described his career (Burt had begun in the mine at the age of ten), and how he had entered Parliament as Radical Member for Morpeth. Then he added, 'Had Mr. Burt been born into a middle-class family, the chances are that he would have been an honest, conscientious Conservative, such as all admit, the late Sir Stafford Northcote to have been. As it is, circumstances have made him an extreme Radical in all matters of Reform but more than half a Conservative on all matters affecting the interest of Capitalists.'

'It is just possible,' he went on, 'that Mr. Burt has a little too much of the philosopher about him.'

On the whole it was not too unkindly an article about Burt, for whom Hardie had a good deal of respect, but it indicated the difference in outlook and temperament between the old generation and the new.

Burt and Hardie had entirely different ideas as to what Parliament was for.

Written by Jas K Hardie, Born Augt 15th 1856. Married, Augt 3rd 1879. Began work as a message boy in Glasgow when 8 years and 9 months old; wrought for some time also in a printing office in Trongate, in 1 Brassfinishing shop of 1 Anchor Line Shipping Co.; also as a rivet heater in Thompsons boatyard. Left Glasgow in 1 year 186_ and went into No 18 pit of 1 Moss at Newarthill, from thence to Quarter Iron works & again one or two other Collieries in neighbourhood of Hamilton. Was elected Sec to miners assn in 1878, and for 1 same position in Ayrshire in 1879. Resigned April 1882 when got appointment, unsolicited y Correspondent & C news. Brought up an Atheist. Converted to Christianity in 1878.

Entry in Keir Hardie's diary.

I detest funerals. Besides, I have no black clothes & never intend to have any more, & to go without them might offend the proprieties. I will be in some time to morrow, most likely the afternoon. faithfully James

Postcard to his brother David in 1898.

FEBRUARY, 1884.

THURSDAY, 21. *Lodge meeting to night read Essay was Burns Drunkard & Concluded he was not Conclusion open to question, even in own mind, but always like to be charitable.*

Another diary entry.

LONDON OFFICE—
53 FLEET STREET, E.C.
GLASGOW OFFICE—
4 WEST NILE STREET.

The Labour Leader.

LOCHNORRIS,
OLD CUMNOCK,
SCOTLAND.

9 . 2 . 98 189

Dear Dave,

I travelled down last night to escape the waste of another day in the train. Saturday, monday, & Tuesday were spent either in trains or hanging about do forsaken junctions waiting connection

Letter to David Lowe, Hardie's assistant on 'The Labour Leader'.

Far from taking Burt's advice, Hardie and three other miners' agents from Scotland decided to go to London to lobby, to get their amendment limiting miners' hours to eight in the Government's Mines Regulation Bill, and, if they could not get it for men, they would at least try to get it for boys.

They interviewed the Scottish M.P.s and were even received by the Home Secretary, to whom they were introduced by Cunninghame-Graham, who had been returned as a Liberal M.P. for North-West Lanarkshire the previous year. Hardie found he had far more in common with Cunninghame-Graham than he had with the Liberal Labour miner M.P.s.

Robert Bontine Cunninghame-Graham was half-Scots, half-Spanish, the son of a Scottish landowner, descended from the Scottish aristocracy. He had been educated at Harrow, had spent much of his youth in South America and by temperament was a romantic and a revolutionary. He was tall, dark and handsome, with a pointed beard, looking every inch of him the Spanish grandee. Cunninghame-Graham had been on holiday in Ayrshire at Ballochmyle House and created a stir by riding into Cumnock on a magnificent black horse which he halted outside the modest tenement building where the Hardie family lived in a room and kitchen.

They talked about miners' conditions and the Eight Hours question, and Hardie had asked him if he would like to see a coal mine. Cunninghame-Graham agreed and Hardie took him to what he thought was one of the worst mines to work in, an old pit at New Cumnock. The two men crept on hands and feet through a long subterranean passage to the coal face where a man, stripped to the waist, his body covered with sweat and coal dust, was working alone. When the two men came out into the fresh air Hardie said, 'Cunninghame-Graham, there's no muckle in our civilisation after a'.'

Cunninghame-Graham and Hardie became close friends and Hardie found him a reliable ally in the Parliamentary fight for the miners' Eight Hour Day.

Cunninghame-Graham was a natural rebel and he had not taken kindly to Parliamentary life. He had scarified Liberals and Tories alike with his sardonic speeches. Ignoring the convention that a maiden speech must not be controversial, he had delivered himself of numerous barbed witticisms and had ended by attacking:

'The society in which one man works and another enjoys the fruit—the

C

society in which capital and luxury makes Heaven for 30,000 and a Hell for 30,000,000, that society whose crowning achievement is misery, its want and destitution, its degradation, its prostitution and its glaring social irregularities—the society we call London—that society which, by a refinement of irony, has placed the mainspring of human action almost the power of life and death, and the absolute power to pay labour and to reward honour, behind the grey tweed veil which enshrouds the greasy pocket of the capitalist.'

This was good going for a maiden speech and in that Parliament Cunninghame-Graham followed it up with a series of attacks not only on the political set-up at Westminster but on the social system that it represented. Sitting in the seat under the gallery, Hardie and his miner friends from Scotland watched the House of Commons at work. He remembered the story of how Carlyle had brought Emerson to the gallery and after listening for half an hour to the proceedings had whispered to the American, 'Do you no believe in the Devil now?' Occasionally Cunninghame-Graham would come and talk to them and explain the procedure and point out the notabilities. Cunninghame-Graham had not been impressed or subdued by Parliament himself. He called it the 'Thieves' Kitchen', and the 'National Gas Works'.

Cunninghame-Graham had none of the Englishman's reverence for the established institutions and looked upon the Mother of Parliaments with a mixture of scorn and contempt. He had been elected as a Liberal and a Radical, but had come to the conclusion that the Grand Old Man, the revered Mr. Gladstone, was a grand old humbug.

He looked upon the Tories as fools and the Liberals as knaves.

'If a hat were dropped from the House of Commons gallery on to the Liberal benches,' he had declared, 'it would fall on the bald head of a millionaire.' 'There was no difference between the Liberals and Conservatives,' he said, 'except the better cut of the Conservatives' boots. All that is required of a man to make him an efficient Member of Parliament is that he has a good pair of legs to enable him to trot in and out of the Division Lobby at the call of the Party Whip.' Both Gladstone, the Liberal Leader, and Lord Salisbury, the Tory, were to him just a pair of political cheapjacks. 'The strife of parties means nothing but a rotation of rascals in office.'

Cunninghame-Graham explained the proceedings to Hardie in a series of acid and ironic running comments.

During his brief Parliamentary career Cunninghame-Graham was to be the crusader for the underdog, and he found no enthusiasm for the underdog in the Parliament of 1887. Later on he was to have his head broken in the Trafalgar Square Riots and go to jail, to figure in stormy scenes in the House of Commons, be named by the Speaker and stride out of the House declaring, 'Suspend away! I do not care a damn!'

'The House of Commons,' wrote Bernard Shaw about Cunninghame-Graham, 'did not understand him until, in an inspired moment, he voiced a universal impulse by damning its hypocrisy. Of all the eloquence of that silly Parliament, there remains only one single damn. It has survived the front bench speeches of the 'eighties as the word of Cervantes survives the oraculations of the Dons and Deys who put him, too, in prison.'

Hardie and Cunninghame-Graham, poles apart in upbringing and temperament, had found a lot in common between them. Hardie liked the way that Cunninghame-Graham, who loved horses, had championed the cause of the pit ponies, and he found Cunninghame-Graham wholeheartedly with him in his campaign for the Eight Hours Amendment which the Scots wanted inserted in the Mines Bill.

They wanted a lot of other amendments, too, and found that Cunninghame-Graham could be relied on to support them all the time.

Cunninghame-Graham was far nearer them than were Burt, Fenwick, William Abraham ('Mabon,' the Welsh miner M.P.), and the other trade union, Liberal-Labour M.P.s—the Lib-Labs as they came to be known. They were either indifferent or hostile to the amendments that Hardie wanted and terribly afraid of voting against the Government and defying the Liberal whips.

Sitting there under the gallery, hour after hour, listening to the superficial speeches and the servility with which the Liberal-Labours accepted the smallest concessions and compromises, Hardie's conviction that the time had come for a Labour Party independent of the Liberals and fighting determinedly for justice for the working class, grew stronger and stronger.

How remote this Parliament was from the shabby men with the mufflers and the pale pinched faces with the marks of the mine on them as they looked up at him in the Quarry, from the men at the meetings at the pithead, and the strikers, and the pickets as they had marched behind the pipers through the mining rows!

Hardie returned from London more determined than ever to carry on the agitation for a Labour Party.

In the July issue of *The Miner*, he wrote a long front-page article on 'Labour Representation'.

'Do either of the existing parties,' he asked, 'fairly represent the desires and aspirations of working men?' He ruled out the Tories because all they stood for was 'twenty years resolute government for Ireland', and 'keeping Mr. Gladstone out of office'.

'But had the Radicals and Gladstonian Liberals in their programmes anything likely to benefit, say, the miners of the country?

'There was some vague talk about allotments and "among the extreme men, Disestablishment and free education, with a graduated income tax, and perhaps a revision of the death duties, are spoken of frequently, be it said with bated breath".

'And even among Labour representatives in Parliament what sign is there to indicate that the working classes are not happy, contented and prosperous? What programme have they put before the country, likely to benefit the constituent?' The answer was emphatic. 'Absolutely none.'

He went on to criticise a book called the *New Liberal Programme*, to which Mr. Burt, M.P., Mr. B. Pickard and Mr. B. Howell, all miners' M.P.s, had contributed:

'In Mr. Burt's opinion every question likely to cause dissension ought to be carefully excluded; but he thinks such questions as Local option, County Government Reform and Home Rule for Ireland might safely be introduced.'

'Imagine,' was Hardie's comment, 'a miner drawing up a programme which does not even touch the question of Mining Royalties, under which mining admittedly groans!'

'It is the half-heartedness of the present leaders which keeps our cause from progressing,' he concluded. 'What was the Parliamentary Committee of the Trade Union Congress doing about it?' he asked. They had summed up their programme in the words: 'To promote the return of working men to Parliament.'

'Undoubtedly a very good object,' continued Hardie. 'But what difference will it make to me that I have a working man representing me in Parliament, if he is a dumb dog who dare not bark and will follow the leader under any circumstances? There is something even more desirable than the return of working men to Parliament and that is to give working men a definite programme to fight for when they get there and to warn them that if they haven't the courage to stand up in the House of Commons and say what they would say in a miners' meeting, they must make room for someone else who will.'

Hardie found the T.U.C's 'apologetic tone very objectionable'.

He proceeded to outline the sort of programme that the Parliamentary Committee of the T.U.C. should advocate. It not only included the political items of Payment of Members, Adult Suffrage, Free Education, and local option to prohibit the liquor traffic but the Nationalisation of Land, Railways, Mines and Mineral Rights, a Legal Eight Hour Day, a National Insurance Fund, compulsory erection of houses for working people, Direct Taxation and abolition of all taxation on food.

He did not think this programme was perfect but he suggested it as a basis for discussion.

It was far away in advance of anything that had ever been approved of by the T.U.C. It certainly would not have been agreed to by the Liberals who would have regarded it as wildly and extremely revolutionary.

Every issue of *The Miner* became more challenging to the Liberals and the Lib.-Labs. Hardie 'to his sorrow' found that Charles Bradlaugh who as a Radical had created a political sensation by refusing to take the oath, had soon been subdued by Parliament. He had become 'more and more peaceful and temperate and devoted to Blue books and other innocent literature' and had opposed the Miners Eight Hour Bill. 'The worst thing that ever happened to Mr. Bradlaugh was his admission to the House of Commons. His only ambition now is to catch the ear of the House and show he is not the wild demagogue he is supposed to be.' He had introduced 'a miserable shadow of a Truck Bill 'promising in the name of the working classes to oppose all amendments distasteful to the Government, that is to say all amendments likely to be of service to the working men.'

The fate of Bradlaugh, he quoted, as an awful example to future Labour M.P's.

'There is an influence about the House of Commons,' he wrote, in a sketch of 'Mabon' 'the Welsh miners M.P.', 'which is apt if allowed to operate, to become fatal to a man's usefulness. That Mr. Abraham may be preserved free from it must be the wish of all who know him'. He noted with disapproval that Mabon, 'although an advocate of an Eight Hour Bill, spoke against it and refused to vote for an amendment limiting the hours of labour for boys to eight hours a day'. He could not understand why a miner's M.P. should do this and noted reproachfully, 'Like most of those who have risen from the ranks he was a total abstainer. Now, however, he drinks wine though we trust it will not be for long, as nobody knows better than himself how far the force of example goes in one who is a recognised leader of his fellows.'

Hardie was unable to attend the first annual meeting of the Scottish Miners' Federation owing to the death of his little daughter, a loss which affected him deeply.

But he sent a lengthy report of his year's activities. The Federation had 13,000 members, he had attended 77 meetings of which 37 had been mass meetings of miners. 'There is scarcely a district in Scotland where my voice has not been heard,' he wrote, 'with what effect it is for others to say. The formation of a Labour Party in the country has hitherto been looked upon as a dream of the enthusiast. It would appear as if the miners of Scotland were to have the credit of transforming it into a reality. . . . Ours is no old fashioned sixpence a day agitation. We aim at the complete emancipation of the worker from the thraldom of wage slavery. Co-operative production, under State management should be our goal: as never till this has been obtained can we hope for better times for working people.'

In September he began what was to be a series of attacks upon Henry Broadhurst, the secretary of the T.U.C. who in the name of the working classes opposed the eight hour proposal, 'pompously posing as the high priest of Trades Unionism'. 'Mr. Broadhurst must either be prepared to advance with the times or fall out and make room for those who will. . . . The strongest objection which can be taken to most of those now at the head of the Labour Movement is that they are not leaders but move just in proportion to the strength of the pressure from behind.' Hardie was doing what he could to supply that pressure. The Eight Hours for miners had been defeated and for this he laid a lot of the blame on the hostility and indifference of the miners M.P's.

To his critics who objected to State interference Hardie replied: 'Gentlemen, we can do with State interference if the homes of the people can be improved, or work be given to the unemployed, or bread to the hungry or hope to the uncared for poor of our large towns. State interference has assisted wealth, monopoly and privilege long enough. Let it now be used to help the poor, the downtrodden, the ill paid and overworked toilers. . . . It is to the interests of the capitalist to divide the forces of Labour, hence we have this bogey press picture of Continental Socialism—and that profession of interested advice from capitalist sources to avoid the foreigner and all his snares.

Gentlemen, Socialism has lost its terrors for us. We recognise our most serious evils in the unrestrained unscrupulous and remorseless forces of capital.'

By the end of 1887 *The Miner* upon which Thomas Burt had bestowed his benediction in January was declaring 'For Mr. Burt we have respect, esteem and love. This does not, however, blind us to the fact that he is not advancing with the times, and however much we regret this, we would regret still more that personal respect should be allowed to stand in the way of what we consider to be the true progress of the working classes.'

Hardie had become an avowed Socialist, declared open war on the old leaders and was advocating an independent Labour Party.

CHAPTER 5

MID-LANARK AND THE SCOTTISH LABOUR PARTY

HARDIE had made up his mind that at the first opportunity he would stand for Parliament. The Ayrshire miners adopted him as their candidate for North Ayrshire, which was a traditional Liberal seat, and there was an outcry from the *Glasgow Daily Mail*, a Liberal paper.

It charged him with 'being a mere tool in the hands of the Tory Party'. Hardie replied in *The Miner*:

'A capitalist Press may howl and open its floodgates of abuse; half-hearted and unsympathetic Labour reformers may stand in the way but a Democratic Labour Party is now one of the certainties of the future. The working class and the unemployed could not look for help from the Tories or from the Whigs, nor from any other party now in existence, but from the Democratic Labour Party of the future, composed of men in earnest, men who have suffered and who, having a heart and a brain to plan, will go to Parliament not to ape the manners of the classes, but to bring relief to the suffering masses.'

North Ayrshire was not, however, to be Hardie's first Parliamentary fight.

Early in 1888, the Liberal Member for Mid-Lanark resigned. It was the constituency in which Hardie had lived and worked and begun his career as trade union leader, and where he was well known, especially among the miners.

He was urged to stand and an appeal signed by electors in the Division was presented to him requesting him to stand as Labour candidate.

In *The Miner* he explained his position.

'For the first time, as far as Scotland is concerned,' he wrote, 'a serious attempt is to be made to run a genuine Labour candidate in the constituency; and my own name has been put forward in that connection. I desire to define my position clearly. I earnestly desire to see Labour represented in Parliament by working men. Should the choice of the electors fall on me, I am prepared to fight their battle. Should another be selected by them, I will give that other as hearty and ungrudging support as one man can give another. The constituency is essentially one for a Labour candidate. Much depends on the position taken up by the Liberal Association. It may not select a Labour candidate. In either case, my advice would be that the Labour candidate should be put forward. Better split the party now, if there is to be a split, than at a General Election, and if the Labour Party only make their power felt now, time will not be wasted when the General Election comes.'

On March 15th he wrote to the Mid-Lanark Liberal Association in much the same terms. A week later he withdrew his name from their official list. 'The Executive of the Association,' he wrote, 'has made its choice without giving the electors a chance of deciding on the merits of the respective candidate or who he is to be.' The Liberal Headquarters in London had decided that Mr. J. W. Phillips, a young Welsh lawyer had been chosen to stand as the official candidate. Phillips, who in later life was to become a well-known shipowner and become known as Lord St. Davids, was typical of the young politicians who were then flocking into the Liberal Party believing that it offered them the best opportunities of a political career. He had fought a previous election when he was twenty-six and was now hoping to get his reward in a safe Liberal seat. He was the son of a vicar, and had just been called to the Bar.

Hardie met his supporters and decided that they would fight the seat, and it was announced he would stand as a Labour candidate. There was an active Scottish Home Rule Association in the West of Scotland which resented the fact that a young unknown Welsh lawyer had been foisted upon a Scots constituency, and it announced that it would support the local man. From London came offer of support from a newly-formed body called the Labour Electoral Association, which held Radical views and during the election assumed the title of 'National Labour Party'.

There was a Scottish Home Rule Association in London, too, and its secretary was a young man called Ramsay MacDonald, who wrote to him saying:

41

'I cannot refrain from wishing you God speed in your election contest. Had I been able to have gone to Mid-Lanark to help you—to do so both by word and deed—would have given me very great pleasure indeed. The powers of darkness—Scottish newspapers with English editors (as the *Leader*), partisan wire-pullers, and the other etceteras of political squabbles—are leagued against us.

'But let the consequences be what they may, do not withdraw. The cause of Labour and of Scottish Nationality will suffer much thereby. Your defeat will awaken Scotland, and your victory will reconstruct Scottish Liberalism. All success be yours, and the National cause you champion. There is no miner—and no other one for that matter—who is a Scotsman and not ashamed of it, who will vote against you in favour of an obscure English barrister, absolutely ignorant of Scotland and of Scottish affairs, and who only wants to get to Parliament in order that he may have the tail of M.P. to his name in the Law Courts.'

The Parliamentary Committee of the Highland Land League, through its chairman, J. Galloway Weir, also supported Hardie. So did the Glasgow Trades Council and the Executive of the British Steel Smelters' Association. Cunninghame-Graham, although a Liberal M.P., sent a message which concluded, 'A good coat is useful enough against the weather, but how poor men should bow down and worship one knowing that it will not warm their backs passes my comprehension.'

There had been five candidates at the previous election and the Liberal Headquarters was anxious that Hardie should withdraw in order not to split the vote, and an emissary from London arrived in Glasgow in order to persuade him to retire.

The Secretary of the Labour Electoral Association, a Mr. T. R. Threlfall, was sent north to take part in the election.

The campaign had begun, but one evening Threlfall did not turn up at the meeting for which he had been advertised. He was waiting to meet Hardie at the hotel and was bubbling over with excitement.

'I've settled it,' he cried excitedly. 'I've been in conference with them all the evening.' 'With whom?' asked Hardie. 'With the Liberals,' said Threlfall, 'at the George Hotel, and you've to retire.'

Hardie knew nothing about political wire-pulling and was dumbfounded. Threlfall had negotiated some kind of political deal and had come to some understanding with Schnadhorst, the Liberal National Agent who had come down from London.

As far as the Labour Electoral Association was concerned the election was off and Threlfall departed the next day. He had completely failed, however, to understand the character of Keir Hardie, who bluntly declared that he had not the slightest intention of withdrawing. Sir George Trevelyan, M.P., one of the leading Liberals, was also staying at the George Hotel. He asked Hardie to meet him, was very polite, explained how unfortunate it was that Liberals and Labour should fight each other. He agreed that they wanted more working men in Parliament but this was not the occasion. If Hardie would only stand down in Mid-Lanark he would give him an assurance that at the General Election he would be adopted somewhere, the Liberal Party paying his expenses and guaranteeing him a yearly salary—three hundred pounds was the sum hinted at—as they were doing for others.

It was a tempting offer to a young man like Hardie, living from hand to mouth on a meagre salary. To his surprise, Trevelyan received an abrupt and emphatic 'NO'. The fight was going on. The Labour Electoral Association had withdrawn its offer of financial support but the problem of how to pay for the election expenses was solved by Miss Florence Harkness, who wrote under the pen name of 'John Law', and who had just published a novel entitled *Out of Work*. She had money and paid the election expenses, which came to £270.

Hardie had had his first experience of how the daily Press could misrepresent him. He had told the editor of the *Glasgow Daily Mail* where the money to pay for his election was coming from but he deliberately and persistently attacked Hardie, stating that it was the Tory Party that was paying him to stand in order to split the Liberal vote and that he was in receipt of 'Tory Gold'. There was no secret at all about it and Miss Harkness herself wrote to the Press stating that she was not a Tory but a Socialist. But long after the Mid-Lanark election the myth of Keir Hardie and the Tory gold persisted.

Hardie was the only local candidate; the Tory candidate, W. R. Bousfield, was a political hack sent down from London Tory Headquarters in the same way as the young Liberal barrister had been sent down by the Liberals. This had roused some resentment among Scots Radicals and a Highland M.P., Mr. Galloway Weir, who was chairman of the Scottish Home Rule Society, sent a telegram to Mr. Gladstone, the Leader of the Liberals, whose name was one to conjure with, urging him not to attempt to influence votes from the Scottish Labour candidate to the Welsh Liberal lawyer. Gladstone ignored the telegram and sent his blessings to the official Liberal.

But it was not only Scots sentiment that mattered. There was a considerable Irish working-class vote in the constituency and it could be swayed by the United Irish League, which was solidly behind Gladstone and Home Rule for Ireland. The Liberals understood these things and sent down some Irish nationalist M.P.s to sway the Irish vote. Every vote given to Keir Hardie, they were told, was a vote against Ireland.

Compared with his Liberal opponents, Hardie was only a novice. He knew nothing about electioneering in the 'eighties and had never taken part in an election before. His followers were mostly young enthusiastic miners and the correspondent of *The Times* noted with surprise that all those who signed his nomination papers were working miners.

In the first paragraph of his election address Hardie gave the figures of landlords, lawyers, shipowners and businessmen who represented Scotland in the House of Commons.

'You will see that the working men of Scotland,' he wrote, 'have no representatives to urge their claims. It is in order to remedy this admitted grievance that I now claim your support.'

He went on to express his support for Home Rule for Ireland and for Scotland and for the rest of the items on the Liberal programme, urged the need for the nationalisation of land and mining royalties, for an Eight-Hour Day for miners, taxation of land values and anti-liquor legislation. He wanted the abolition of the House of Lords which he described as 'effete anachronism' and denounced the national expenditure on Royalty as 'a disgrace' and added, 'From the Crown downwards I would insist on the introduction of strict business principles in the payment of duties.'

'I know intimately the needs of the working classes,' he added, 'and would agitate for every reform likely to promote their welfare. I hold my principles not as "pious opinions"—good enough for believing in but not for acting on—but as principles worth fighting for. Herein lies the chief distinction between myself and the other gentlemen whose names are now before you. They would follow their leaders right or wrong; I, on the other hand, would press upon them the claims of the people.'

Hardie's election address was by no means a revolutionary document, but no printer in the constituency would print it and it had to be printed in Ayrshire by the *Ayrshire Post*.

Mid-Lanark in 1888 was a widely-scattered industrial constituency, and included several large towns and areas which are now constituencies on their own. But there were only 9,143 voters on the roll. There was a property qualification. Only householders with houses valued at £10 a year were qualified and so the young miners had no votes.

He issued a manifesto denouncing the local Liberal Executive:

'The attitude of the official Liberals makes it unmistakably clear they care nothing for the interest of Labour, except in so far as they can be made subservient to those of the middle class. Liberals are eager to use our political power as a weapon against Tory landlords, but they are afraid that, in the hands of consistent and independent men, the same weapon may be turned against the social injustice of which Labour is the prey. We do not intend any longer to be merely tools of political tricksters. As the Irish have, by opposing them, forced the Liberals hastily to find "political salvation" as to Home Rule, so we can, and will convert them to a belief in the direct representation of Labour, and the addition to their official programme of measures which will benefit the class to which you and I belong. If Liberalism will not accept co-operation on fair and reasonable terms, then Liberalism must in the future reckon with our hostility.'

His speeches consisted mainly of pleas for Labour representation in Parliament when Labour M.P.s would represent working men. He was frequently interrupted and there were some stormy scenes at his meetings, especially at Wishaw, near Motherwell, where the Irish turned up in force and where only half a dozen hands were raised for a vote of confidence.

He had more support in the Hamilton district, where he was known and where a young miner called Robert Smillie, who was one of Hardie's closest friends, moved the vote of confidence. 'It is being said,' Hardie declared, 'that I am poor. I plead guilty to that. If I were a man of wealth I would not be a fit representative for a constituency composed of working men. I plead guilty, too, to a charge that I am a working man. Men of wealth may have sympathy for the workers, as they have sympathy for a suffering animal, but they cannot understand like those of us who have worked and suffered. I do not want to be sent to Parliament by the money of rich men, nor to be kept by them. I want to be sent to Parliament by working men, to be paid by working men and kept by working men to speak for working men.'

He had no election organisation worth speaking about except his band of young miners. The local paper on the day of the poll reported: 'Mr. Bousfield, the Tory candidate, and Mr. Phillips, the Liberal candidate, had numerous gigs and carriages but Mr. Keir Hardie had none.' The most interesting item that *The Times* recorded was that 'some of the miners went to work at 4 a.m., in order to leave the pit to vote before the poll closed'. But Hardie was at the bottom of the poll. The result was:

PHILLIPS (Liberal)	3,847
BOUSFIELD (Tory)	2,917
HARDIE (Labour)	617

Hardie had been overwhelmingly defeated but it had been a significant and historic election. It was the first time Labour had stood independent, defiant, as a separate political party with its own programme and policy. 'In days to come,' wrote Hardie to his followers in the next issue of *The Miner*, 'the great Liberal victory in Mid-Lanark will be remembered only in connection with the stand you made'.

To the 'Gallant Six Hundred' who had voted for him he addressed the following manifesto:

'Men, in my own name, and that of the poor and needy everywhere, I thank you for your votes. You have shown that there are still a remnant left of these whose hearts beat true to humanity's cause. At Balaclava six hundred men faced five thousand. To-day the name and fame of the six hundred live in song and story: but the five thousand—?

'In days to come the great Liberal victory in Mid-Lanark will be remembered only in connection with the stand you made. Your vote marks a turning point in history. You have raised the "conditions of the peoples" question to a first place. The meaningless drivel of the ordinary politician must now give place to the burning words of earnest men, whose hearts are on fire with love to their kind, men who believe in the Fatherhood of God, the brotherhood of man.'

It was an election long remembered in Lanarkshire.

Many an old collier declared with pride in later years, 'Aye, I voted for Keir Hardie in Mid-Lanark in 'eighty-eight. I was one of those whom he called the "Gallant Six Hundred".'

Keir Hardie had lost the by-election but he had created a new party. The Mid-Lanark by-election had one immediate result. Those who had watched Keir Hardie's fight and approved of his challenge to the orthodox Liberals decided to come together to form a Scottish Labour Party. On May 19th, 1888, a group of twenty-seven men who had supported Hardie were called together in Glasgow and a committee was formed to arrange a conference for a Labour Party in Scotland. The members of the committee were Duncan McPherson, Keir Hardie, Charles Kennedy, George Mitchell and Robert Hutchinson.

Three months later, on August 26th, the conference was held at the Waterloo Rooms, Glasgow, and the Scottish Labour Party was born. R. B. Cunninghame-Graham was elected honorary president and the hon. vice-presidents were Dr. Clark, M.P., and John Ferguson. The chairman of the executive was J. Shaw Maxwell, later to become the first secretary of the Independent Labour Party, George Mitchell was the treasurer and Keir Hardie was appointed secretary.

The Conference decided immediately to form a Scottish Labour Party, whose object would be 'to educate the people politically and secure the return to Parliament and all local bodies of members pledged to its programme'.

The programme included, among other items, the prohibition of the liquor traffic; abolition of the House of Lords and all hereditary offices; nationalisation of land and minerals; free education; Boards to have power to provide food for the children; State acquisition of railways, waterways and tramways; State banking; and graduated income tax on all incomes above £300. An addition to the programme was to the effect that the ultimate object of the Party was 'to secure the nationalisation of all the capital used in production'.

The amendment was withdrawn on the understanding that the executive would embody it in a statement of first principles. 'The Labour Party in Scotland,' wrote Hardie jubilantly, 'is now fairly on its feet and ready for action. It will embrace within its ranks not only those working men who have grown tired of playing at politics as a game for the amusement of the rich, and who want to see social legislation pushed to the front, but also such men as have shown by years of devotion to the cause that they are worthy of trust.'

He was dealing with the Press criticism that had immediately been voiced that 'certain of the office bearers are not *bona fide* horny-handed sons of toil'.

Cunninghame-Graham was an aristocrat and a landlord and Dr.

47

G. B. Clark, the Radical and land reformer M.P. for Caithness, came from the Clark family of cotton manufacturers of Paisley.

'These critics,' replied Hardie, 'go on the assumption that a Labour Party should consist of the begrimed ones only. Those who argue thus are for the most part those who hope to create feeling against the new movement by appealing to the prejudices of the working class.'

He knew quite well the role that had been played in revolutionary movements in the past by middle-class people and aristocrats who, while not born among the workers, had identified themselves with their struggles and voiced their aspirations, and indeed often become their leaders. Poets like Shelley and William Morris had not come from the working class but had been in revolt against the cruelties and inhumanities and sordidness that had come with the industrial revolution. Neither Marx nor Engels had been manual workers, nor had many of the Chartist leaders and innumerable others who had played prominent parts in democratic movements. 'It is just as well,' he continued, 'that this matter should be fixed at once, and made clear to all whom it may concern. If therefore, anyone, peasant or peer, is found willing to accept the programme and work with and for the Party, his help will be gladly accepted. It would be a strange Labour Party, indeed, which would shut out from its ranks such Labour leaders as Cunninghame-Graham, Dr. Clark, John Ferguson and Shaw-Maxwell have proved themselves to be.'

From now on it was to be war on the Liberals who were opposed to Labour. 'The weapon has been forged,' he continued. 'A General Election will come, and it is for us to see that no Liberal gets returned who is not with us. Better a thousand times an open foe than a secret enemy. The wolf in sheep's clothing is always most to be feared, and the man who poses as a Liberal and yet refuses to support shorter working hours, an improvement in the homes of the people, the organisation of relief works for the unemployed and the restoration of land to rightful owners, may call himself what he pleases, but he is an enemy and as such is to be opposed.'

Both Cunninghame-Graham and Keir Hardie had now become so well known that they could draw a crowd in any of the big towns in Scotland. The Mid-Lanark election and Hardie's campaign had roused widespread interest and Cunninghame-Graham's unorthodox speeches in the House of Commons had been widely reported.

They were in striking contrast, the debonair, well-dressed descendant

Keir Hardie was a founder member of the I.L.P.

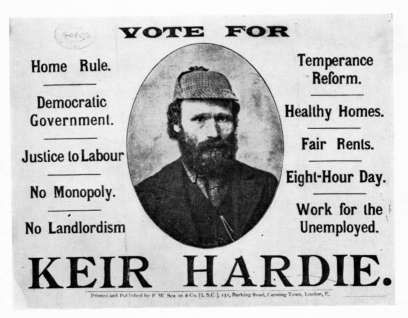

Published during the election campaign at South West Ham, 1892.

Dined with Rosebery on Friday at the Welsh Parliamentary dinner & he found in the "good Scotch face at the end of the table" the one only link which now bound him to Wales. He had a long steady look in my direction as he declared that "Parliamentary courage, too rare a Quality in our political life" needed to be held in check sometimes lest it do harm. Now for the fund again.

faithfully J Keir Hardie

Letter to David Lowe, 1900.

of the Scottish kings and the sturdy, dour, simply-clad miner, each in their own style, forthright and effective, fiercely unconventional, eloquent and earnest, quite capable of dealing with questioners and interrupters, convincing the doubters, and making converts.

They went to halls and market places, conferences and street corners and dock gates, anywhere where they could get an audience.

There was one memorable meeting in the Camlachie Division of Glasgow when it was expected that Keir Hardie was going to be howled down by the Irish, who did not know his attitude towards Home Rule. The hall was packed when Cunninghame-Graham, who arrived first, went on to the platform, and pandemonium broke loose. He retired into the ante-room behind the platform, called two of the door attendants and asked them to bolt the doors of the hall.

Then he appeared on the platform for the second time with a dummy six-shooter pistol which he had seen lying among the belongings of a theatrical company in the ante-room. Pointing the formidable-looking weapon at the noisy crowd below, he shouted for order.

Silence fell as if by magic, and then he told his startled audience that the doors had been locked and that if anybody moved from his seat or interrupted a speech he would blow his brains out. 'I am going to speak for half an hour,' he announced, 'and then I shall introduce my friend, Keir Hardie, and until he has finished his address not a man will interrupt him, or try to move, unless he wishes to be carried out of the hall as a corpse.' For a moment one could have heard a pin drop, but then the audience, having a sense of humour, roared with laughter and everybody applauded the solitary figure on the platform, and when Keir Hardie appeared, immediate silence reigned in the hall. When the listeners heard that both Cunninghame-Graham and the principal speaker strongly favoured Home Rule for Ireland they applauded wildly. Only when the meeting was over did they discover where Cunninghame-Graham had found his formidable gun.

'I first met Hardie,' wrote Cunninghame-Graham, recalling those days in later life, 'about the year 1887 or 1888 when he and Chisholm Robertson were the chief miners' leaders in the West of Scotland.

'I first saw him at his home in Cumnock. I spoke to him for the first time in the office of a paper he was connected with. I think *The Miner* or *The Cumnock News*. He was about thirty years of age, and I should judge but old for his age. His hair was already becoming thin at the top of the head and receding from the temples. His eyes were not very strong. At first sight he struck you as a remarkable man. There was an air of great benevolence

49

D

about him but his face showed the kind of appearance of one who has worked hard, and suffered, possibly from inadequate nourishment in his youth. He was active and alert, though not athletic. Still he appeared to be full of energy, and as subsequent events proved, he had an enormous power of resistance against long, hard and continuous work. I should judge him to have been very serious and of a highly strung temperament. He was a very strict teetotaller and remained so to the end but he was not a bigot on the subject and was tolerant of faults in his weaker brethren. Nothing in his address or speech showed his want of education in his youth. His accent was Ayrshire. I think he took pride in it in his ordinary conversation. He could, however, to a great extent, throw his accent aside but not entirely. When roused or excited in public or in private speech it was always perceptible. His voice was high pitched but sonorous and very far carrying at that time.

'He was then, and, I believe always, an extremely abstemious eater and in the long peregrinations about the mining villages of Lanarkshire and Ayrshire when I was a young unknown M.P. and he equally unknown miners' leader, in rain and wind and snow, an oatcake, a scone, a bit of cheese, always contained him. He would then sit down by the fireside in the cottage in the mining row and light up his corn cob pipe and talk of the future of the Labour Party, which in those days seemed to the miners a mere fairy tale. Now and then I have seen him take the baby from the miner's wife and dandle it on his knee while she prepared the tea. He had the faculty of attracting children to him and most certainly "he forbade them not". They would come round him in the miner's cottages and lean against him for the first few minutes. One felt he was a family man and so did the children.'

The Ayrshire miners had joined up with the Trades Union Congress and in 1887 Hardie was sent to the annual conference at Swansea. The Secretary to the Congress was Henry Broadhurst, suave, experienced at handling trade union conferences, complacent, and pompous, one of the Lib-Labs of the old school, friendly-disposed to the big employers of labour who patronised him and very conscious of the fact that he was a Member of Parliament and that the leaders of the Liberal Party consulted with him and approved of him.

Hardie went to the rostrum and attacked him for supporting Liberal capitalist candidates at election times. It was the first clash with the old leaders at the T.U.C.

Charles Fenwick, the leader of the Northumberland miners whom Hardie had nettled by his attacks on him over his attitude towards the Miners' Eight Hours Bill, scornfully replied from the platform, 'There are some men and some movements who are like Jonah's gourd, in this, that they spring up in a night and wither in a night.' The old leaders laughed and applauded. Who was this young raw Scots fellow from Ayrshire, anyway, and what right had he to question the conduct of Broadhurst?

Fenwick's reference to him stuck in Hardie's memory, and he was to remind Fenwick of it in later years. For Hardie's appearance at the T.U.C. was not just an incident to be forgotten. It was just the beginning of a long struggle and a battle of men and ideas which was to last for years and which Hardie, after defeat after defeat, was ultimately to win. But at the Swansea Congress he was no match for Broadhurst and the old school. They were too strongly entrenched.

Hardie continued to attack them in *The Miner*. 'It is difficult to write temperately of a man like Broadhurst,' he wrote.

'The other day he had a motion before the House of Commons referring to the condition of the poor.

'Presumably he had, to some extent at least, considered the question and when he came to propound his remedies he had nothing to propose except free education and one free meal a day for poor children. Little wonder that members laughed immoderately at this vain display of contemptible fooling with a serious problem.

'Mr. Broadhurst has thus again given a glaring illustration of his total lack of qualification for the position he occupies. So long as he holds the position of secretary to the Trades Union Congress, he will be recognised as an exponent of the views of trade unionism. I put it to the members of our leading unions. Can they afford to pay a man £200 a year for misrepresenting their views in Parliament?

'If not, there is but one remedy. Henry Broadhurst must be replaced by a man in touch with the people. If he has not the good grace to resign at the Dundee Congress, he must be voted out. The former will be the most dignified course, though the latter will be the most effective. He must make his choice, but one or the other it must be.'

The Ayrshire miners tabled a resolution for the Dundee Conference of the T.U.C. condemning Broadhurst 'for having supported at election times, those who were sweaters and unfair employers of labour by his declaration that he would continue in this course in the future, by the fact that he had admittedly held shares in a company where men are shamefully overworked and underpaid and declares that he is not a fit and proper person to act as secretary of the Parliamentary Committee of the Trade Union Congress.'

Hardie had discovered that Broadhurst was a shareholder in the chemical company of Brunner Mond and that these shares had been allotted to him after speaking for Sir John Brunner at election meetings, for which he had also received a fee of £20.

It was a direct personal attack in a conference where Broadhurst had many friends, which he dominated and which he could handle. Hardie, moving his resolution, was frequently interrupted and jeered at.

'Men coming into a movement and selling themselves for gain corrupted it, polluted it and ate out all that is best and noblest in trade unionism,' he said. 'All we ask for is that the men who stand on our platforms as trade union leaders shall know no party except the party of Labour in this country, which Whigs and Tories are seeking to oppress, keep down and trample underfoot.'

Broadhurst fought back cynically and cunningly, admitting that he held the shares and that he had a right to invest his savings where he liked. The Conference supported him by 177 votes to 11. Hardie had lost again, but his reputation as a fearless and uncompromising fighter against the old school had grown. He had become known as one of the stormy personalities of the T.U.C.

But if he had made enemies at the T.U.C. he had made friends too. There were other rebels like Tom Mann and Ben Tillett who wanted a more aggressive trade unionism taking an active and independent line in politics. They met together at the T.U.C. and co-operated against the platform and discussed with each other the line they should take next.

CHAPTER 6

SOUTH WEST HAM
FIGHTING ALONE IN PARLIAMENT

THE Mid-Lanark election, the activities of the Scottish Labour Party, the conflicts at the T.U.C. with the old school, had now made the name of Keir Hardie known south of the Border. In South West Ham there were a group of working men Radicals who had captured the local Liberal Association.

They wrote to Hardie asking him if they should nominate him as their candidate. Dr. G. B. Clark had advised him to contest a London constituency and so Hardie went down and was adopted. His chief supporters were a local doctor and a shoemaker who had got on to the Town Council. This was a problem for the Liberal Headquarters and Schnadhorst, their National Agent, was by no means pleased that the stubborn Scotsman who had caused all the trouble in Mid-Lanark had now arrived in London. Still those fellows at S. W. Ham were an awkward lot and it was not an easy matter to persuade Hardie to withdraw from a fight. And there was the precedent of John Burns at Battersea. The discreet line would be to leave Hardie to be defeated at S. W. Ham and not to interfere in case the trouble spread to other London constituencies. Schnadhorst invited Hardie to meet him at his office and met with a refusal. Later they met on neutral ground in the presence of a third party. Schnadhorst, wishing to placate Hardie, asked what he could do to aid him in S. W. Ham. 'Nothing,' was the reply, 'except to keep out of the way.'

This ended the interview, they were able to raise the money among themselves and not a copper of the expenses came from the Liberal funds. Liberal Headquarters thought that Hardie would be defeated and that would end the problem.

Hardie, however, was convinced that the seat could be won and addressed a series of open-air meetings at the dock gates, many of them at 5.30 in the morning when the dockers went to their work.

Cunninghame-Graham went to help him and wrote a vivid description of the district of Canning Town, 'a very microcosm of the nineteenth-century world. Street upon street of half-cooked, brick abominations, falsely called houses; here and there a "Little Bethel" chapel, in its hideousness making sweet religion a rhapsody of bricks and stucco. Row upon row of open stalls at night when the stale vegetables are sold under the flare of naptha lights. Public houses not a few. An air of desolation over the whole place that only modern civilisation gives, an air which makes a .... in Texas or a windswept pampas infinitely more habitable and human. On one side, lines of endless docks and on the other, lines of endless misery.'

The people had become interested in 'the northern miner, shaggy of head, earnest in manner and perfervid, like the Scots of old before the days of Knox, of Kirk, of whisky and commercialism'. 'No one can take a stroll through Canning Town,' continued Cunninghame-Graham, 'and fail to see that there commercialism has done its worst. Thus it seems to me that folk there are drawn to Hardie as to a man from another world. So strange to see a man in earnest; so strange to hear a man with aspirations and theories of a new life, even if one hardly comprehends them all oneself. So unusual to be addressed as "Men", and not "Gentlemen", so beyond all one's everyday experience to see the speaker so moved by the strange inward somthing that makes his colour come and go, makes his hands clench, and sends you from the meeting with a choking in your throat, making the dirty streets look strangely different, and the feet step light giving a sort of exultation. In Canning Town there are many poor enough to inherit the earth, though at present they lack achievement as to their inheritance and this explains, I think, he had got hold of them. Not that he is a demagogue, but that he makes them feel there is sunshine somewhere if they could but come at it.

'It is difficult to make out exactly whether it is the socialistic programme or the clear grit of the man that has impressed them. I incline to think the latter as programmes are many, men are few. Less eloquent than Burns, less dogmatic than Mann, less of a preacher than Tillett, Keir Hardie has, nevertheless, some qualities which none of them possess. He alone of Labour leaders known to me, at any rate, has something poetic about his personality and his speeches.'

Hardie speeches at S. W. Ham were very similar to those he had made at Mid-Lanark, only now he had more experience of addressing crowds and spoke easier. The men that gathered round his soapbox at the docks and looked up at him when he was speaking moved him in the same way as the crowd of miners had done at the Quarry. They interrupted him and asked him questions in broad Cockney which he had some difficulty in understanding, and they were amused, too, at his strong Scots accent, although he spoke slowly and clearly. Many of them were big casual labourers who had come from Ireland and had found themselves working a couple of days a week, and sometimes unemployed for long periods when there were no ships to be loaded and unloaded at the docks.

'It is not my fight, men, it is yours,' he had told them. 'It is you who will lose or win. If you return me to the House of Commons, I will fight for you. I have seen men waiting for work at the dock gate, standing there as if they were so many heads of cattle. "One man one vote," as John Burns said, is good but "One man, one job, and a job for every man is better".

'If the Liberals are prepared to accept our principles, we are prepared to work with them. If they are not prepared to accept our principles they are no more our friends than the Tories.'

He had been attacked by his opponents because he was not a Londoner but had come from Scotland. 'I am a Scotsman,' he replied, 'and you may be Scots, or Irish, or English, but you are all labourers.'

The topics that Keir Hardie talked about were not those which they usually heard about at election times. There was nothing of the political cheapjack about him. He appealed to their manhood and their self-respect; he wanted to make unemployment, low wages, bad housing, the real issue of politics. He wanted a new party, a party that would fight in Parliament for the working class—a Labour Party!

Later on, when the election was won, he said it had been won by these meetings at the dock gates.

When the poll was declared, Keir Hardie had been elected M.P. for S. W. Ham. The figures were:

KEIR HARDIE (Labour)	...	...	5,268
MAJOR G. E. BANES (Tory) ...	...		4,036

At thirty-six Keir Hardie had won his way into Parliament.

At the docks next morning there was great rejoicing and when Keir Hardie arrived at 5.30 to thank them they carried him shoulder-high. He was now Keir Hardie, M.P. for S. W. Ham—their M.P.—and they decided to celebrate their victory.

Most of the other M.P.s would be going to Westminster in their carriages, many of them with their coachmen and footmen.

Why not hire a carriage for Keir Hardie? They were able to get a large-size wagonette and a lot of the enthusiasts squeezed in. They would take him in style to Parliament. One of them had a cornet and played it lustily at intervals on the way up from Canning Town. They were celebrating their triumph and having a day out. They were stopped by the police at the gates and Hardie stepped out, and while they cheered he made his way into Palace Yard.

The next day the Press announced that Hardie had vulgarly and ostentatiously arrived at Westminster escorted by a brass band. The legend persisted for years.

But it was Hardie's dress that scandalised the House of Commons. In his election campaign at S. W. Ham he had worn the brown home-spun tweed suit in which he had arrived from Scotland. It was the usual kind of suit worn at the time by a Scottish working man.

But it was not so much the suit that caused the consternation but the cap. It was a tweed cap with flaps, like a deerstalker's cap. Nearly all the other M.P.s wore frock coats and top hats. John Burns and some of the Lib-Lab M.P.s wore bowlers, which were hardly the correct thing, but nobody before had arrived at Westminster in a cap!

Hardie had not deliberately set out to flaunt the conventions. 'I had always worn a tweed cap and homespun clothes,' he explained, 'and it never entered my head to make a change. My wife in Scotland had thought about it and had sent on a soft felt hat, but it had not arrived. I received eight or ten top hats from good-hearted people in the country afterwards and several people sent me orders to their tailors to get a suit of clothes.' John Burns had come with a brand new suit of navy blue serge which had been made by a foreman cutter who was an admirer and presented to him by his supporters.

'It was a beautiful suit, a perfect fit,' wrote William Kent in his biography of Burns. When Burns entered the House, one Lambert, the dandy of the Parliament, said what a fine suit it was and asked who his tailor was. 'Just then Keir Hardie appeared. He had come in a brake, the kind of thing, Burns told me, you saw going to Epping Forest, an old deerstalker cap and check suit, you could have played draughts on it. Lambert said, "Here is a Labour man dressed like a gentleman, but look at that bugger".' What Keir Hardie thought of the dandy is not recorded. He was probably not interested at all in

Lord Salisbury's Trust in the People
"If we were out of the way the first
thing you fellows would do would
be to help yourselves out of the Treasury"

A Tory view of Hardie.

Cartoon by F. Carruthers Gould from 'Westminster Gazette'.

him. But he was interested in Burns and what he intended to do in the new Parliament. For Burns had called himself a Socialist and had a national reputation as a strike leader and as a critic and rebel at the T.U.C. He was the most popular working-class orator in London. He had the record of a fighter outside, but what was he prepared to do inside?

Hardie suggested to Burns that they should sit on the opposition side of the House and thus show at the beginning that they were not going to be subservient to the Liberal Government. Burns would not agree. He had apparently already made up his mind that he was going to work with the Liberals. Now that he had got into Parliament he was not prepared to take any risks.

They looked upon Hardie as if he were the emissary from another world, as indeed he was. There were all sorts of exaggerated stories about him in the Press the next day. Hardie had to contradict them later. 'The statement that I perambulated the floor of the House in my offensive cap until recalled to orderliness by the awful tones of Mr. Speaker Peel was without any foundation in fact. I was walking up the floor to take the oath in conversation with Sir Charles Cameron, then one of the Glasgow Members, who with hands deep-plunged in his trousers pockets, *was* wearing his hat. He did not realise that the Speaker was addressing him and when I called his attention to it he at once removed it. It sufficed for some of the more imaginative gentlemen in the Press Gallery that I was there, and next day there were long descriptions of the "truculent" way in which I had defied the conventions and the stern rebuke which the Speaker had administered. All pure fiction! In fact Mr. Speaker Peel expressed to me personally his surprise and regret at the injustice which the Press had done.'

But the cap had become a symbol, a symbol that something different and defiant had arrived to upset the tranquillity of Westminster.

They wondered what would happen when this strange apparition addressed the House, and had not long to wait.

Hardie decided to move an amendment to the address to the Queen's speech.

It read:

'And further, we humbly desire to express our regret that Your Majesty has not been advised when dealing with agricultural depression to refer also to the industrial depression now prevailing, and the widespread misery, due to large numbers of the working class being unable to find

He carried the plight of the unemployed to the House of Commons.
Cartoon by 'Jordie' from 'The Labour Leader', 1894.

employment, and direct Parliament to legislate promptly and effectively in the interests of the unemployed.'

The Members crowded in to hear what the strange man had to say. They expected fireworks and a row, a tub-thumping oration, something full of sound and fury that they could expect in Trafalgar Square or Hyde Park.

Keir Hardie had been portrayed as such a truculent fellow that they were prepared for anything. He spoke at first slowly, quietly, almost hesitatingly, carefully marshalling his figures of the numbers of the unemployed in London, Liverpool, Glasgow, Birmingham and the other big cities.

The figures that he had been able to obtain showed that there were about 1,300,000 people out of work, and behind them were their wives and children and dependants. Then there were the casual and part-time workers, a considerable army—about 300,000. But it was not just the number of unemployed, it was the social misery that resulted from unemployment.

'Remember,' he said to them, 'that this question not only affects those out of work but also those workers in employment. I believe all the horrors of sweating, of low wages, of long hours, and of deaths from starvation, are directly traceable to the large numbers of people who are totally unemployed or only casually employed. The worker in the workshop is fettered by the thought that outside his workshop gates there are thousands eager and willing to step into his shoes should he be dismissed in consequence of any attempt to improve his position.'

He developed his argument, examining some of the remedies that were sometimes proposed. Protection, emigration. The Government was a large employer of labour itself; it could initiate work schemes, develop the land, reduce working hours, so that there would be more jobs. Members on both sides whispered to each other. He was making a good speech. He had never been to school but he spoke faultless English. He spoke for about forty minutes and ended his speech with a challenge: 'It is said that this Amendment amounts to a vote of "Want of Confidence in the Government", and that therefore Honourable Members opposite will not vote for it. The Government that does not legislate for the unemployed does not deserve the confidence of this House. If the Queen's Speech contained a reference to this question of anything like a satisfactory nature I would not have raised it on this occasion, but not having it, I will take the sense of the House upon it.'

He appealed to the Irish. There were nearly as many unemployed with their dependants as there were people in Ireland. 'If the honourable gentlemen who represent the cause of Nationalism in Ireland would have felt justified in risking the life of the Government on the question of Home Rule, I claim to be more than justified in taking a similar risk for the unemployed.'

John Burns would not second Hardie's amendment. He did not agree that the Government should be embarrassed. Hardie's motion was seconded by Colonel Vincent, a Tory. Some of the Irish and a number of the Tories supported him in the division lobby, his amendment being defeated by 276 votes to 109. He had impressed the House with his earnestness, ability and courage but the Liberals and especially his Lib-Lab enemies were angry with him for forcing the division and making it appear that they had voted against the unemployed.

In the country Hardie's reputation went up. The Socialists were disappointed with John Burns. 'In spite of his queer dress and rough appearance,' wrote H. M. Hyndman, 'some of us felt that a little of what we had so long been fighting for might possibly be realised. For there was no laughing-down of Hardie. He had the matter at heart and had made a very good speech. It undoubtedly influenced the House of Commons, for the time being, and gained for the Ayrshire miner the undisputed leadership of the Independent Labourites, as distinguished from the revolutionary Socialists, who, however, were quite ready to back him so long as he continued on that line. Hardie did, in fact, champion the cause of the class from which he sprang in the calm, deliberate manner and phraseology of a man who meant serious business. The Grand Old Man (Gladstone) himself paid Hardie the doubtful compliment of listening to him. The Tory leaders hearkened also. But to do Hardie justice these little attentions and compliments he received had not the slightest influence in turning him away from his independence. He went his way in House and Lobby in the same solitary fashion he had adopted from the first.'

Punch christened him 'Don't Keir Hardie'. They also called him 'Queer Hardie' and he became known, too, as the 'Member for the Unemployed'.

But the speech in the 1892-95 Parliament which attracted most public attention was the one he made on the motion, 'That a humble address be presented to congratulate Her Majesty on the birth of a son to His Royal Highness the Duke and Her Royal Highness the Duchess of York'.

This was the child that was destined to become King Edward VIII and the Duke of Windsor.

Hardie was theoretically a Republican but it was not just Republican sentiment that made him protest. On the same day that the Royal baby was born, June 23rd, 1894, there had been a big mining disaster at the Albion Colliery, Cilfynydd, in South Wales. Nothing had been said about this, but it had greatly affected Hardie. The following night the French President, Carnot, had been assassinated. The Press was far more interested in the Royal event and in the assassination in France than in the tragedy in Wales. Hardie had written in *The Labour Leader*:

'Never in the history of British journalism was there anything more offensively snobbish. Everyone will mourn with Madame Carnot, and rejoice in a subdued kind of way with the Duke and Duchess of York in the birth of their child, but it is to the sore-stricken poor of that Welsh valley that the true hearts of this great nation will turn with overwhelming sympathy. For the lickspittles of the Press, who have no ears for the cry of the poor widow and orphan, and who attempt to see in the birth of a child to the Duke and Duchess of York an event of Divine significance to the nation, there can be nothing but contempt. The life of one Welsh miner is of great commercial and moral value to the British nation than the whole Royal crowd put together from the Royal Great Grandmama down to this puling Royal Great Grand-Child. . . .

'Two hundred and fifty human beings, full of strong life in the morning, reduced to charred and blackened heaps of clay in the evening! Woe, woe unutterable everywhere all through that fair Welsh valley. Only those who have witnessed such scenes, as I have twice over, can realise what they mean. Only those who know, as I know, that these things are preventable and solely due to man's cupidity, can understand the bitterness of feeling which they awaken. We are a nation of hypocrites.'

Aflame with such thoughts, Hardie made his way to the House of Commons to hear Sir William Harcourt move an address of congratulation to Her Majesty on the birth of an heir to the Duke of York. Mr. Balfour had no sooner finished a speech of happy phrases when Hardie rose to enter his protest. A hush fell over the House, but the hush did not last long.

He began by saying that the resolution 'seeks to elevate to an importance which it does not deserve, an event of daily occurrence', and added, 'I have been delighted to learn that the child is a fairly healthy one and had I the opportunity of meeting its parents I should have been pleased indeed to join in the ordinary congratulations of the occasion. But when we are asked as a House of Commons representing the nation to join in the congratulations then in the interests of the House I take leave to protest. He went on:

'It is a matter of small concern to me whether the future ruler of the nation be the genuine article or a spurious imitation. Now Sir, this proposal has been made because a child has been born into the Royal Family. We have the right to ask what particular blessing the Royal Family conferred upon the nation that we should be asked to take part in the proceedings to-day. We have just heard it said that Her Majesty has ruled for over half a century. I would correct that, Sir, by saying that Her Majesty has reigned but not ruled. I remember, in reading about the proceedings in connection with the Jubilee, that one point made was that during the fifty years of Her Majesty's reign the Queen had not interfered in the affairs of the nation. That may be reigning but it is certainly not ruling.

'Then, there is the Prince of Wales. What high dignity has His Royal Highness conferred upon the nation?'

COLONEL SANDERSON (Armagh) rose to protest: 'I rise, Sir, for the purpose of moving that the hon. Member be no longer heard.'

SIR WM. HARCOURT: 'I hope that the hon. and gallant Member will not press his motion. I do not think it would tend to produce the result he desires and which I think we all desire—namely, the prevention of disorder.'

MR. KEIR HARDIE: 'I was about to observe that I know of nothing in the career of the Prince of Wales which commends him especially to me. The "fierce white light" which we are told "beats around the throne" sometimes reveals things in his career it would be better to keep covered. Sometimes we get glimpses of the Prince at the gaming tables, sometimes on the racecourse. His Royal Highness is Duke of Cornwall, and as such he draws £60,000 a year from the Duchy property in London, which is made up of some of the vilest slums.' (Cries of 'Question'.)

MR. SPEAKER: 'The hon. Member must keep to the terms of the resolution.'

MR. KEIR HARDIE: 'I will bow to the ruling, Sir, and proceed to the subject of the resolution. We are asked to rejoice because this child has been born, and that one day he will be called upon to rule over this great Empire. Up to the present time we have no means of knowing what his qualifications or fitness for that task may be. It certainly strikes me— I do not know how it strikes others—as rather strange that those who have so much to say about the hereditary element in another place should be so willing to endorse it in this particular instance. It seems to me that if it is a good argument to say that the hereditary element is bad in one case, it is equally good argument to say that it is bad in the other. From

his childhood onwards this boy will be surrounded by sycophants and
flatterers by the score. (Cries of "Oh! Oh!") A line will be drawn between
him and the people whom he is to be called upon some day to reign over.
In due course, following the precedent which has already been set, he
will be sent on a tour round the world, and probably rumours of a
morganatic alliance will follow (loud cries of "Oh!" "Order!" and
"Question!"), and the end of it all will be that the country will be called
upon to pay the bill. (Cries of "Divide" "Divide!").

'As a matter of principle, I protest against the motion being passed, and
if there is another Member of the House who share the principles I hold
I will carry my protest the length of a division. The Government will not
find an opportunity for a vote of condolence with the relatives of those
who are lying stiff and stark in a Welsh Valley, and, if that cannot be done
the motion before the House ought never to have been proposed either.
If it be for rank and title only that time and occasion can be found in
this House, then the sooner that truth is known outside the better for the
House itself. I will challenge a division on the motion, and if the forms of
the House permit, I will go to a division in the hope that some Member
at least will enter their protest against the mummery implied in a resolution
of this kind.'

MR. SPEAKER: 'The question is that a humble Address be presented
to Her Majesty on the birth of a son to His Royal Highness the Duke and
Her Royal Highness the Duchess of York.'

The putting of the question was followed by loud cries of 'Aye' from
all parts of the House, Mr. Keir Hardie alone replying in the negative.
Mr. Speaker again putting the question, Mr. Keir Hardie challenged
the statement. The House cleared for a division. On Mr. Speaker
again putting the question Mr. Keir Hardie repeated his negative, but
did not challenge Mr. Speaker's words, 'The Ayes have it.'

The Address was accordingly agreed to.

A writer in the *West Ham Herald,* describing the debate, wrote:

'I've been in a wild beast show at feeding time. I've been at a football
match when a referee gave a wrong decision. I've been at rowdy meetings
of the Shoreditch Vestry and the West Ham Corporation, but in all my
natural life I have never witnessed a scene like this. They howled and
yelled and screamed, but he stood his ground.'

When the Duke came to write his memoirs, half a century later, he
recalled that when he was born 'at least one grumpy voice made itself
heard'.

He added, 'The impress of Mr. Keir Hardie's doctrines now lie
heavy on Socialist Britain, and even as a prophet of Royal destiny he
has proved himself uncannily clairvoyant.'

But there were more truths than that in the speech that shocked the
House of Commons.

CHAPTER 7

I.L.P. 'THE LABOUR LEADER'

HARDIE'S stand in the House of Commons had given encouragement to those who believed the time had come for an independent Labour Party.

In Scotland there was already the Scottish Labour Party and in other parts of the country, especially in Lancashire and Yorkshire, there were groups who thought the time was ripe for a national organisation which would fight elections independently on a Socialist programme.

This had been strongly advocated by Robert Blatchford in *The Clarion* and by Joseph Burgess in *The Workman's Times*.

At the annual meeting of the T.U.C., held in Glasgow in September 1893, the resolution in favour of independent Labour representation which had been passed at three previous conferences was re-affirmed. Following this decision a meeting of delegates and others eager to see a new organisation was held and it was decided to call a national conference to discuss the setting up of a new party.

The Conference was called for Bradford on January 13th and 14th, 1893. Bradford was chosen because it was thought the most convenient centre for Scotland and the industrial north, from which most of the delegates would attend. It had been the centre of a Labour Church and Labour Club movement with radical traditions. Hardie and Burgess also held the view that it was better to hold the conference out of London, where it was less likely to be influenced by either the dogmatic Social Democratic Federation or the middle-class Fabian Society. Keir Hardie was elected to preside over the conference. One hundred and twenty-one delegates attended from branches of the Scottish Labour Party, Labour Clubs and trade unions, and a few delegates from the Social Democratic Federation and the Fabian Society. Bernard Shaw turned up and took part in the discussions after there had been some question about his credentials. Robert Blatchford

E

made the dramatic declaration, 'I regard Liberals and Tories as enemies of the people. When I say a man is my enemy I mean I hate him and will fight him to the death. I cannot understand why I should take that man's hand. I would consider it a stain on the Labour Party to have any dealings with the Liberals. I would as soon have dealings with the devil.' Ben Tillett attacked 'the Continental revolutionaries' in a speech which showed Bernstein, the German representative of 'Vorwarts' how insular the British Labour Movement was. But although the conference showed no enthusiasm for the doctrinaire socialism of the S.D.F. it declared that the objective of the Party should be 'To secure the collective and communal ownership of all the means of production, distribution and exchange'. An amendment to this which defined the objective of the Party 'To secure the separate representation and protection of Labour interests on public bodies' was defeated by 91 votes to 16, the minority consisting of trades council and trade union delegates.

Hardie, recalling this later, wrote: 'This, I hope, disposes once and for all the fiction that the I.L.P. was ever a half-way house between Liberalism and Socialism. Had it been such I would never have been its chairman.'

The conference adopted the following programme: Abolition of child labour under 14 years of age; a legal eight-hour maximum working day; State provision for aged, sick and disabled workers, and for widows and orphans; abolition of indirect taxation, and taxation to extinction of all unearned incomes; work for the unemployed; every proposal for extending political rights and democratising the system of government.

The new party was to be called the Independent Labour Party, only a small minority voting for the more aggressive-sounding name of Socialist Labour Party.

The Times gave lengthy reports of the proceedings and pointed out that a new force had emerged in British politics which was likely to be a danger to the Liberal Party.

Hardie had been asked to write an article on the I.L.P. Conference to the *New Review* which had been founded by a group of Liberals.

He explained why the I.L.P. had come into existence. 'The mighty unseen forces which make for progress have decreed the commencement of a new era and the Liberal Party is endeavouring to live and flourish on what were the big reforms of twenty-five years ago.

Liberalism, even in its most advanced form, is a quarter of a century behind the times.' He went on to stress that while political reforms were necessary, a change in the economic system which created unemployment and poverty was also necessary and the Liberal Party showed no sign of realising this. 'The I.L.P.,' he concluded, 'is the outcome. It sees and chafes at the impotence of Liberalism either to deal in drastic fashion with political reforms or even to understand the new desire for economic change.

'Our aim is to create a genuinely Independent Labour Party to take charge of the revolution to which economic conditions are leading us, and its object is to build up an industrial commonwealth in which none will suffer want because of the over abundance of others.'

The formation of the I.L.P. and the interest taken in his activities in Parliament encouraged Hardie to embark upon a venture which he had been contemplating since he had changed the name of his monthly journal, *The Miner,* into *The Labour Leader.*

Why not change it into a weekly?

He could edit it from London and it could be printed and published in Glasgow where there was already the nucleus of a circulation. He decided to take the risk. *The Labour Leader* made its first appearance as a weekly on March 31st, 1894. The London office was at 53 Fleet Street, in an ancient building which had been designed by Sir Christopher Wren. 'The floor sloped, the walls bulged, but the chimney drew,' wrote David Lowe. 'The bulges in the walls were flattened and the office furniture was designed to suit the slope of the floor.' 'You can call if you are not over sixteen stone,' was Hardie's invitation to provincial readers. In Glasgow the office was situated in 66 Brunswick Street, and the printing house address was 48 New Wynd.

Bruce Glasier, who was more of a poet than a practical journalist, took charge at Glasgow and Hardie himself, with some assistance from London Socialist friends, did the editing from Fleet Street. Altogether the weekly wage bill apart from the printing came to £750 a year.

'I determined when the idea of starting a paper first took definite shape in my mind,' wrote Hardie in the first number, 'I would make it worthy of the Labour Movement.' 'There was no lack of journals in London or elsewhere catering for the working man,' he went on. 'These start from the assumption that the working man is a lower order of creation solely interested in the details of divorce, breach of promise and affiliation cases . . . I have had to stop taking in one

democratic paper in my day because my boy was getting old enoug
to read and I did not care to have him polluted by the nasty stuff
contained. I will not insult the class to which I am proud to belong b
offering them anything which would tend to degenerate young or old

The first issue of the new weekly contained a typical article fro
Cunninghame-Graham in which he contemptuously dismissed th
Liberals as 'the free trade, cheap labour Liberals, the modern Nor
conformist sweaters, the party bolstered up with the money of soa
and mustard men'. 'Liberalism, having done good work in its day,' I
concluded, 'must decay, as newer issues needing newer and mor
vigorous men appear. Therefore Socialism, which being of a differen
constitution can never recede, is the hope of all men.'

When *The Labour Leader* began as a weekly, another by-electio
was pending in Mid-Lanark, with Robert Smillie standing as th
Independent Labour candidate, and Hardie devoted a leading artic
outlining the familiar arguments why the working class should vo
Labour.

The new paper started off by selling 57,000 copies and had a bac
page of advertisements. Hardie went to Glasgow to see the first issu
off the press. The folding machine broke down every ninety minut
and ultimately the papers had to be folded by hand with the enthusia
tic editorial staff, including Hardie, taking their coats off and joinin
in the work.

But the new weekly had been launched and Keir Hardie had ever
reason to be gratified at its reception although he was to discover late
that it was easier to start a Socialist paper than to continue running
when the advertisers discovered exactly what it was.

Robert Smillie was heavily defeated at Mid-Lanark, the Irish vo
going to the Liberal. *The Labour Leader* consoled itself with the fa
that his vote of 1,221 almost doubled that of Keir Hardie's five yea
before.

This election was to be the pattern of other by-elections that th
I.L.P. were to fight. An I.L.P. candidate always meant splitting th
Liberal vote and it was not to be wondered at that the Libera
regarded Keir Hardie and the I.L.P. with apprehension, especiall
when they saw in *The Labour Leader* that, far from being discourage
Hardie was appealing for an election fund of £20,000 which coul
enable the I.L.P. to fight 80 seats at the General Election.

The I.L.P. tactics of running Socialist candidates at by-elections an orcing three-cornered fights irrespective of what happened to the Liberals had become one of the most interesting developments in British politics and the London Fabian Society, some of whose leaders believed in the policy of permeating the Liberal Party rather than opposing it, invited Keir Hardie to address it.

Ramsay MacDonald presided and Bernard Shaw and the Webbs were present. Hardie dealt with the political situation and went on to argue at length for the I.L.P. point of view. He had become a member of the Fabian Society himself and paid his tribute to the educational work it was doing. But he went on to attack the idea that it was possible to permeate the Liberal Party and capture it for Socialism. 'What was the Liberal Party,' he asked, 'that they were invited to capture?

'It had great wealth behind it and social influence, for he noticed that even the Dukes were coming back to it: they recognised it was a harmless sort of animal, not likely to do them such injury. It had behind it a powerful and unscrupulous press, and the legal intellects were at its service and it used them in thwarting the path of the workers. They were asked to capture this party, upheld and supported by such men, and use them for their own purpose to bring about their own destruction.'

Hardie went on to examine and reject the Fabian Society's theory that the Liberal Party could be permeated and captured for Socialism.

'What they required,' he said, 'was not a permeating policy not pledging Liberal candidates to support that or the other measure, but uncompromising hostility to Liberalism and Toryism . . . From all points of view the line of action which the I.L.P. and the S.D.F. had pursued was the only consistent line for Socialists who meddled with politics at all. To perpetuate the fiction that Liberalism, any more than Toryism, was going to help to realise Socialism was but to play into the hands of monopoly . . . The Liberals would shortly discover that without the growing Socialist Party they were helpless. They would then come their way or go to the Tory way and defend privilege and monopoly. The only possible policy which would make for the union of all sections of Socialists was resolute, fighting independence until they had realised the object they had in view.'

'In conclusion he wished to say to the superior persons who bossed the Fabian Society in London that they were rapidly bringing upon themselves the position of being generals without followers.

'He spoke with knowledge when he said that members of the Fabian Societies in the country were as strongly I.L.P. as the I.L.P. itself. If they, in London, cared to stand alone and fill the gap in the interests of Liberalism, they were welcome, but he hoped they would find that the Society to which they belonged which had done so much for Socialism in the past, would not tolerate the spoiling of its good work by playing into the hands of the enemies of Socialism, no matter how plausible might be the arguments put forth.'

Hardie's outspoken remarks were punctuated with applause, so he must have had a good many sympathisers even among the London Fabians.

At question time Bernard Shaw asked if the I.L.P. disagreed with the latest Fabian Manifesto, critical of the Liberals, entitled *To Your Tents O Israel!* which was critical of the Liberal's Newcastle programme.

Hardie replied that he agreed with the Fabian manifesto but that the Fabians were not prepared to carry their criticisms to the logical conclusion of opposing the Liberals.

Mrs. Webb noted that Hardie had made 'an unfavourable impression' on her.

Hardie for his part was not enthusiastic about Mrs. Webb and regarded her as a middle-class intellectual who had tried to be patronising. He got on better with Bernard Shaw, who had realised by now that the I.L.P. was not another edition of the S.D.F. Bernard Shaw, however, was not as convinced as Hardie was that Socialism would gain much by capturing the trade unions. He argued that there were so many Tory working men in the trade unions, and so many reactionary trade union leaders, that they might turn out to be a Conservative influence.

Hardie had a new kind of audience when he went to speak at Oxford University. Balliol College refused to allow him to speak within its precincts but Manchester College came to the rescue and he had a good audience.

He wrote:

'There were some hundreds of young men just about to begin life in earnest and who amongst them have an ideal which will carry them safely across the dirty places of life's road.

'And yet, in the days to come they will be the leaders of the intellectual life of the nation. At Oxford they will learn all that books have to teach. They will also get to know many things not to be gleaned from books:

but they will go out into the great world as unfitted for their task as if they were inhabitants who had suddenly been transplanted from another planet . . .

'These students, like all young men, are full of generous impulses, and mean to do the right thing. The sense of honour and chivalry is strong. But these qualities do not make good the lack of that experience which can only be gained from having lived with and among, and been part of, the common people. For, after all, a nation is not founded on its aristocracy, nor even its prosperous middle class, but on the poor o'erlaboured wights who to-day require to beg a brother of the earth to give them leave to toil. It is here where the philosophy of Socialism teaches a more profound truth than that taught in any of the accepted schools.'

Hardie thought that the students at Oxford were isolated and insulated from the realities of the outside world.

'For generations the very atmosphere of the place has been saturated with the teachings and the air has rung with controversies of the intellectual giants of their day. And yet, smoking the pipe of peace in the rooms of a young giant, heir to an estate, the blare of the Salvation Army trumpets came grating harshly on the senses, and later in the evening the loud, coarse laugh of the outcast was borne up on the chilly night air. What have the teachers and guides of English youths been about at Oxford all these centuries that the Salvation Army became a necessity of the religious life of the people, and why are there, at the end of the nineteenth century of the Christian era, girls who require to sell their souls into a bondage of shame that they may obtain bread for the body? These questions await reply.'

Later in the same month he visited Cambridge. 'Oxford,' he wrote. 'must look to her laurels.

'There was a great crowd, and an audience which, if not friendly, was far from being hostile. There had been rumours of organised disturbances, but as is often the case, these proved foundationless.

'The questions were of the kind one associates with places where the propaganda has been neglected. It is astonishing how old dogmas retain their hold over the minds of the young as well as the old. Some of the young men present were alarmed lest "capital" should be driven away by Socialism. Others were afraid that if interest were abolished the stimulus to industry would disappear. One bumptious person walked ostentatiously on to the platform amidst the cheers of the exuberant spirits present who expected to see some fun as a result. He wanted to know whether I desired to see more working-men than middle-upper-class persons in Parliament, and seemed considerably astonished at my temerity and perversity in saying that I did. He collapsed completely under the audacity of the proposal.

'After the meeting the fellows of Queen's, where I went to spend an hour, gathered in the Quadrangle and sang, "FOR HE'S A JOLLY GOOD FELLOW", after which there were tobacco, coffee and talk.'

In the House of Commons he continued to use every opportunity to draw attention to the treatment given to the privileged and the poor. He could find nobody to second his amendment in opposition to the resolution for a pension of £4,000 a year to the late Speaker (Lord Peel).

Hardie had continued to raise the question of the unemployed on every possible occasion and finally in 1895 his pertinacity was rewarded by the Government's decision to set up a committee of inquiry into the problem of unemployment. He again put down as an amendment to the address on the Queen's Speech the same amendment that he had moved at the beginning of the Parliament. Hardie's attitude in the House of Commons and his agitation in the country had made an impression on public opinion and the Liberal Government came to the conclusion that it would be unwise to take up a purely negative attitude.

It was announced that the committee would be set up and Hardie was given the assurance that it would get to work immediately and publish an interim report. He had forced the Government's hand. A grant of £100,000 to relieve unemployment for the period until the Committee report was announced. A sum which Hardie thought was ridiculously small was announced. But the Government had been forced to depart from the position that Gladstone had taken up in 1893 that unemployment was not a subject with which Parliament should be called to deal.

Parliament was dissolved shortly afterwards and Hardie was not there to continue with his agitation.

But he had brought the question of unemployment to the forefront of politics and had earned the title of 'Member for the Unemployed'.

Hardie had looked forward to the 1895 General Election with confidence, believing that he would be returned again and that some of the twenty-eight candidates that the I.L.P. had decided to run would be returned also.

He was over-optimistic and over-estimated the strength of the I.L.P. The time had not come when the British working class was prepared to abandon its faith in the Liberals and return a new party which had no friend in the daily Press and had been branded as extremist, Socialist and revolutionary. The Liberal penny Press specially concentrated on Hardie and denounced him as the wild man of British politics.

This had its effect at West Ham. His speeches were boycotted and the Liberal *Daily Chronicle,* which was widely read in the constituency, attacked him in a leading article on the day of the poll.

The Liberals themselves did not run a candidate but they worked for the Tory and did everything in their power to swing the Irish vote away from Hardie.

A meeting of Irish voters was addressed by two local priests and a resolution was passed, which called upon the Irish to refrain from voting for him, and a special leaflet was circulated.

Hardie replied in an eve of the poll speech at Canning Town.

He dealt with the leaflet that had been issued by the Irish priests.

'This handbill is issued,' he said, 'in the name of the Irishmen of South West Ham.

'There is one section who will not obey it. Those Irishmen of West Ham who are true to the memory of their great leader, Charles Stewart Parnell. The Irishmen who think more of their country men rotting in prisons than they do of the Liberal Government will not obey.

'The Irishmen of West Ham are asked by the priests either to abstain or to vote for Major Banes against me. The Handbill contains at the bottom this statement: "Irishmen, act on this and do not allow Keir Hardie to put your country at the tail of the Socialist programme." Well if Major Banes is returned by Irish votes, the Irish movement will be dragged at the heels of the capitalist and landlord movement, the publican and "Free Labour" movements. Are you Irishmen of West Ham prepared to drag the cause of Ireland through the mire?

' "Do you say that it is a case of Home Rule first? I can understand an Irishman in Connemara saying that, but here in the South West Ham it is Labour first. I want to see the English Democracy stretch hands across the channel and join with you in a common crusade against your common enemy—the landlord and the capitalist. I want to see the people of these Islands united in one great final campaign for the overthrow of economic injustice." '

Hardie had enthusiastic meetings but a large number of Irish followed the advice of the priests and did not vote for him. The Tory vote went up by 714 and Hardie's vote went down by 1,293.

The result was:

MAJOR BANES (Tory)	...	...	4,750
KEIR HARDIE (Socialist)	...	...	3,975
Majority	...	...	785

In a letter to the South West Ham electors he thanked them and explained his defeat. 'By a combination as strange as ever was witnessed in politics I failed to secure re-election. Every section of the community contributed its quota to the majority by which my opponent was returned. Teetotallers worked hand in hand with publicans; some Trade Unionists with free labourers, Liberals with Tories; priests and professed Home Rulers with Coercionists; and all to secure the defeat of the representative of Labour.

'On the other hand, Churchmen and Nonconformists, Socialists, most of the Trade Unionists, and all that is best and worth having, rallied to the cause of humanity as represented for the moment in myself. I thank my friends for the zeal with which they worked. The triumph of our Movement has not been delayed, we have but purified it by purging it of unworthy elements.

'Let the friends of our cause be of good cheer.'

The I.L.P. candidates did not do well in the election. Twenty-eight candidates went to the poll. All were defeated. Two prominent Liberals, John Morley and Sir William Harcourt, had lost their seats as a result of the I.L.P. splitting the vote and the Liberals had lost votes through the I.L.P. urging abstention where there were Labour candidates.

Ramsay MacDonald had stood as an I.L.P. candidate at Southampton but had only polled 867 votes in an electorate of 14,000.

MacDonald was bitterly disappointed that he had not been returned at the first time of asking. In his biography published in 1945, Viscount Samuel, then Herbert Samuel, a promising young Liberal, quotes a letter that MacDonald wrote to him on August 16th, 1895, from Lossiemouth. MacDonald then seems to have been on more friendly terms with Samuel than with Hardie. He wrote:

' "Don't mistake our position because Hardie, by his own incapacity lost his seat and none of us being scapegoats got in." The letter ended: "Meanwhile the party of progressive ideas is being so badly handled that it is almost suicide to join it. Off to golf. Always yours. J. R. Macdonald." '

What MacDonald meant by Hardie's 'incapacity' was not quite clear. He had perhaps been over-confident at South West Ham and had spent some of the time helping I.L.P. candidates in other parts of the country. It was not Hardie's 'incapacity' that had lost South West Ham but his attitude towards the Liberals which had resulted in the alienation of the Irish. Had Hardie compromised with the Liberals in

Hardie and John Burns. A cartoon from the 'Westminster Gazette'.

the 1892-1895 Parliament he might have saved his seat. But in that case he would have become like John Burns—just another Lib-Lab. At the beginning of his letter MacDonald had complained to Samuel: 'We didn't have the Liberals. They threw us out and slammed the door in our faces. A little generosity on their part at the election would have gone a long way in building a bridge of understanding between the parties.' MacDonald seems then to have been thinking of 'bridge building' then—a rather ricketty bridge it turned out to be in later years. 'The Liberals,' he continued, 'chose to stick to their purses and official votes.'

If MacDonald had entertained the delusion that the Liberals were prepared to finance independent-minded Labour men and Socialists,

Hardie certainly had not. He knew his Liberals. At that election the Liberals had no more wanted MacDonald in Parliament than they had wanted him. So MacDonald had reluctantly to conclude: 'There can be no going back now, unless of course circumstances change greatly and then the change will not be so much on our side (at least of those who have not plunged into the excesses of the I.L.P.) as on the Liberal side.'

What MacDonald called Hardie's 'incapacity' was his refusal to compromise with the Liberals, who according to MacDonald's own story were not ready to compromise anyway, except on their own terms.

Hardie's reaction to the election defeat of 1895 showed the difference in the character of the two men. 'Despondency?' wrote Hardie. 'No, no. Rather proud, savage elation. Half the battle won first time and that too the most difficult half. But we must learn to fight elections.'

John Burns, who had kept in with the Liberals, was quite pleased at Hardie's defeat, took up a 'I told you so' attitude and described the I.L.P.'s election defeat, which had cost £4,000, as 'the most costly funeral since Napoleon's'.

Mrs. Sidney Webb wrote: 'The I.L.P. has completed its suicide. Its policy of abstention and deliberate wrecking has proved to be futile and absurd.' Altogether the I.L.P. had polled 44,594 votes. Bernard Shaw took the view that 'the party which, on the whole, had polled so well, had justified its campaign'. A young journalist, J. L. Garvin, writing in the *Fortnightly Review*, expressed a view that was not widely shared when he wrote that the results pointed 'not to the elimination of the Independent Labour Party from practical politics but to its permanence as an increasingly powerful and disturbing factor in British politics'.

CHAPTER 8

OUT OF PARLIAMENT

HARDIE accepted an invitation from the American Labour Day Committee to attend the Chicago Labour Congress on September 2nd, 1895. It was a welcome change after the election campaign and a respite from the worries of *The Labour Leader*. A group of friends came to St. Enoch's station, Glasgow, to see him off, and as the train went out, sang *Auld Lang Syne* to the disgust of the Sheriff of Ayrshire who ostentatiously put his fingers to his ears and muttered uncomplimentary remarks before leaving the compartment in disgust at Kilmarnock. But this was more than compensated for at Liverpool by another hearty send-off from the local Socialists who not only marched in procession to the quayside but chartered a tug which accompanied the *Campania* some miles out to sea.

He was accompanied by Frank Smith, a Londoner, who had been prominently associated with the Salvation Army, and who was to become Hardie's lifelong and devoted friend.

These were the days of mass emigration to America and many people had come to the quayside to bid their relatives farewell. Hardie noted in his diary:

'Looking from the deck of the *Campania* as she majestically steamed out of her moorings at the sea of faces on the quay—extending over half a mile—one fell a moralising. Some on the ship were on pleasure bent, but others were going forth heavy of heart to seek a new home across the waves. Their native land had no place for them, no room for them. They were being driven out as cumberers of the ground, cleared out as lumber —rubbish. And yet these young fellows with their well knit frames, and frank open countenances were worth their room and keep.

'Britain, however, the prolific mother of empires, has no room for them, and here they are, going to other lands where labour is not yet the drug in the market it is at home.

'Poor mother! And poor wife, who looks through her blinding tears at the husband and the father of her children. He is going out in the hope

77

that he may one day be able to send for her. And poor country, which thus acts the stepmother to her sons and daughters.'

Another note ran:

'What a microcosm of society we are! The saloon passengers, railed and fenced off from the rest of their fellows include a duke and duchess, an archbishop, a bishop, and any member of respectabilities, clergymen, professors, and agitators. Among the steerage passengers were a great many Italians, the women with their kerchiefs and olive skins; the children dirty, ragged, unkempt, curly black-eyed urchins: the men with their shoulder blankets and their gaunt eager-looking faces making a motley group. The Britishers in the steerage were mostly Irish, though there were a sprinkling of Englishmen and Scotsmen.

'All those are going out as outcasts from their native land.'

Hardie and Smith spent fifteen weeks in the States. They spent nearly a week in New York, where Hardie addressed several meetings and then went on to Chicago. They visited Eugene V. Debs, the American Socialist who was in prison on a charge arising out of the part he played in the Pullman strike. They travelled as far west as San Francisco speaking at trade union and Socialist meetings en route.

At San Francisco, Hardie addressed a meeting of the local Municipal Socialist League, where a Scottish Presbyterian minister took the chair.

Among those who attended was the Mayor of San Francisco, known as the 'Silver King' from the fact that he had amassed millions of dollars out of silver speculation.

He approached Hardie with a view to enlisting his help in a campaign in Britain for popularising bi-metalism which would have meant a big demand for silver. If Hardie would persuade the I.L.P. to declare in favour of bi-metalism he would give him a cheque for 100,000 dollars, at that time about £20,000. And if he would make a pronouncement as Chairman of the I.L.P. at its annual conference which could be used in Bryan's presidential campaign he would give him 20,000 dollars for that.

' "He very candidly explained," wrote Hardie, "that it was a purely business proposal, and no questions were to be asked as to how the money was disposed of. Smith and I laughed across the table at each other at the very astute way in which the whole thing had been led up to, and the Rev. Mr. Scott who had introduced the Mayor, thought I was a good bit of a fool in thus laughing the idea out of court.

' "The Mayor looked blankly the surprise he felt. That a Labour leader should turn such a business proposition down was beyond the grasp of his comprehension." '

Hardie returned from America to find that the I.L.P. had not faded away after its overwhelming defeat at the General Election. Within a week after his arrival at home he received forty-three letters asking him to lecture in different parts of the country. 'Not this year, comrades, at any rate,' replied Hardie (it was December 14th). 'Not that I mean to shirk my share of the work' . . . He went on to explain why he was compelled to charge the modest sum of £3 10s. as a fee for lecturing. 'I have endeavoured, not with much success, to clear my out-of-pocket expenses from these talking engagements. Train fares and travel mean money, so does postage, so does the loss of time involved in connection with the work, which in the case of a man living by his pen, as I do, comes to a serious item. The return journey between Scotland and London costs about £3 10s. in fares and food. To some parts of the Kingdom it costs more, to some less. I found two years ago that a fixed uniform fee charge of £3 3s. for all meetings in the provinces enables me to meet all expenses. The charge covers everything—hotel bill, travelling and all other outlays. It is not a big one, and can with a little management be raised from the meeting. When branches have any difficulty in the matter there is an end to it, as I have no idea of placing any burden upon them. When I am living in Glasgow or London those places have all the meetings they want, and there is no question of fee or expenses.'

Every political columnist short of an idea or paragraph, vilified, attacked, sneered at and abused Keir Hardie. This was so general and universal that when something appeared moderately fair about him he used to ask, 'What have I done wrong now?'

People came to his meetings out of curiosity, to see him and to listen to him. They came expecting to hear a fiery mob orator, a tub-thumping demagogue, and to be entertained. They found instead that they were listening to an earnest speaker whose sincerity commanded their respect, who spoke faultless English and who argued his case reasonably and sensibly, who scorned rhetorical tricks, did not tell funny stories, nor march up and down the platform tearing a passion to shreds. There was something about the man that made them listen to him. By the time he had finished they realised that he was not at all like the Keir Hardie that had been vilified by the Press.

This man had a mission and a message. Many of those who had come to scoff remained to start a branch of the I.L.P.

Among them were active trade unionists and co-operators, Radicals, disillusioned with the Liberal Party, idealists and intellectuals prepared to join together to run Socialist candidates at Parliamentary by-elections and municipal elections, to sell *The Labour Leader* and other Socialist papers and pamphlets, and to carry on the work of converting and educating others.

And it was not just another political party that Hardie was out to establish, it was not just an organisation for getting people into Parliament, it was a campaign against poverty and unemployment and social injustice, a crusade for the establishment of Socialism and a new society.

To build up the I.L.P. had now become the dominating purpose of Keir Hardie's life. He was out of Parliament and there would not be another General Election for five years. He recognised that he had been optimistic about the immediate success of the I.L.P. as a new political party. But that did not daunt him. He did not want to get back to Parliament again alone. Indeed he had felt 'a sense of relief', as he put it, 'at having been released from three years' solitary confinement'. He would carry on the work of agitation in the country.

By his voice and pen he would do his utmost to build up a movement which would not only capture Parliament but lead the way to a social revolution in Britain. For the next twenty years Keir Hardie was Britain's most tireless and determined agitator.

In addition to his speaking in the country, he continued his editorship of *The Labour Leader* at Glasgow. David Lowe, a Socialist journalist who had come to join him from Dundee, did most of the actual work of bringing out the paper. Hardie wrote weekly articles and comments on current affairs. He persuaded prominent people to contribute to it and whenever he was not on the spot in Glasgow, sent on instructions and advice.

On March 28th, 1896, he was able to boast that *The Labour Leader*, on entering its third year, 'is now paying its way. That is to say with the help of these contributors who serve their cause by their pen without fee or reward, the sales cover the cost of production.

'So far as I know this beats the record in Labour journalism in this country.'

Keeping *The Labour Leader* going was indeed a feat in itself. It was he who had begun it and it was he who shouldered the responsibility of keeping it going. At one time he mortgaged his modest life insurance policy to pay the printer's bill. Once, the Ayrshire Miners' Union, which had the greatest confidence in him, showed it by helping him out of his difficulties by lending him £100 which he soon repaid. Sometimes well-to-do friends like T. D. Benson, the estate agent of Manchester, who had become treasurer of the I.L.P., Adam Birkmyre, the mill owner of Glasgow, and Dr. G. B. Clark came to the rescue and so in one way or another *The Labour Leader* bills were paid and the paper came out.

Hardie had to travel a great deal and much of his weekly writing was done in the train and 'in dreary waiting-rooms at God-forsaken junctions'.

David Lowe preserved many of the letters that Hardie sent him with his copy. From Newcastle on October 29th, 1898, he wrote:

'You might go over this carefully and make corrections and amendments. It is 2.30 a.m. and I got drenched returning from Stockton, and having no change and no fire in my room I am beginning to feel the effects.

' "Hardie," wrote Lowe, "was careless about his health and seemed to think his iron constitution could stand any strain. Perhaps the pit conditions under which he had worked in his early manhood made him indifferent to weather. Looking back on these days I cannot remember him ever wearing an overcoat. Usually a heavy woollen muffler slung loosely around his throat was his extra protection against cold. On a bitter frosty night and very late—I once conveyed him to the railway station from whence he was facing a long wintry overnight journey in jacket and muffler. Having a heavy ulster, I took him in hand and literally forced him to use it, which he did more to please me, I fancy, than out of concern for himself. In that letter one can see him sitting alone in a bedroom of some cheap hotel writing through the early hours of the morning wet to the skin in view of a fireless grate." '

He had an enormous correspondence, most of which he dealt with himself.

He coped with it as best he could, but he sometimes found it necessary to apologise in *The Labour Leader* for what were after all under the circumstances no long delays.

Hardie had declared that the I.L.P. would fight every by-election it could. The first opportunity came with a vacancy in North Aberdeen. It was decided to nominate Tom Mann, the engineer and fiery orator, who had become the organising secretary of the I.L.P. In *The Labour Leader*, Hardie appealed for £300 and himself went north to assist. There were only nine days for the campaign but Mann polled 2,497 votes. The Liberal majority dropped from 3,458 to 430. 'That,' commented Hardie in his notes, 'effectively disposes of the pessimist. It is for us to prove our capacity to fight'.

The Liberals had now to face the possibility of elections becoming three-cornered fights. The nomination of an I.L.P. candidate might lose them the seat. This, of course, did not worry Hardie. He had lost all confidence in the Liberal Party and welcomed these opportunities for educating the working-class voters to the need of building up a Party of their own.

He, himself, took on the candidature at a hopeless by-election in East Bradford in July 1896. 'This,' he wrote, 'is a vacancy which the I.L.P. must contest. Not as one who would but as one who must, that is the guiding principle, and so I go'.

He was obviously not expecting to win. 'But,' he added, 'we will make a fight of it and the I.L.P. has never yet had occasion to regret its by-election results. Neither will it be in East Bradford. All other engagements fixed or in process of arrangement are hereby cancelled until the campaign is over.'

He and his band of volunteers addressed many open-air meetings. Among them were Bernard Shaw, Tom Mann, Bruce Glasier, Joseph Burgess. Hardie was at the bottom of the poll.

The result was:

GREVILLE (Tory)	...	...	...	4,921
BILLSON (Liberal)	...	...	...	4,526
HARDIE (I.L.P.)	...	...	...	1,953

The Tory major had won by the small majority of 395 over the Liberal manufacturer. As a result Hardie wrote in *The Labour Leader*:

'For concentrated bitterness the conquest stands unrivalled. Curses loud and deep, were, according to the London correspondent of the *Bradford Observer* showered upon my head in official Liberal circles when the result was made known. That I don't wonder at. Liberalism was fighting for its existence. The official ghouls of the T. P. O'Connor type who grew rich by abusing the workers whilst the Liberal sweater robs his victims had staked their all in West Bradford. "Keir Hardie had to be fought,' said T. P. O'Connor, in his account of the election. It was not Captain Greville who had to be fought by the Liberals. I could have done that and done it handsomely. But it was not the Tory that had to be fought—it was Keir Hardie!

'I hope the official Liberals are satisfied with the result! They have secured the return of the Tory aristocrat, heir to a rent-roll of £18,000 and a seat in the House of Lords.

'Flouted, jeered at, blackguarded, libelled, lied about, the I.L.P. has nevertheless grown until it is indispensable to the Liberals. The moment it becomes so, offers a compromise and arrangements begin to be made. They fought us in the past because they hated us and our principles; they hate us and our principles still, but they must pretend otherwise, else they can't get office. If they had believed in our principles in the past, they would have supported them, which they didn't; if they believed in them now, they would come and join us, which they don't. Sit firm is the word.'

Once again the Irish Nationalist vote had gone against him. One of the Irish Nationalist M.P.s declared that he would prefer to vote for the Devil than Keir Hardie.

But Hardie had his Irish supporters, too. James Connolly, later to be shot in the Easter rebellion of 1916, had become a strong supporter of Hardie and contributed a series of articles, 'Ireland for the Irish', in *The Labour Leader*. Hard-up as Hardie was, he lent Connolly £25 to start a paper, *The Workers' Republic*, in Dublin.

At Barnsley, Pete Curran, an Irishman, stood as I.L.P. candidate but was heavily defeated. Every by-election meant a financial crisis for the I.L.P. Hardie told in later years how they raised the money to fight Barnsley:

'A vacancy occurred at Barnsley and the National Council of the Party had a meeting to consider it. We had not one penny in the funds; in fact we were in debt. There was only one small struggling I.L.P. branch in the constituency, which was many miles in extent, and included about a score of towns and villages. I was deputed by the council to visit Barnsley and consult with the local members about the vacancy. The meeting was held in a small evil smelling upper room and there were present fourteen members all told. The election we knew, would cost three or four hundred pounds, and I suggested that the first thing to be done was to find out what funds could be raised. Each member present was asked to guarantee a certain sum which he would raise by hook or by crook before election day and when these promises were all totalled up, we found we had sums promised amounting in all to £2 12s. 6d.

'A majority of the members were against fighting until one comrade, a Swiss, who had been in a good way of business but was then earning his living as a working jeweller drew off a massive solitaire diamond ring which he was wearing and putting it on the table said, "There, that will fetch £25 in any pawn shop; that is my contribution to the fight."

'That settled the matter, and we straightway adopted Pete Curran as the candidate, and the next day the campaign was in full swing. Every parson, in the constituency, every newspaper, every trade union official of any standing was against us. We were stoned by the miners, who formed the bulk of the electors, and hooted by women and children in the streets. We had to be our own chairman at meetings, and seldom found a

83

supporter with sufficient courage to move the resolution of confidence in the candidate.

'But we went through with the contest, polling over 1,000 votes, and to-day the Barnsley division is almost solid for Socialism. It was thus, by clean hard fighting, leaving consequences to look after themselves, that the I.L.P. was built up.'

Tom Mann was selected to fight Halifax by the Halifax Trades and Labour Council.

Two of the Liberal-Labour M.P.s went to Halifax to speak for Billson, the Liberal manufacturer. Hardie drew attention to the fact that both of them sat in the House of Commons as Trade Unionists. One of them was Henry Broadhurst, the Secretary to the Parliamentary Committee of the Trade Union Congress, and another old enemy, Charles Fenwick, was the paid representative of the Northumberland miners.

Hardie wrote:

'I put a straight question to the trade unionists of Leicester and Wansbeck. Did they in voting for Broadhurst and Fenwick ever expect to find them using their position to oppose the return to Parliament of a fellow unionist? When a strike is declared the trade unionist who goes back to work is called a blackleg. Are not Broadhurst and Fenwick blacklegging at Halifax?

'Those questions will not bear shirking. In a straight-forward fight with Liberal and Tory, Mr. Broadhurst may earn the twenty-five pounds a week, which was at one time, at least, paid him for speaking for the Liberal, but where there is a genuine trade unionist in the field the trade unionist who opposes him is playing a traitor to the cause of Labour. That is what these men have done.'

Tom Mann was defeated as usual, polling 2,000, but the action of the Lib-Labs had caused considerable resentment. Billson, the lawyer and company promoter, had been elected with their support.

Hardie elaborated his cause against the Lib-Labs in a further long article which was reproduced and widely distributed throughout the country in a leaflet called *Trade Union Politics*.

' "These men," he declared, "are sent to Parliament to represent Trade Unionists. They are paid for representing trade unionism in the House of Commons. At Halifax they became the hirelings of the Liberal manufacturer and lawyer."

'In America, there is a set of professional Labour politicians, whose services are hired by one or the other of the political parties. Republicans and Democrats have exiled their "Fakers", as these men are called. Are we to have a similar class in this country?'

Hardie recalled that Broadhurst had received shares in the Brunner

Mond Company for his services at the time when the workers were working twelve hours a day, and went on:

'There is a good reason why Broadhurst, Fenwick, Wilson, Pickard, etc. oppose Tom Mann. If we succeed, their comfortable fat sinecures are gone. In Parliament they would disappear. In opposing the I.L.P. they are fighting for their very existence. They are in Parliament to represent Labour. But how do they do it? By a smug, obsequious imitation of respectability. Above all things they must be like "the gentlemen" with whom they associate—like them in dress, in habits, and in manners. This is not Labour representation, it is the betrayal of Labour interests and it is because their caste is in danger that these men turn their backs on the Trade Unionists of Halifax and elsewhere and support a man whose only object in seeking admission to Parliament is to enable him and his class, the more effectually to fleece the workers of the country.'

This was damaging to the Lib-Labs, both in their own constituencies and in their own unions. Those who read *Trade Union Politics* found difficulty in answering Keir Hardie's case that the time had come for Trade Unionists to have their own Party in the House of Commons.

The position of the Lib-Labs was slowly and surely being undermined.

CHAPTER 9

CAMPAIGNS FOR THE
BOTTOM DOG

HARDIE'S home was still at Old Cumnock in Ayrshire. There he had succeeded in building a house of his own. He had known what it was to be evicted and he had long wished to have a home where his wife and three children could live in security and from which he could not be driven. One of his supporters and admirers was a wealthy Port Glasgow businessman named Adam Birkmyre. He knew that Hardie was poor and also proud. He took the risk of rebuff and asked Hardie if he could help him financially. Hardie declined an offer of money but when Birkmyre approached him again he said he would accept a loan in order to build a home from which no landlord could evict him. Birkmyre offered to give him the money but Hardie insisted that he wished to pay the money back and it was finally agreed that it should be an interest-free loan of £600 with which Hardie would build his house, the money to be repaid over a period of years.

With the money Hardie acquired a site at Cumnock on the main road between Kilmarnock and Dumfries and built the house which he called Lochnorris, the name of an old ruined castle owned by the Marquis of Bute. It had a garden which sloped down to the River Lugar which had been immortalised by Burns. This was to be Hardie's home, his retreat, when he could snatch time to be at home, for his life was to become a long series of pilgrimages and wanderings, and he found little time for relaxation and rest. But he was always glad to arrive back at Cumnock, even for a few days to work in his garden, to get the sun and breathe the fresh air, to go for walks with his collie dog and renew his friendships with his miner friends.

Hardie had been lucky in his wife. She had the difficult task of keeping the home going on the very small weekly sum that he could afford to send her. The two boys and the girl were growing up. They

86

lived thriftily and frugally and could not afford luxuries. He was very fond of his daughter, Nan, who was very like him in appearance.

He could not afford to give them any more education than what they received at the elementary school. The boys left school to become engineers and the girl helped the mother at home. When he was away there was always a letter or a postcard for one of them and they always looked forward eagerly to his return.

Sometimes he arrived tired and worn out from long train journeys and days and nights of incessant work. Hardie was a man who could not spare himself; there was always the inner force within him which drove him on. There were long intervals when they did not see him at all.

For although he was out of Parliament and not so often in London he was always travelling to speak somewhere for the I.L.P. He was its best-known national speaker and from all parts of the country came letters asking him for meetings. 'There is so much to be done and so few to do it,' he wrote. He found it impossible to refuse any invitation to speak for some struggling I.L.P. branch carrying on its propaganda work for Socialism against heavy odds.

Then there was *The Labour Leader*, which after its earlier success had now run into difficulties in the political apathy that had followed the election of 1895.

These were indeed the difficult years but Hardie went on with his work, 'still nursing the unconquerable hope', eagerly watching for signs of an awakened interest in politics, confident that the time was coming when the working class would be roused from its apathy and listen to the message of the I.L.P.

Hardie followed the activities of the trade union movement with great interest and in article after article in *The Labour Leader* impressed upon trade unionists the importance of political action.

The year 1897 was a year of chronic industrial unrest and a long and bitter struggle in the engineering industry.

There was a national lock-out and for many weeks Hardie's weekly articles stated the case for the men. The politicians were disclaiming any responsibility. 'Lord Salisbury's Government is not losing sight of the dispute,' wrote Hardie. 'Mr. Opposition Morley doesn't seem to have come in sight of it yet. Herbert Gladstone goes to Leeds, and opens Liberal clubs and makes speeches, and although thousands of his constituents are in the street locked out by Sir James Kitson, the

Liberal M.P., Mr. Gladstone never once refers to the matter. At Barnsley, the Liberal candidate begs votes as a friend of the workers; but no reference to the lock-out crosses his lips—even though he is supported by Mr. B. Pickard, M.P., the Secretary of the Miners' Union.'

Hardie wanted the T.U.C. to rally to the engineers and save them from defeat, to pool all the Union funds in a fighting fund to help the men locked out, and even 'to proclaim a general strike to bring the trade of the nation to a standstill'. The spectacle of men on strike always moved Hardie. He wrote: 'One hundred thousand men are locked out and side by side with these are a hundred thousand women enduring bravely.

'Looking up in mute appeal are three hundred thousand children— five hundred thousand in all. As I pen these words the bitter winds without are howling dismally as sleet-laden they rush by in their cruel fury. And I think of the home with the furniture gone and the cupboards empty and the fireless grates and the coverless beds, I think of the children—and I can write no more.'

He wrote bitterly in the Christmas number of *The Labour Leader*:

'The season's greetings to all who are remembering that Christ came "not to send peace but a sword" against wrongdoing in all its forms. There can be no peace so long as gaunt hunger stalks the land.

'I am afraid my heart is bitter to-night, and so the thought and feelings which pertain to the Christmas season are far from me. But when I think of the thousands of white-livered poltroons who will take the Christ name in vain, and yet not see His image being crucified afresh in each hungry child I cannot think of peace. I have known, as a child, what hunger means, and the scars of those days are with me still and rankle in my heart, and unfit me in many ways for doing the work waiting to be done. A holocaust of every church building in Christendom to-night would be as an act of sweet savour in the sight of Him whose name is supposed to be worship within their walls.'

The engineers were forced to return to work after having been out for seven months. 'For seven long weary months,' wrote Hardie, 'the men fought grimly. Gaunt poverty, like a hungry wolf, was the constant occupant of tens of thousands of homes. Hunger had gnawed at the vitals of the children whilst despair tugged at the heartstrings of the parents.' 'What had Parliament been doing?' he asked. 'The engineers have probably noticed that these working men who go to Parliament, by the grace of the Liberal Whip, are not so very different from the other men who are there. May that not be the reason, why there is no burning desire anywhere to send more working men to Parliament?' The lesson of the engineers lock-out was that the workers should create a new party, composed of Socialists, to capture Parliament, to prevent engineering employers imposing their will on the men. Hardie contrasted the indifference that Parliament had displayed towards the engineers lock-out to the enthusiasm with which it was turning to celebrate Queen Victoria's Diamond Jubilee.

The engineers had hardly returned to work before the Welsh miners came out on strike. Hardie went down to South Wales to speak at meetings in the mining valleys and *The Labour Leader* opened a relief fund to collect money for the soup kitchens.

After travelling the long train journey from Scotland he arrived in Merthyr late on a June evening.

' "After a wearisome journey," he wrote, "I at length found myself among comrades. Travelling up from Newport one realises how peaceful life might be here. The everlasting wood crowned hills near their summits up into the mist as the train creeps up the valley. . . . How it jars on one to see the virgin beauty of Nature outraged by ugly pit heaps which have been left after the mineral wealth has been exhausted." '

He found the soldiers walking about the streets at Merthyr, 'beardless boys', some of them working men for whom the labour market offered no useful opening and who, as a consequence, have hired themselves out to the killing trade for a few pence a day. They are here, if necessary to shoot other working men who are struggling to make the conditions of their toil a little easier.'

He spent a fortnight in the valleys addressing mass meetings of the men on strike. He wrote:

' "At every one of the thirteen open-air meetings it rained. Sometimes it was merely a drizzle, at others a deluge. If moisture is good for growth we all ought to be growing here. In common with the band, I have a double supply, sweat from within, rain from without. Despite the fact that June is nearing to its close, there is a keen cold wind on these hillsides which finds out the weak spots. The men, however, are used to the wet and don't mind the wind. They are in good heart and spirits and have but one fear and that is that the leaders may sell their pass." '

He made a careful calculation of the wages young men of thirty had been able to earn the previous year. It worked out at about a pound a week and men were striking for another two shillings a week.

Hardie reported that some of the prominent owners who were refusing the men their 22s. 6d. a week were making £3,000 a year.

'As a rule these men are Christians, and like Mr. Richard Cory of

Cardiff, take an active part in evangelistic work and they never tire of warning the workers against Socialism, because all Socialist are atheists! William Abraham, M.P., the miners' leader, has ceased to lead.

'He believes the men to be wrong and wishes them back at work. He does not seem to realise that the grievances of the men are deep seated and that dissatisfaction is widespread. When at work the men are robbed on every hand, deductions—some legal, many illegal—are made from their wages. House rents are going up, earnings are going down. No wonder that the men have risen in revolt. For their paid leader in such a crisis to say that he doesn't know who is to blame is nonsense.'

'Leaderless Wales' was the title of a long article in *The Labour Leader*.

'The meetings which I addressed revealed how eagerly the people will drink in the teachings of Socialism, when placed before them in language which they can understand. At Peny-daran and Troedyrhiw the muster was very large. Five brass bands of music turned out, and played the men up from Merthyr, Dowlais, Treharris, Merthyr Vale, and the surrounding districts generally. A platform had been erected in the stone-yard, with a flagpole, from which the Union Jack proudly floated. It was significant, however, that side by side with the Union Jack floated the "Red Flag" so dear to the hearts of Socialists. The rain came down in torrents, and whilst the meeting was going on a veritable deluge lasted, but not a soul budged. Patiently the thousands stood and listened.

'A male voice choir sang a grand old psalm tune, and the soul stirring anthem, "The Crusaders".

'House after house we visited, and found starvation—in every one. In several we saw baskets of crusts which the children had been to beg, and in one we tasted the bread pudding which the careful and thrifty mother was baking for the children.

'A big strong clean-limbed fellow, a widower whose house was kept by his daughter, made complaint that, as his wife was dead, he did not receive the same pay from the stoneyard as those who had a wife. In another case, where the husband had gone no one knew, while the son refused work in the stoneyard. This place, including Dowlais probably touches the lowest depths of poverty and suffering to be found in the valley. In one of the houses a coloured portrait of the Right Hon. Joseph Chamberlain adorned the wall on one side of the fireplace and over the cupboard, on the other side, was proudly suspended a marriage certificate.'

Hardie had no idea as he addressed these strikers' meetings on the mountain side at Merthyr that, later, he was destined to represent them in Parliament.

All that he knew was that they were miners on strike. As he talked to them on the Welsh mountain side in the rain, his memory went back to similar meetings in Lanarkshire and Ayrshire when he, too, had been out on strike and had been hungry and cold.

The Welsh miners held out until September. Hardie had done what he could to help. The I.L.P. followed up his tour by sending down an organiser into South Wales, and other speakers followed. *The Labour Leader* fund helped.

Money came in in small sums from many parts of the country as a result of Hardie's descriptions of what he had seen in the Welsh valleys. Lace workers from Barcelona sent money. Walter Crane, the artist, sent a cheque, Sir Thomas Lipton supplied 2,000 pound packets of sugar. George Cadbury sent £100 worth of cocoa. Alderman David Morgan, known in South Wales as Dai O'r Nant ('David of the Brook'), aged 65, was sent to prison for two months' hard labour for being in a crowd which booed some blacklegs, although evidence was given at the trial that he had tried to stop the booing as soon as it had started.

Hardie had met Dai O'r Nant and thought he was a much better leader than Mabon. D. A. Thomas, the coalowner, had said of him that 'although he did not always agree with Alderman Morgan, for straightforwardness and honesty of purpose there was no man in South Wales superior to him and that was why he respected him. If there was one leader more than another who could not be bought it was David Morgan.' This was Hardie's idea of what a trade union leader should be. He quoted it with pride in *The Labour Leader*.

Hardie's next battle was for a different class of workers. It was for the men and women employed in the chemical industry of Glasgow.

He went to visit Lord Overtoun's works, where they worked a twelve-hour shift and Sundays as well, among the foul, poisonous vapours, and wrote a vivid detailed criticism of the place which was a veritable hell upon earth. There was not even a meal-hour and they ate before the furnaces with their dirty hands stained with the poisoned chemicals with which they worked. 'There is no rest for these men,' wrote Hardie. 'If a man dares to stay away from work on Sunday to attend church or chapel he is punished by losing Monday's wages also.'

The owner of the chemical works was Lord Overtoun, a leading Scots philanthropist, prominent in the Sunday Observance and Sunday Rest societies. Hardie was scathing in his denunciation of Lord Overtoun:

'When the Glasgow Corporation proposed to run Sunday cars to enable the citizens to get out from the streets and slums to spend a few hours in the country, a deputation from the societies named above waited upon the Town Council to enter an indignant protest against this desecration of the Lord's Day. Lord Overtoun headed that deputation!'

Yet Lord Overtoun's workers were forced to work on Sundays.

Hardie quoted a passage from the 23rd chapter of Matthew:

'Woe unto you Scribes and Pharisees, hypocrites, for ye are like unto whited sepulchres, which indeed appear beautiful outward, but are within full of dead men's bones and all uncleanness. Even so yet also outwardly appear righteous unto men, but within ye are full of hypocrisy and iniquity . . . Ye serpents, ye generation of vipers, how can ye escape the damnation of hell!'

Hardie thought that Christ's attack on the Pharisees of his day admirably described Lord Overtoun, the Christian philanthropist who owned the Shawfield Chemical Works.

He went on:

'I expect some good, pious Christians will be shocked at this "irreverent" quotation of Scripture. Heard read from the pulpit, and applied to the religious hypocrites of 2,000 years ago, they would esteem it most excellent. May I remind these good souls that Christ spoke these words, not of dead hypocrites, but of those by whom He was surrounded — the Lord Overtouns of His day, of those who took part in foreign missions, and were the religious leaders of the times, but whose lives were driving the people to atheism. I presume Christ would say the same to the religious leaders of these times, but whose lives were driving the people to atheism.

Hardie concluded:

'I am not attacking religion, but I mean to try whether the conscience of the Christian Church cannot be so stirred up on this matter so to insist on men who make so much profession of Christianity as Lord Overtoun makes, first of all giving some evidence of the faith that is in them by their treatment of their workpeople. If they will not treat these humanely, then the Church should not accept for its altar the blood-stained gifts which have been procured by the destruction of men, body and soul. Lord Overtoun I don't know, and have no personal animus against, and as soon as he puts his works at Shawfield in order on lines which everyone will admit to be fair, I will cease from troubling. Until he has done so, I will do my best to make it impossible for him to appear on a public platform in Scotland. If we both live he will find this no vain boast, no idle statement.'

Hardie gave details of the wages, which were shockingly low. Labourers were paid threepence an hour and furnacemen paid fourpence an hour. 'Think of it. A human being made in the image of God toiling in a hell-hole for fourpence an hour.'

Hardie said that it was estimated that Lord Overtoun gave £10,000 a year to charity; which 'worked out at twenty-two shillings and ten

ence an hour in furtherance of God's work, while to his workmen he
ave fourpence'.

The Labour Leader created a sensation in Glasgow and the articles
vere reprinted in pamphlet form.

Nobody had ever written about the great Christian philanthropist,
.ord Overtoun, like this before.

But there was no support for Keir Hardie's crusade from the
Glasgow pulpits. On the contrary, his pamphlet was denounced as the
work of 'an anti-religious atheist' and he found it necessary to reply
n another series of articles and a pamphlet entitled *More About
Overtoun*.

He wrote in an introduction:

'The proposed six month's revival campaign is as good as dead.
D. L. Moody and John McNeill may come and use all their platform arts
and gifts but Glasgow will not be moved, unless it be to ribald mirth.
Whilst they talk, the thoughts of the listeners will be on Lord Overtoun
and his slaughterhouse at Shawfield.'

Many people in Glasgow thought that Lord Overtoun might take
action for libel, but he remained discreetly silent. And Hardie's campaign had its effect. Not only were steps taken to reduce Sunday labour
in the Shawfield works but there were increases in wages and changes
in the conditions which Hardie had so effectively exposed.

CHAPTER 10

FIGHTING THE BOER WAR

THE Boer War broke out in October 1899 and Hardie found himself ranged alongside the Radicals in the Liberal Party who had strongly opposed the Tory Government's policy in South Africa. The I.L.P. took a strongly anti-war line, declaring it to be 'a war of aggression and an outrage on the moral sense of a civilised community'. It denounced 'the criminal conduct of the Press and the leading politicians in misleading the public and rousing the passions of war'. The S.D.F., with the exception of Hyndman, also opposed the war but the intellectuals of the Fabian Society were divided, took a referendum as to what was to be the Society's attitude and decided to make no official pronouncement. Ramsay MacDonald, who was then the chairman, and fifteen other prominent members resigned. Sidney Webb attacked the I.L.P.'s attitude of opposition to the war as 'ultra Nationalist, ultra Gladstone, as old Liberal to the finger tips'.

Blatchford, the old soldier, declared: 'Until the war is over I am for the Government.'

Some of the Liberals, including Haldane, Grey and Asquith, were for the war, but John Morley, John Burns and Lloyd George were against. A South African Conciliation Committee was formed and at its meetings in the country the anti-war Liberals and the anti-war Socialists spoke on the same platform. They were labelled Pro-Boers and were bitterly attacked in the popular Press.

In *The Labour Leader* Hardie wrote a series of articles outlining what he thought should be the Socialist attitude towards the South African war. They were factual, well informed, a closely-reasoned analysis of how the war had come and the part that the big capitalist vested interests had taken in the events that had led up to it.

'It was a capitalist's war,' he argued, 'out of which the British capitalists hoped to make money by exploiting cheap labour in the

94

old mines of South Africa.' 'As Socialists,' wrote Hardie, 'our sym-
pathies are bound to be with the Boers.'

For the first time *The Labour Leader* came out without celebrating
Christmas. 'To make pretence of honouring the season of peace and
goodwill whilst we are carrying death and heartache into thousands
of homes in an endeavour to enforce wrong would be a mockery,' was
his explanation.

Hardie went on to describe how the gentlemen on the Stock
Exchange were making money out of the war:

'But, as usual, it is to the Stock Exchange we have to go to sound the
depths of unscrupulous callousness. On Thursday, 14th, a rumour was set
afloat on the Exchange that Buller had relieved Ladysmith and captured
2,000 Boers. South African shares immediately stiffened in price. On
Friday, the mysterious whisper again went round, this time he had
captured 10,000 Boers. The result was something like a boom in African
stock, and those who had been buying heavily at a low figure sold out at
a handsome profit.

'On that very day, whilst business patriots who sang "Rule Britannia"
and "God Save the Queen", the day war was declared, were making
thousands, General Buller was seeing his men go down in hundreds before
the enemy, and finally had to retire defeated. Next morning, when the
truth was known, the market dropped lower than ever, and the scoundrels
who sold high the day before bought again, and are doubtless holding
for the next rise. These are the men for whom our brave soldiers are
waging war against the Transvaal Republic. They prey upon the vitals of
the nation in times of peace, and pile up fortunes out of her blood in time
of war, and yet are accounted honourable men.

'In any self-respecting state they would be hanged for despicable
traitors.'

Hardie had no illusions that the war was a just and necessary war.
He went on:

'Over 1,000 men dead and buried in the veldt, 5,000 wounded and in
hospital, 3,000 prisoners in Pretoria, and the real fighting not yet begun.
And for what? That knaves grow rich. Coalmasters, iron and steel
masters, shipbuilders, and shipowners, Stock Exchange swindlers and
business gamblers are all growing rich out of the war. Prices and conditions of life are steadily rising, meaning increased profits all round.

'How did the working class benefit?' he asked, 'If the worker gets a five
per cent increase in his wages, it will be more than absorbed by the
increased price he will have to pay for everything he uses. But then, who
cares for the working man? He is a neglible quantity. Business men have
to be catered for, argued with, and convinced by the politician who seeks
their votes. The worker is content to be flattered and cajoled. Were it
otherwise he would hurl into oblivion the unholy brood of bloodsucking

vampires who batten on his misery. As it is, he hugs them to his bosom as his best friends. God pity and have mercy on him.'

Hardie wrote scathingly of the House of Commons that allowed the war to go on:

'More and more the House of Commons tends to become a putrid mass of corruption, a quagmire of sordid madness, a conglomeration of mercenary spiritless hacks, dead alike to honour and self-respect. It has become a machine for registering the decisions of the Stock Exchange. Intellect which will not be subservient, courage which cannot be bought—qualities which ought to be primed above all else—are feared and hated.'

During the war the cheap British capitalist Press had sunk to its lowest depths.

H. W. Massingham, editor of the Liberal *Daily Chronicle*, had not always agreed with Hardie but when he was forced to resign his editorship because he disagreed with the war, Hardie paid him a tribute:

'Mr. H. W. Massingham has been dismissed from his position as editor of the *Daily Chronicle*. He has bravely taken his stand. The proprietor of the *Daily Chronicle* is an ambitious man, one of the modern hypocrites of commerce, who gives tens of thousands of pounds to cathedrals and public parks and dismisses old men, pensioners who have helped to build up their millions. He has an ambition to shine in Parliament as a Liberal friend of the people, and Mr. Massingham was imperilling his chance by writing against the war. So Mr. Massingham has had to go. Nothing in his career, meteoric as it was, rebounds so much to his credit as this giving up a well-paid position of power and importance rather than betray the dictates of his sense of justice. The Press is controlled by the war gang.'

Drunken patriotic mobs were openly incited by the Press to break up anti-war meetings.

Hardie wrote:

'The mobs who howl down speakers and go mad with frantic delight at the sight of a red-coat are, as Tolstoi has shown, literally bereft of reason. They howl for war because it is war and means bloodshed, apart from any question of principle involved. I saw a young Scots lad in the dress of a Highland regiment in Fleet Street the other day the centre of an admiring crowd. He was too drunk to stand and had cut his face badly in falling. But bloodstained and besotted as he was, he was the popular idol of the city man in the tall shiny hat who vied with the street arab in doing him homage. It was a humiliating spectacle.'

A big anti-war meeting was arranged for Glasgow, and Lloyd George, who had succeeded in escaping from a riotous mob at Birmingham dressed as a policeman, was billed as one of the Glasgow speakers.

Hardie was not one of the speakers himself but helped to organise the stewards.

David Lowe described what happened:

'Sandy Haddow and I addressed the Irish Nationalists and received a guarantee that the meeting would be defended. And it was. The City Hall was packed to its utmost capacity. Even before Bailie John Ferguson took the chair, the stewards had as much on hand as they could manage, yet the disorderly crowd were kept in subjection and several flags were captured. The oratorial triumph of the evening was the speech of Lloyd George. For a peace meeting it was a hot engagement.

'At the close of the City Hall meeting a riot outside seemed imminent and a few of the speakers and their friends had to recourse to police protection.

'Foiled in their attempt to wreck the meeting and to assault the speakers, the crowd of students and patriots marched to *The Labour Leader* office and smashed the plate glass windows and carried off books and pamphlets. However, it was not all lost because the students lifted a poster board on which was a *Labour Leader* contents bill and gleefully paraded the streets prominently exhibiting their trophy. From an advertising view, the thing should have been done weekly.'

Hardie had many similar experiences during the Boer War. He never knew when attempts to smash up the meetings would be made by patriotic roughs and drunks. Yet he found the clergymen who were using their pulpits to glorify the Boer War more nauseous than the drunken hooligans or the super-patriotic comedians of the music hall. He wrote in his notes:

'The clergyman who supports, much more advocates, war, by that very fact puts himself out of court. The politicians, the financiers, the business men may plead that war will benefit them, and that they are therefore justified in advocating and encouraging it. But for the minister of Christ there is no such justification. He, by his office, stands forth as the representative of Him who taught the doctrine of non-resistance, even when attacked, as an integral part of His philosophy of life. The clergy take upon themselves the duty of carrying on the work which Christ begun, and claim for themselves the title of His representatives.

'Nowhere is Mammon more firmly seated than in the Church.

'All the cold, sterile apathy of the age finds its home in the pulpit. The roystering, human weaknesses of the libertine, the drunkard, and the gambler are as virtues compared to the gilded, cold heartlessness of organised Christianity. The proud, bombastic, self-righteous spirit of Phariseeism dominates the Church and all its works. The modern Christian Church is a reflex of the modern business world, only more hateful because of the garb of unconscious hypocrisy in which it is arrayed.'

Of Joseph Chamberlain, who was the popular hero of the moment, he wrote:

'The glorification of Mr. Chamberlain proceeds apace.

'In the early eighties he was the idol of Radicalism, after '86 he became the mainstay of Unionism, now he is the only adequate instrument of Capitalism. Your Campbell-Bannermans and Harcourts lack the grit and the audacity; your Salisburys and Balfours retain too much of the ancient flavour of *noblesse oblige*; and it is your Chamberlain and Asquith type alone which has sufficient lack of honour and absence of moral conscience-ness to make them callous enough for the dirty work of the magnates of the Stock Exchange.'

It had been unpopular enough to be labelled Socialist, but now the I.L.P. was being denounced as 'Pro-Boer' too and its membership had gone down. Hardie's hopes of seeing an Independent Labour Party winning many seats at the General Election receded. Everything decent in British politics seemed to have disappeared in the madness of the war.

Yet in the midst of this, Hardie persistently went on with his campaign for the organising of a Labour Party. Even John Burns admitted to a friend: 'Hardie is a dour, dogged fellow. If I were a general I would give him a lonely outpost that should be held to the death.'

CHAPTER 11

BEGINNINGS OF THE LABOUR PARTY

ᴡɪᴛʜ the attention of the country taken up by the South African War
did not look as if much progress was likely to be made on the politi-
al front. But a General Election seemed imminent and Hardie was
oing what he could to get the organisation going which would enable
abour candidates to challenge again the orthodox parties.

He was out of the T.U.C. but he still took a keen interest in its
roceedings and he had inspired and drafted a resolution which
ppeared on the agenda of the 1899 Congress in the name of the
ᴀmalgamated Society of Railway Servants, later to become the
ᴺational Union of Railwaymen, which was regarded as one of the
ᴹore advanced unions.

It read:

'That this Congress, having regard to the decisions of former years, and
ᴠith a view to securing a better representation of the interests of Labour
ɪ the House of Commons, hereby instructs the Parliamentary Committee
ɔ invite the co-operation of all Co-operative, Socialist, Trade Union, and
ther working-class organisations to jointly co-operate on lines mutually
greed upon in convening a special congress of representatives from such
f the above same organisations as may be willing to take part, to devise
ays and means for the securing of an increased number of Labour
ᴹembers in the next Parliament.'

This resolution was carried on a card vote by 546,000 to 434,000.
ᴵt was a victory for those who had persistently advocated that the
rade unions should embark on political action.

A preliminary move was made in Scotland. On January 6th, 1900, a
onference was called at the Picardy Place Hall, Edinburgh, with
ᴿobert Smillie, Hardie's staunch friend and ally, in the chair. A large
ᴺumber of invitations had been sent out to trade unions, co-operative
ocieties and to I.L.P. and S.D.F. branches, and 224 delegates were
resent. Hardie was on the platform.

It was agreed to set up a Joint Committee representative of the organisations present to proceed with the work of screening independent Labour representation in Parliament.

Hardie was delighted with the result of the conference, which he described as an unqualified success, but was not so sanguine about the results of a conference of the same kind which was due to take place in London the next month. He appealed to the English delegates:

'Saturday's conference at Edinburgh shows what can be done when the right spirit prevails, and considering the momentous issues at stake, it is incumbent on everyone holding a position of responsibility to put aside all personal bias and past differences of opinion as to make success certain in a matter where success means so much to the toiling millions.'

At Edinburgh there had been a slight clash between the ultra moderates, who were afraid to go too far, and the doctrinaires of the Social Democratic Federation, who were concerned that the conference would not go far enough. Hardie was afraid that this might happen again on a bigger scale and wreck the London Conference.

But the London Conference turned out better than Hardie, usually an optimist on these questions, expected. It was held at the Memorial Hall, Farringdon Street, London, on February 27th, 1900. One hundred and thirty delegates attended, representing 116 Trade Unions, seven represented the I.L.P., two the L.P., five the S.D.F. and there was one from the Fabian Society, representing a total affiliated membership of 568,177.

Hardie, Ramsay MacDonald, Philip Snowden, F. W. Jowett and Joseph Burgess were among the I.L.P. delegates.

The first clash of opinion came when R. W. Jones, the delegate from the Upholsterers' Trade Union, moved a resolution that the Conference 'was in favour of the working classes being represented in the House of Commons by members of the working classes as being most likely to be sympathetic with the aims and demands of the Labour Movement'.

To this George Barnes of the engineers, and a close friend of Hardie's, from Glasgow, moved an amendment to the effect that the representatives in Parliament should not be just members of the working class but also sympathetic with the aims of the Labour Movement and whose candidatures were promoted by an affiliated organisation. Very much the same issue had been raised at Bradford when the I.L.P. was formed. The Barnes amendment was carried with John

Burns, who had rather unexpectedly turned up, also representing the engineers, speaking for it.

The delegates from the S.D.F. wanted to commit the Conference to a definite declaration in favour of Socialism and 'a recognition of the class war'. It read:

'The representatives of the working class movement in the House of Commons shall form there a distinct party based upon the recognition of the class war and having for its ultimate object the socialisation of the means of production, distribution and exchange. The party shall formulate its own policy for promoting practical legislative measures in the interests of Labour, and shall be prepared to co-operate with any party that will support such measures or will assist in opposing measures of an opposite character.'

This went a good deal further than the trade union delegates were prepared to go and A. Wilkie, for the Shipwrights, moved an amendment making a selected programme the basis of the party and leaving members free outside the items it contained. This was carried by a big majority against the S.D.F. resolution. This was exactly the danger that Hardie had foreseen. He then moved a further amendment on behalf of the I.L.P. It read:

'This Conference is in favour of establishing a distinct Labour Group in Parliament, who should have their own Whips and agree upon their policy which must embrace a readiness to co-operate with any party which, for the time being, may be engaged in promoting legislation in the direct interest of Labour and be equally ready to associate themselves with any party in opposing measures having an opposite tendency: and, further, no member shall oppose a candidate whose candidature is being promoted by any organisations coming within the scope of Resolution No. 1.'

George Wardle (Amalgamated Society of Railway Workers) seconded it.

Wilkie then withdrew his amendment and Hardie's amendment became the substantive resolution.

The delegates of the S.D.F. were very angry about the defeat of their resolution and blamed Hardie. But it had been defeated before Hardie's amendment had been moved, for the majority of the trade union delegates were dead against it.

Hyndman kept up the criticism of Hardie for years. In his autobiography he wrote: 'The issue was as plain as it could be: should the party representing Labour be a Socialist Party, or should it be an intriguing, programmeless, go-as-you-please group adding yet another purchasable faction to other purchasable factions in the House Hardie solemnly proposed it should be the latter from the beginning and all through. And it was so.

An I.L.P. amendment was carried to reduce the size of the proposed Executive Committee from 18 to 12, seven from the Trade Unions two from the I.L.P., two from the S.D.F. and one from the Fabian Society. Originally the Fabian Society was to have two members on the Executive, of whom Bernard Shaw was one. In later years Shaw gave, in a letter to Lord Elton, Ramsay MacDonald's biographer, his version of what happened.

'The Labour Representation Committee was formed by the Socialist societies and their leaders, with its doors open to the trade unions as such no matter what their opinions of Socialism (most contemptuously hostile) might be.

'As their voting numbers were overwhelming and their money indispensable, they would have swept out all the Socialists and replaced them with old Conservative or Lib-Lab trade union secretaries if the L.R.C. had been democratically established. So we fell back on the good old Tory device of *ex-officio* members. The Fabian Society with less than 2,000 members, all middle class to the marrow of their bones, was actually allowed two members *ex-officio*. I was one of them, Edward Pease was the other.

'Keir Hardie was determined to get rid of this clever bourgeois element and more especially of me. Besides K.H. had learned from experience, as I also had, that mixed committees of clever bureaucrats and journalists and of genuine Labour men will not work; their words do not go at the same speed or in the same channels. Accordingly he carried the reconstitution of the Committee with only one Fabian *ex-officio* and thus got rid of me (with my cordial consent), leaving Pease, as the Fabian secretary, in possession. Pease liked being on the L.R.C. and could see nothing wrong in any of its proceedings, an attitude which suited Hardie and MacDonald exactly . . . '

Shaw's comments are interesting in the light of later developments and controversies in the Labour Movement.

Hardie may not have been enthusiastic about having Shaw directing and permeating the Labour Representation Committee as soon as it was born. He knew from experience what could happen when the S.D.F. and the Fabian Society clashed. He knew his trade unionists. If they were to play their part in the new Independent Labour Party they had to be persuaded that it was neither revolutionary doctrinaire nor bossed by the superior middle class.

The Press gave only the briefest reports of the Conference. *The*

102

Times gave it only a quarter of a column, considerably less than it had given to the first I.L.P. Conference seven years before. The political correspondents had not realised the significance of what had been done and that the establishment of the Labour Representative Committee marked an important new development in British politics.

Keir Hardie, however, was elated at the decisions of the Conference, about which he had not been too optimistic. He wrote a long three-column article in *The Labour Leader* stressing its significance. At the Conference John Burns had said that a Labour Group in Parliament already existed. Burns's speech he described as 'a comic interlude', for if there had been an active Labour Group in Parliament, there would have been no need for the Conference. Hardie went on:

'A Labour Party which requires to remind a Labour Conference of its existence is altogether too modest for the bustling age. It may be retorted that what is wanted is quiet work, not loud advertising. I do not endorse this view. A Labour Group in Parliament should be militant, and this it could not be without meeting with the hostility and abuse of the Press, which would effectively advertise its existence. Nothing would please the party politicians more than to have a Labour Group willing to work along orthodox lines in constitutional fashion. In my judgment such a group would not be worth its room. Parliament responds to pressure, not to argument, and the constituencies need to be stirred and quickened into activity, as they were of old by militant work on the floor of the House of Commons.'

He went on to stress the importance of the setting-up of the new party and its implications. A shilling a year from the affiliated membership represented at the Conference, including the 500,000 trade unionists, would bring in £25,000 a year. Such a sum was not immediately required but only 3d. a member would bring in £6,250 and that was a substantial beginning to enable the new Labour Party to become established. He replied to the S.D.F. criticism by pointing out that if their resolution had been carried the position would have been exactly as it was before the Conference met with this difference, 'that there would have been suspicion and bad blood where there is to-day cordial harmony'. Each organisation is free to maintain and propagate its own theory, bring forward its own candidates in its own way, the object of the Conference being to secure a united Labour vote in support of these candidates and co-operation amongst them on Labour questions if they were returned to Parliament. The only element required to ensure success is all-round confidence and from that, everything else will grow in 'time'.

Hardie resigned from the chairmanship of the I.L.P. at its Annual Conference held in Glasgow at Easter 1900. The I.L.P. was now firmly established and he thought the time had come when he could safely relinquish the chairmanship which he had held since the Party had been formed in 1894.

During the session the business was suspended in order to present him with an address in which it was sought to express 'with gratitude and pride our recognition of the great services he has rendered to the Independent Labour Party and the national cause of Labour and Socialism'.

His successor in the chair was Bruce Glasier, also a Scot. Glasier said :

'In the House of Commons and in the country he has established a tradition of leadership which is one of the greatest possessions of the Socialist and Labour movement in Britain. His rock-like steadfastness, his unceasing toil, his persistent and absolute faith in the policy of his party are qualities in which he is unexcelled by any political leaders of our time. He has never failed us. Many have come and gone but he is with us to-day as certainly as on the day when the I.L.P. was formed. By day and by night, often weary and often wet, he has trudged from town to city in every corner of the land bearing witness to the cause of Socialism and sturdily indicating the cause of Independent Labour Representation.

'On the N.A.C. his colleagues are deeply attached to him. He is always most amenable to discussion with them. They do not always agree with his views, but they have been taught by experience to doubt their own judgment not once but twice and thrice, when it came into conflict with his.

'Hardly in modern times has a man risen from the people who, unattracted by the enticements of wealth or pleasure and unbent either by praise or abuse, has remained so faithful to the class to which he belongs. His career is a promise and a sign of the uprising of an intensely earnest, capable and self-reliant democracy.

'He is a man of the people and a leader of the people.'

These words were not flattery. The Conference knew that they were true. Without Hardie's work and inspiration the I.L.P. would not have become a force to be reckoned with in British politics. And those nearest him and who had worked with him most knew how selfless he was and how devoted to the cause.

The Labour Representation Committee had been formed just in time. The General Election came in September before the new party had had time to get into its stride. The Boer War was still raging and it was a difficult election. Only twelve candidates who ran under the

banner of the Labour Representation Committee went to the poll,
and eight of these were I.L.P. nominees.

All the constituencies did not then poll on the same day and so it
was possible for a candidate to contest two seats.

Hardie fought both Preston, in Lancashire, and Merthyr Tydvil, in
South Wales.

There had been some delay at Merthyr and Hardie himself at first
declined, thinking that Preston was the seat more likely to be won, but
finally the Merthyr enthusiasts persuaded him to agree to nomination.

He went first to Preston.

Hardie addressed numerous meetings at Preston between the Monday and the Thursday, speaking many times in the open air as well as
indoors, went down to Merthyr by train on the Thursday and was
back in Preston for meetings on the Saturday and the Sunday. He left
Preston on the morning of the poll to start another campaign at
Merthyr.

He was at the bottom of the poll at Preston, the result being:

R. W. HANBURY (Conservative)	...	8,944
W. E. M. TOMLINSON (Liberal)	...	8,067
J. KEIR HARDIE (I.L.P.)	... ...	4,834

Both Liberal and Tory Headquarters in London gave a sigh of
relief. Keir Hardie had under the circumstances polled a good vote
but he was out.

A few days later, when the Merthyr result was known, they discovered that Hardie was in. The result was:

D. A. THOMAS (Liberal)	... ...	8,598
KEIR HARDIE (I.L.P.)	... ...	5,745
PRITCHARD MORGAN (Liberal)	...	4,004

At Preston Hardie had run in opposition to the Tories. At Merthyr
he had opposed the Liberals. Merthyr Boroughs returned two members
and Hardie had succeeded in winning one of the seats, defeating the
Liberal company promoter, Pritchard Morgan, by 1,741 votes.

Tired out but triumphant, Hardie wrote to *The Labour Leader* vivid
descriptions of the elections.

Fighting two elections was a tremendous physical effort. About
Preston he wrote:

'I have dim notions of weary hours in a train, great, enthusiastic open-
air crowds in the streets of Preston, and thereafter oblivion. Jack Penny
tells me that my open-air performance in one afternoon included almost

continuous speaking from three till eight, with a break of an hour for tea. It is said that 12,000 people were addressed from four platforms, which had to be erected in the market place. What I remember of the business is a great concourse of people, of whom I was a unit. Time and space and individuality had all gone, and we were a mass unified by sympathy and floating somewhere in space. I could feel the people throb responsive to my every thought. In all these years of public work, I remember no similar experience. And that, too, in Tory Preston.'

In 1900 motor cars were still a novelty and Hardie had never been in one until an enthusiastic supporter drove one for him at Merthyr where he arrived the day before the poll.

'It was my first experience of a motor. I don't say it will be my last. More cheering, laughing crowds in the open air, indoors, everywhere. Consultations and arrangements for the poll next day, and then to bed. I had visited about one-third of the constituency. The outlook to me was not hopeful. How could men be expected to vote for a candidate whom they only knew from a villainous portrait which adorned the walls? But Tuesday, the polling day, was to change all that, for had not Parker and Shallard, the demons of the play, engaged a motor-car, which was guaranteed to work wonders . . . The sky was dismal and rain was falling freely. I had neither coat nor umbrella. Neither had I any voice.'

Then came the count.

'The Drill Hall, the genial presiding officer, the anxious faces of the watchers at the tables, as the voting urns were emptied, and their contents assorted. Joe Burgess, confident from the start: St. Francis, strained to a tension which threatened rupture; Dai Davies, drawn 'twixt hope and fear; the brothers Parker, moved to cavernous depths of their being. Dai looked up and nodded, whilst the shadow of a smile twinkled in his eyes. At length came the figures, and Dai found vent for his feelings. Who can measure the intensity of feeling bottled up in the heart of the Celt? A great cheering crowd, a march to a weird song whilst perched on the shoulders of some stalwart colliers, I tried vainly not to look too undignified. A chair helped considerably. That night, from the hotel windows, in response to cries loud and long-continued, I witnessed a sight I had never hoped to see this side of the pearly gate. My wife was making a speech to the delighted crowd.

'All this, however, does not tell how it happened. I only spent eleven waking hours in the constituency previous to the opening of the poll, which perhaps is one way of explaining it.'

Hardie was back in Parliament again, the Member for Merthyr Tydfil, which he was to represent for fifteen years.

Hardie took no rest but immediately went further into Wales to speak for John Hodge, the Scots secretary of the Steel Smelters' Union, who was unsuccessful. Returning to Scotland, he had an enthusiastic welcome at his home town at Cumnock where the local miners met him at the station, took the harness off the horses and dragged the cab in triumph through the streets of the little town. It was only when he reached home that he discovered how exhausted he was.

At Cumnock he was the guest of honour at a reception in the Town Hall, where his older miner friends entertained him with great enthusiasm. James Neil, who had been associated with him for twenty years, took the chair and many of the veterans of the Ayrshire miners were there to join in the celebration of his victory.

CHAPTER 12

BACK IN PARLIAMENT

PARLIAMENT opened in December and on the following evening a meeting was held in the Memorial Hall to congratulate John Burns, Richard Bell and Keir Hardie on their return. John Burns had been at the formation of the Labour Representation Committee but was not enthusiastic about it and preferred to remain closely associated with the Liberals. Richard Bell was an official of the Amalgamated Society of Railway Servants, who admired Hardie and his stand in the previous Parliament. He said he would try to continue in the House of Commons the work he had been doing outside and, as a novice in Parliamentary procedure, he relied upon Hardie to help him.

They had, that day, consulted as to how they should take the oath, and Hardie decided to affirm, because he feared he might by chance kiss the same book that Chamberlain had used.

On his way home he addressed meetings in Yorkshire. At the Corn Exchange, Leeds, Robert Blatchford presided over two large meetings. Blatchford had attacked Hardie in the *Clarion*. The Socialism of the I.L.P. was not strong enough for Blatchford. But they continued to appear on the same platforms.

Hardie wrote to Lowe:

York, 7.12.1900.

'I meant to have sent to-day copy for political notes, but am too tired to do anything this forenoon and evening . . . We had a big turnout here last night, and the great man (Blatchford) announced that, having got through his sulks, he would again take a turn at writing about Socialism, whereupon the Democracy cheered. But it was to the educated, not the working class, that we must look for our salvation—whereat there was grim silence. For the moment, however, there is harmony and he grew quite pathetic as he lectured his hearers on the iniquity of overworking and underpaying, and thus prematurely ageing *their leaders*, Mr. Hardie in particular. Now for dinner, then for word grinding.'

Blatchford's advice against overworking Socialist leaders was, however, sound advice. Hardie had clearly been doing the work of half a dozen men and he was feeling the strain of the election campaigns.

The Khaki Election of 1900 had established a Tory Government in power with a substantial majority. The Liberals were split on the issue of the Boer War and there was a critical Radical Left, the ablest Parliamentarian of whom was David Lloyd George. Then there were the eighty Irish nationalists whose main interest was Home Rule for Ireland and who were anti-Tory and also against the South African War.

The Liberals claimed Burns and Richard Bell, but Hardie was not recognised by anybody. Nobody sent him a whip and so he was not even informed personally when Parliament was to meet. He wrote:

'Leaders of Parties, it seems, send out notices to their followers concerning when Parliament is to meet, and the fact that John Burns has not yet taken to fulfilling that part of his duties, accounts for me having been unsummoned. It may be further noticed that as the Labour Party has not yet appointed its Whip, I am an unwhipped Member of Parliament. Does the House contain another?'

There was no response to Hardie's suggestion. Burns was as averse as ever to break with the Liberals and be in a group with Hardie. So when Parliament met Hardie found himself once again alone, as he had been when he was the M.P. for West Ham. Bell sometimes supported him but he was not of great assistance in the Parliamentary conflict. Hardie had more support from the Irish, some of whom were no more enthusiastic about the Parliamentary conventionalities than he was.

On the first day of January 1900 the *New York Times* had put to several of the best-known public men in Britain the question: 'What is the chief danger, social or political, which confronts the new century?'

Hardie replied:

'Militarism! It distracts attention from social questions, subordinates the rights of the civilian to the imperious rule of the soldier, increases taxes, interferes with trade and commerce and glorifies war, which in all its aspects is a reversal to barbarism. It is, besides, a menace to political freedom, and in essence and fact, a contradiction of the principles of Christianity.'

At the first opportunity in the new Parliament, in the debate on the Address, Hardie made a speech denouncing the Boer War. 'I am one of those,' he said, 'who have been saying things, outside the House, about the war because I hold strong opinions about it. I am opposed to

109

war in the abstract. The civilisation and the Christianity of the nine-teenth century should have produced some other method of settling disputes than an appeal to brute force.' He made a lengthy attack on the Government for its conduct of the war. He believed that 'the nation was led into the war, bluffed through the war and tricked into endorsing the war before it had time to consider its sanity.' He pro-tested especially against the burning down of Boer farms and urged that there should be an armistice.

John Burns spoke on December 13th and some of the Tories tried to shout him down. Hardie had not intended to speak again but he joined in 'because of the unmannerly interruption from the opposite benches when the Member for Battersea was speaking'. 'Although,' he said, 'in the streets the myrmidons of the war party may smash our heads and sometimes close our lips, yet in this House we should insist upon freedom of speech for even the smallest minority.' He declared that the soldiers in South Africa were sick of the war. 'There are three classes in the country who still favour the war. These are those who make something out of it, either as contractors or shareholders in companies—these are the people who know nothing of the facts, the "men in the street", as they are called—and there are those who are lost beyond all redemption to all sense of honour and truth.'

Queen Victoria died in January 1901 and Hardie commented: 'The sycophancy of the Press has been sickening, the columns of graphic lying about London's tears and the nation's mourning are simply the products of a diseased imagination.'

When the House of Commons met in March he made, amidst con-siderable interruption, a protest against the military display at the Queen's funeral.

'The leading characteristic of the Queen,' he said, 'was domestic simplicity, and it seems to me a mockery that the last ceremony in con-nection with her passing should have taken the form of a huge military display, a pageant, a show, from which all simplicity was absent. The dead body of England's Queen was made a recruiting sergeant to help the military business.'

Hardie's amendment to the address, 'We humbly express our regret that your Majesty's advisers have not availed themselves of the oppor-tunity which the demise of Her late Majesty Queen Victoria affords to recommend the office of hereditary rule be abolished' was ruled out of order by the Speaker, who pointed out that whilst it would be quite in order to discuss the abolition of Royalty in the form of a motion

r a bill, it would be rather out of place to try to do so on the Address.
o Hardie let the matter drop.

A few months later the Government introduced the Civil List which
rovided generously, Hardie thought too generously, for King Edward
1e Seventh and the Royal Family. Hardie joined Henry Labouchere,
1e Radical M.P., as teller in opposing the Civil List which had been
1creased from £553,000 to £620,000 a year. Speaking in the debate
e said that:

'When taxes were being increased, when trade was depressed, when
rages were going down, when thousands of the employees of the State
ad clamoured in vain to have their wages increased from 19s. a week to
4s. a week, it was not a suitable time to ask the House to vote what
mounted to an increase of £100,000 a year to the income of the King and
1ueen. If an example of economy was to be set, for which the Chancellor
f the Exchequer pleaded so eloquently, that example should be set in high
laces. It could not be expected that the other spending departments of
1e State would pay much regard to the Chancellor's warning on economy
rhen they found the highest officers of the State increasing their expendi-
1re in connection with the occupants of the Throne to an extent which
ad never occurred before.'

A Liberal M.P., Mr. J. H. Yoxall, who had been lucky in the ballot
1r Private Members' Bills, introduced a Miners' Eight Hours Bill. It
ras opposed by a coalowner Tory and Mr. Charles Fenwick, the
iberal-Labour miners' M.P. from Durham. Hardie intervened in a
1ort speech and after replying to Fenwick, who had argued for non-
1terference in the mining industry, remarked:

'If the angels in Heaven do weep it must be when a representative of
rorking men, paid by the working men to come to this House to protect
1e interests of working men, gets enthusiastic cheers of employers of
1bour in opposing a measure introduced for the benefit of working men.'

He had persuaded the Irish to go into the Lobby in favour of the
ill. He had much in common with the Irish and when a number of
1em were suspended and ejected by the police he defended them in
'he Labour Leader. It was quite a capable piece of Parliamentary
:porting.

'Mr. Speaker named the Members and called upon them to withdraw.
hey refused. He asked the Sergeant to evict them and the Sergeant
1arched up to Mr. J. F. Flavin, six feet four, all muscle and bone, touched
im on the shoulder with his finger and requested him to leave the House.
[r. Flavin respectfully declined, and the Speaker ordered the Sergeant to
pply the necessary force. Then began the pantomime. Half a dozen
:tendants, wearing gold badges with expensive shirt fronts and evening
ress, approached Mr. Flavin, and for ten minutes they wrestled pantingly

with their burden. Mr. Flavin smiled cheerfully at them, assuring them from time to time he would not hurt them and begging them not to injure themselves by over-exertion.'

Then the police arrived.

'All of a sudden, there was a murmur of excitement: half a dozen constables had appeared in the House, and these, under the instructions of the Home Secretary, proceeded to carry out the Members who had been named. Mr. Crean was the first to be tackled, He has no great stature but an indomitable spirit. Despite his qualities, however, he was over powered and carried out. Member after Member followed in the same manner. This is the first time the police have been permitted to enter the House of Commons on duty. Mr. Speaker informed the House at a subsequent sitting that he was responsible for calling them in, and no one challenged his authority for doing so . . . the House of Commons has always been regarded as the institution which represents in the highest degree the nation as a whole, and the person of a Member of the House of Commons inside the Chamber itself has hitherto been regarded as sacred. By this incident it has been degraded to the level of a pot house in which the chucker-out is employed. And the responsibility does not rest with the Irish Members. The root of the original trouble was the closuring without discussion of a proposal to spend millions of public money. Some form of protest was demanded . . .

'Not one in ten seemed to see that the responsibility for the real disgrace lay elsewhere than on the Irish benches. The real offender was first the Chairman of Committees, Mr. Lowther, who accepted the closure and the Speaker, who called in the police. It is to the everlasting credit of the Irish Members that they had enough public spirit left to protest against these unconstitutional acts.'

When the Chancellor of the Exchequer proposed in his Budget that there should be a tax on sugar to pay for the Boer War, Hardie opposed it on the ground 'that the bulk of the tax would fall on the very poorest section of the community.'

'Everyone who understands the condition of life of the very poor knows that tea and bread form their staple diet and every sweated victim in London and in every other centre of industry will be taxed to pay for the war. The Chancellor of the Exchequer tells us that the income of the country liable to be assessed for income tax has risen during the last twelve years by £120,000,000. If that is so, surely some other means might have been found of securing a proportion of this rather than having to put this burdensome and iniquitous tax on sugar and thereby inflict injustice on the poorest of the poor.'

Years after, when people asked Hardie why he took his tea without sugar he would reply, 'I gave it up because I didn't want to pay for the Boer War.'

The Irish M.P.s opposed a Bill which had been promoted by the

At work at Neville's Court, 1902.

Keir Hardie and his wife at home at Cumnock, 1902.

Labour Party Executive, 1909.

Front row: J. R. Clynes, M.P.; Ben Turner, M.P.; J. Ramsay MacDonald, M.P.; Keir Hardie, M.P.; Arthur Henderson, M.P.; Stephen Walsh, M.P. Second row: W. Barefoot; Philip Snowden, M.P.; W. Walker; J. J. Stephenson; W. C. Robinson; W. Hudson, M.P.; John Hodge, M.P. Back row: E. R. Pease; Harry Orbell; G. H. Stuart; J. S. Middleton, *Assistant Secretary*; Arthur Peters, *National Agent.*

London and North Wales Railway Company moving a motion challenging the right of M.P.s who were railway directors to vote. Hardie joined in to say:

'The House existed to protect the public, the directors of a railway company existed to protect their own interests. Every Member of the House knew that, nineteen times out of twenty, the interest of railway directors conflicted with those of the public at large . . . The power of the railway companies was growing in the House and if they did not pass the motion it would go out that the House was less concerned about its own honour than about the interests of the railway companies. Some Members were aware that there could be no more serious charge levelled against politicians than that the House of Commons was simply an annexe of the Stock Exchange.'

On April 23rd, 1901, he took advantage of the rules of procedure to move a motion calling for the establishment of a Socialist Commonwealth in Britain.

This was the first time a Socialist resolution had been moved in the British House of Commons. It read:

'That, considering the increased burden which the private ownership of land and capital is imposing upon the industrious and useful classes of the community, the poverty and destitution and general moral and physical deterioration resulting from a competitive system of wealth production which aims primarily at profit-making, the alarming growth of trusts and syndicates able by reason of their great wealth to influence Governments and plunge peaceful nations into war to serve their interests, this House is of the opinion that such a condition of affairs constitutes a menace to the well-being of the realm, and calls for legislation designed to remedy the same by inaugurating a Socialist Commonwealth founded upon the common ownership of land and capital, production for use and not for profit, and equality of opportunity for every citizen.'

It was asking a lot of a Tory House of Commons in 1901 to pass this, but the debate roused so much curiosity that the House filled up. It was half-past eleven before Hardie could move his motion and at twelve o'clock the House adjourned.

'Mr. Keir Hardie,' wrote the Parliamentary correspondent of the *Daily News*, 'had about twenty minutes in which to sketch the outlines of a co-operative commonwealth. He seemed to me to perform this record feat of constructive idealism with remarkable skill and indeed it would be difficult to imagine a creation of human fancy that would produce more deplorable results than the society from which Mr. Hardie in his vivid way, deduced the China Expedition, the South African War and the London slums. Mr. Balfour, coming back from dinner, smiled pleasantly on the Speaker, doubtless calculating that things as they were would last his time.'

113

H

Hardie certainly packed a lot into his speech, concluding:

'Socialism, by placing land and the instruments of production in the hands of the community, eliminates only the idle, useless class at both ends of the scale. Half a million of the people of this country benefit by the present system; the remaining millions of toilers and business men do not. The pursuit of wealth corrupts the manhood of men. We are called upon at the beginning of the twentieth century to decide the question propounded in the Sermon of the Mount, as to whether or not we will worship God or Mammon. The present day is a Mammon-worshipping age. Socialism proposes to dethrone the brute god Mammon and to lift humanity into its place. I beg to submit in this very imperfect fashion the resolution on the paper, merely predicting that the last has not been heard of the Socialist Movement, either in the country or on the floor of this House, but that, just as sure as Radicalism democratised the system of government politically in the last century, so will Socialism democratise the country industrially during the century upon which we have just entered.'

On May 14th he moved the rejection of the Civil List, frankly admitting that working-class opinion at the time was favourable to Royalty. 'It was due to the fact,' he said, 'that they did not understand Royalty. They did not see that it was inconsistent with dignity of manhood to stick to hereditary rule whether of a monarch on the throne or the House of Lords. The object of working-class power should be to purify the system of Government by eliminating whatever could not be supported on grounds of common sense.'

Busy as Hardie was in Parliament, he did not neglect his work outside. In spite of the overwhelming defeat at the General Election and its unpopular role in opposing the war, the I.L.P. was recovering from its temporary setback. George Cadbury the Quaker, who was also against the war, had given £500 to the Election Fund and another anonymous contributor, 'Peace Lover', probably another Quaker, had given £250, and more money was coming in from the branches.

Hardie's reappearance in Parliament and the stand he was making there also acted as a tonic.

After six weeks of the new Parliament he was emphatic that alliance with the Liberals or any other Party was absolutely impossible. He wrote: 'I cling tenaciously to my old faith that alliance with any political party would lead to irretrievable ruin. Our strength as a cohesive and fighting force lies in our isolation. The strongest man, says Ibsen, is he who can stand alone and the same remark is true twice over of political parties. The orthodox politician could only bring us weakness, not strength.'

But there were other organisations in the country with which the I.L.P. should strive to work. He meant the trades unions and the co-operative movement.

'But are there not others, bone of our bone, strength of our strength? Are not the great Trade Union and Co-operative movements children of the same great mother as ourselves? We claim them as more than allies. They are our older Brothers, and as such must fight with us. For our cause is their cause, and their cause is our cause; and united we can win deliverance for all who have been oppressed. Already the Labour Representation Committees have done much to bring us together. But they are only at the beginning of their healing work. There are family differences to be lived down on both sides, family feuds to be forgotten and forgiven. But time and commonsense will work wonders if only we are patient.

'I have the feeling—it may be but the vain imaginings of egotism, that the possibility of a distinct and separate Labour Group has been brought perceptibly nearer. First and most important, it must define its position. Make it clear what it aims at and wherein it differs from existing parties. This well done, and it must seek strength.

'And here let me remark parenthetically that its chief reliance for power must always be upon itself and mainly on the character of its exponents. It matters not how high may be the ideal of underlying a cause. It will assuredly fail if there be even a suspicion of self-seeking or insincerity or lack of staying power on the part of its champions. Character is more to a movement than doctrine—a fact apt to be overlooked. Having found its strength, a movement must have wisdom enough to apply it. Decision of aim, decision of character, decision of application. Therein lies strength and success. No faltering, no temporising, no wool gathering.'

Bitterly critical as he had been of the leadership of the old reactionary, orthodox, Liberal-Labour leaders, he did not give up hope of winning the trade unions; he was confident that in time he could win over their rank and file.

The second conference of the Labour Representation Committee had been held at Manchester and forty-one trade unions with an affiliated membership of 353,000 had now paid their dues. The trades councils of Leeds, Leicester, Woolwich, Bradford, Birmingham, Sunderland and Manchester had also joined up. Here was a solid foundation upon which the new Labour Party could be built.

He went down to South Wales to some more meetings in the valleys. Merthyr realised that it had a new type of member.

At one meeting he told his constituents:

'He had, during the short time he had represented the Merthyr Boroughs, received more appeals for help from churches and chapels than during the three years he had represented West Ham (Shame). It was no shame at all. The constituency had been accustomed to it and had come to look upon M.P.s as milk cows. Even if he were a rich man he would refuse to subscribe a single penny in response to such appeals.'

He went to North Wales, too. Here the quarrymen employed by Lord Penrhyn had been on strike and Hardie addressed a series of meetings in order to encourage them.

Nothing angered Hardie more than the introduction of soldiers and the Government had sent the soldiers to North Wales.

As the 'blacklegs', the men who continued to work, returned home of an evening, 'they are met by booing and ironical cheering from the villagers, the women and children in particular.

'To put down this intimidation extra police were drafted in from all the surrounding districts. But still Colonel Ruck, the chief constable, was unsatisfied. He wanted soldiers. The bench of magistrates decided there was no need for soldiers. There had been no serious crime. The officials of the quarries petitioned the Home Secretary, who had sent down 200 men of the North and South Staffordshires. 200 more were being kept in Aldershot ready to be moved.'

The owner of the quarries was in receipt of an income of £100,000 a year from them, but the quarrymen were fortunate if they made 25s. a week clear all the year round. Hardie appealed for funds to keep the quarrymen going, as he had appealed for funds for the miners.

He went to the Bangor police court to hear the trial of a striker. The prosecutor was Lord Penrhyn's agent and the bench was occupied by magistrates nearly all interested in the quarries. The word of the 'blackleg' was taken against that of the striker, although there was no corroborative evidence and no witnesses. 'The entire proceedings were a biting commentary,' said Hardie, 'on the methods by which justice is administered under the shadow of Penrhyn Castle.'

He was glad to get away for a short break to his home in Scotland.

'Oh, bonnie is the blink o' one's ain fireside.

'After six weeks of hot air and irritated atmosphere and endless repetitions of wordy nothings and glare and glitter and London generally, to get to where the moonbeams can be seen and the silence felt is a luxury. Then to see the sheep sheltering her lambs from the blast with her own body and the kye meditatively chewing the cud and the farmer's boy sauntering past in charge of his easy-going team, and to drive the good steel spade six inches into the brown earth is to get in touch with nature and reality, and the word spinners and all that pertains to them become mere phantoms of some ugly hideous dream and Life begins to re-assert itself.'

There was a week's holiday in Ireland in September. In *The Labour*

Leader he described a visit to a village near Killarney and ended it with the note:

'As we drove off, the kindly "God bless you" of old and young rang in our ears. It was with genuine sadness that we left these people in their loneliness. All around us the bogs, away in front faintly outlined through the gloom the towering peaks of the Rock Mountains, their tops just touched by the departing glow of the sun sinking into the Atlantic beyond. From many a cottage in these wilds, tear-stained eyes would watch the glow thinking that the light of their lives had gone—westwards. Not a hut, cabin or farm-steading here but has sent forth its sons and daughters to America, not because there was no room for them at home, but because the blight of landlordism has laid a curse alike on the gifts and nature of man.'

September saw another by-election campaign on North-East Lanark with Robert Smillie as candidate. The miners' union this time gave substantial aid to the Election Fund. The co-operation between the I.L.P. and the unions was growing but it was not strong enough to secure Smillie's victory.

Then there was a long series of meetings in the North of England and the Midlands before Hardie could relax at Cumnock again. London in wartime was a nightmare to him. The old year was going and he sat up late into the night writing a few last notes for *The Labour Leader*:

'There is so much to be said, and the desire to make Socialism understood is growing into a passion. I see no other chance for redeeming the world from poverty and sin and war and lust and all manner of uncleanness. But my solitary candle is burning low in its socket. Outside the twinkling stars are keeping watch over the silent world. What a blessed thing is the holy calm of this home retreat. Not a sound to be heard save the slow tick of the old grandfather clock on the stairs and the soothing murmur of the Lugar Water at the foot of the garden. London is a place which I remember with a haunting horror, as if I had been confined there once in some long ago stage of a former existence. The weary feet on the pavement, the raucous song, the jingle of the cabhorse, and the babble of St. Stephen's. Were they real? God knows. Enough for the moment that they are not here. Here there are warm hearts and—peace. Where these are, heaven is.'

The reappearance of Keir Hardie in Parliament had put new life into the I.L.P. and the activities of the Labour Representation Committee, with Ramsay MacDonald as its energetic secretary, increased too.

At Birmingham in March 1902, there were 110 delegates representing 456,531 members and it was reported that the engineers and the carpenters, with a further combined membership of 100,000, were joining up too.

George Cadbury, the Quaker, attracted to the I.L.P. by Hardie's opposition to the Boer War, entertained the delegates at Bournville. 'Try to get fifty Keir Hardies into the next Parliament,' he told them.

There was an interesting by-election at Wakefield, with Philip Snowden as I.L.P. and Labour candidate.

Both Snowden and Ramsay MacDonald were now prominent figures on the I.L.P. platform.

Hardie thought that Snowden was the most gifted orator in the Party and that MacDonald was the 'best all-rounder'.

MacDonald had been elected on to the London County Council, where he was doing a great deal of solid work.

'At the last election,' wrote Hardie, 'he was the I.L.P. candidate for Leicester. Should he be returned the nation would be the gainer. With Ramsay MacDonald, George N. Barnes, Philip Snowden, and Fred Jowett working together in the House of Commons, the future of Socialism in Britain would be assured.'

Hardie declared at the I.L.P. Conference at Liverpool that Liberalism in Wakefield had been buried forever. At Liverpool, Mrs. Pankhurst moved a resolution pledging I.L.P. support to women's suffrage. It was unanimously carried and Hardie proudly pointed to the fact that the I.L.P. was the most advanced of the Parties, the only Party in favour of women's suffrage. Mrs. Pankhurst had become an active member of the I.L.P. and so were many of the women destined to play a prominent part in the fight for Women's Suffrage.

The Boer War was over. What had been hailed as a great British victory had brought unemployment and poverty to the workers of Britain.

'The saturation of blood riot in which the nation indulged over the murdering of two freedom-cherishing Republics in South Africa,' wrote Hardie, 'has, during 1902, brought forth after its kind. Gaunt hunger stalks like a grim spectre through the land and the black despair of the workless man is heavy enough to make itself felt in every heart. Crime, drunkenness, and pauperism are on the increase and forty-five years of effort in seeking to humanise and cleanse the life of the nation have been swept away by the war.'

He quoted figures to show that the crime figures had been increased by 50 per cent, that the number of vagrants in the workhouses had increased by 100 per cent and that 31,000 had been added to the pauper roll.

These were grim days in London. Hardie used to find time to give a helping hand to the down-and-out in the Salvation Army shelters.

He wrote:

'Shelters are full to overflowing, and when everything has been done which these agencies can do, there are still thousands of hungry people left to walk the streets of London without a copper in their pocket, with little clothing and with no place of shelter wherein to lay their heads. On Monday at the Salvation Army depot at Stanhope Street were men and youths of all ages, from the slum-bred lad of fourteen up to the decrepit old drayman of sixty. Women were there also. One case, that of a respectable-looking old lady, who is well known as a match seller in Fleet Street, attracted special attention. She is always clean, her profusion of grey hair is kept in good condition, and her aged, wrinkled face has a most benevolent and motherly expression. She was found sitting on a doorstep with a market basket beside her containing a few boxes of matches which the hurrying crowd had not had sufficient time to purchase. She was stiff with cold and on being assisted to her feet, she was just able to crawl with the aid of her crutches into the shelter where the soup was being provided. The whole scene presented a most harrowing spectacle and made up the most emphatic picture which the heart or mind of man could conceive as to the mockery of regarding our country as representing either a civilised or a Christianised society.'

He went on to give further examples of the unemployed printer, workless because of the arrival of the linotype machine, and of the shabby genteel man who carried, in a bag, a clean linen collar, black necktie with scarlet spots and a beautifully laundered handkerchief which he was ready to put on if he were interviewed for a job.

He concluded:

'These are fairly typical cases. Of course, there are loafers and people who do not want to work; but, everyone who has any practical experience of this work knows that the great bulk of the men who are helped are genuine cases, and that those who are not are more to be pitied than blamed. They are the victims of a heartless system and under any decent conditions of society such men as are to-day classed as the very lowest amongst our outcasts would not only be useful but lovable members of their own kind. The one thing that never fails to strike an observer is the large human element this class of people always displays. Wretched and outcast they may be, and yet they display more of the feelings of a common brotherhood in their relation to and with each other than will be found in any other rank or class of life.'

David Lowe left *The Labour Leader* in January 1903 and another Dundee journalist came to take his place, and in announcing this Hardie digressed upon the difficulties of running a Labour paper.

difficulties which were to be understood later by the Labour editors and papers that were to follow him.

The circulation of the paper had gone up. It was read 'literally in every part of Great Britain' but it had practically no advertisement revenue.

'Our advertising agents have reported times almost without number that advertisements have been refused or withdrawn simply and solely because the advertiser, being an orthodox politician, refused to patronise a paper the politics of which were an offence to himself, or were likely to offend his customers. I mention this not by way of complaint—I rather regard it as a compliment—but in order to emphasise the fact that the *Leader,* more than any other paper published, has to rely upon its circulation for its existence. I have no desire that it should be otherwise. As a leader writer on one of the London dailies said to me last week, the newspapers are coming every day more and more under the influence of the advertising manager, and now it is a common instruction to sub-editors to allow nothing to appear which would be likely to scare or offend the big firms who advertise.'

The miracle was that *The Labour Leader* had managed to survive at all.

'The wonder is that it weathered the storm and kept afloat,' he wrote. 'What it has meant to me personally to keep it going is no one's concern but my own. Not only has the *Leader* never paid its editor a brown coin by way of fee or salary, but I have had to draw freely upon my own resources and upon those of more fortunate friends and comrades for assistance. This year, if an extra 5,000 can be added to the circulation, all this will be changed. That this can be done I have no manner of doubt. Whether it will be done is another question . . .

'If success comes this year well and good; if it doesn't, there are more years to come.'

The Coronation of Edward VII had been delayed as a result of the King's illness. Hardie attended the Coronation ceremony at Westminster Abbey, to report it for *The Labour Leader.*

He wrote:

'Inside the Abbey were thousands of dignitaries, notabilities and elected persons. Mayors and Provosts in their robes and chains of office. Peers enveloped in long cloaks which they knew not how to carry, their wise heads surmounted by huge coronets, Peeresses in dresses of barbaric splendour, costing, I am told, £700 each. Here were whole rows of fantastic nobodies, resembling nothing so much as the grotesque get-up of a continental bal-masque, but lacking in gay sprightliness. It was also a gathering of all that is best and worst in our national life; the snob and the saint were there rubbing shoulders, as were also the scheming knaves of politics with the honest mediocrities whose weaknesses they know so well how to harm.

'The occasion of it all was, of course, the Coronation of the King, a meaningless ceremony—serving no other or more useful purpose than an excuse for all this display of vanity and snobbery.

'As grouse shooting begins on the 12th, the King had to be got ready for annointing in time to allow his loyal and patriotic subjects, to whom the slaughter of birds is one of the necessities of life, to be on the moors at the appointed hour. The King, seen at close quarters, does not look well. He is an old man, not so much in years as in looks. His attempts to smile were not pleasant to the beholder.

'Still he has been annointed, the Coronation dresses have been worn. Society has had its orgy, and the mob have had their feelings tickled. What more could the pathetic heart of man desire?'

For several weeks in January 1902 he remained at Cumnock, where his only daughter Nan lay seriously ill. For several weeks Hardie remained at her bedside in great distress until he was able to announce with relief that she was out of danger.

He was an intensely emotional man and when he received a telegram in the House of Commons in July that his mother was dying he left the debate hurriedly and went north by the night train. She had visited him in London the previous winter and he had taken time off from Parliament, showing her the sights of the city and 'looking at it through new eyes—my mother's'. At their home at Cambuslang in Lanarkshire, the old people died within a few hours of each other.

'Closed for ever are the grey eyes which blazed resentment or shed scalding tears when hard, untrue things were spoken or written about me or my doings, stilled the beatings of the warm, impulsive heart which throbbed with pride and joy unspeakable when any little success came her laddie's gait.'

David Hardie died the same evening.

'Having had twenty years of the life of a sailorman; he had learned to the full the vocabulary of the vigorous Saxon. It was part of his speech when breath and articulation were both sorely deficient, he strained both in expressing himself as had been his wont. The last thing I heard him say was, "Tak that damned stuff awa." This was reference to his medicine. He had small faith in doctors and their wares . . .

'Fear of death must have been an invention of priestcraft. He is the grim king for those who are left to mourn, but I have never yet seen a deathbed—and I have seen many—where the White Herald has not been welcomed as a deliverance.

'Those two talked about death as if it were an everyday incident in their lives. They did so without emotion or excitement or interest of any kind. They were dying together and at this they were glad. Had it been a visit to Glasgow, three miles distance, they were planning, they could not have been more unconcerned. They never once referred to any question of the

121

Beyond. As Socialists they had lived for at least 25 years and as such they died and were buried. They had fought life's battle together, fought it nobly and well, and it was meet that they should enter the void together.'

In October there were rumours of an election. Hardie thought it necessary to warn his followers:

'The crying claimant need of the moment will be a Labour group in Parliament which, by its energy, will attract these scattered forces and enlist their active support. The trouble about the Labour member, or candidate, is that he does not understand politics. Labour needs a new type of representative men who will send, men for whom the House of of Commons will not be a place of ease but a workshop, men who will be a vitalising force, not only in Parliament, but in the country; who will spend and be spent in and for the movement, of which they will be the active energising centre and not isolated units living and moving apart as superior creatures. To serve such men is a problem. However few their numbers, they will suffice, if only they are of the right stamp.'

The number of unions affiliating to the Labour Representative Committee was growing.

Hardie went down to address the annual meeting of the Merthyr District of the Miners' Federation and pleaded that the miners as trade unionists should join up too. 'Over a million trade unionists were now affiliated with the Labour Representative Committee but up to the present the Miners' Federation had held aloof and stood outside. (Cries of 'Shame'.) He hoped that statement would not hold out for long. Why should the colliers want to have a separate colliers' party in the House of Commons? They wanted to send collier members there from as many mining districts as possible but when the colliers' member got there he wanted him to join with the engineers' member, the gas workers' member, the compositors' member, and the carpenters' member in forming one Labour Party which would protect the interests of the workers as a whole.'

Hardie was taken suddenly ill during this visit to Wales. He had to be operated on for appendicitis and it left him weak. He pulled himself together sufficiently to write an article for the issue of *The Labour Leader* that appeared in the last week of the year 1903.

His real object in writing was, he said, to bid an official goodbye to the *Leader* and its readers. He could no longer continue as editor and he had decided to hand it over to the Independent Labour Party. It was a wrench for him.

'The thought of parting with it is like consenting to the loss of a dearly loved child. Time was when handing it over would have been a risky experiment. Now with the party organised and consolidated as it is, the risk is reduced to a minimum—for the I.L.P. is no longer a mixed assortment of job lots. It is an organisation in the truest sense of that much misused word. . . .

'It was as a monthly that the *Leader* first came out being 17 years ago and possibly I may live to see it a daily.

'What it has cost me to keep it going no one will ever know and few will be able even to remotely guess. But it has been kept going: and now the Party takes it over as a self-supporting going concern. I am proud of the fact.'

His old political opponent, Major Banes, the Tory candidate for South West Ham, wrote to say:

'As an old opponent of yours politically I learned to respect you and to value not only your openness and earnestness but your desire and efforts to see that your followers should be just in their dealings with those who differ from them—and depend not on violence, noise and abuse but mainly upon the justice of their cause.'

The King, who had been operated on for the same complaint, sent a message of sympathy to him:

' "The King's expression of sympathy which Sir Thomas Barker conveyed to Mr. Keir Hardie is characteristic," said the Pall Mall Gazette. "His Majesty has been that way himself and his is the feeling of one brave man to another."

'About Mr. Keir Hardie as a political factor, opinions may differ, but as to the pluck with which he has continued to work under the shadow of malady and right up to the operating table, there can be only one opinion, and this has now received the highest endorsement.'

A correspondent wrote in *The Labour Leader*:

'When the news came from Wales that Keir Hardie had broken down, it was not unexpected by us. Our only trouble was to know how much of a breakdown it was. We who were close to him had been terrible conscious for a year that our much loved chief was simply staving off the inevitable by the exercise of his will, kicking against the pricks, bluffing Nature as he himself put it. But we knew alas, in a way which we could not make him comprehend! but it was a dangerous process. And so when the breakdown came, and it did not seem to be a bad one, we knew that what we had begged him to do months before would now have to be done, we were rather satisfied. We did not say, "I told you so" but we thought it very loudly.'

CHAPTER 13

LEADER OF THE LABOUR PARTY

THE General Election to which Hardie had looked forward with great eagerness took place in January 1906. The Tory Government had resigned and a new Liberal Government was formed with Sir Henry Campbell-Bannerman as Prime Minister. He chose his Ministry and then called for a Dissolution of Parliament.

Hardie was not enthusiastic about the personnel of the new Liberal Government. Campbell-Bannerman had been cradled in Toryism and had been the chairman of the Unemployed Committee which 'had got the winter over without doing anything for the out-of-works'. 'Perhaps,' thought Hardie, 'he has repented of the apparent callousness which the exigencies of party forced upon him in those days and is prepared to atone for the past by his good deeds in the future'. He was 'shrewd' and 'capable of looking all round a question before taking action'.

There were too many peers in the Cabinet for Hardie's liking and they were mostly landlords who had 'not joined the Government to press for either land nationalisation or for the taxation of land values'.

Hardie wrote of Lloyd George:

'Mr. Lloyd George can be safely described as a politician with no settled convictions on social questions. As a hard working lawyer, a rising politician he has had enough to do to keep abreast of the fighting party line without wandering into the by-ways of social reform.'

The most prominent Radical was John Morley, one of Hardie's old political opponents.

'Morley is philosophic, timid, and pedantic; he is the last of the race of Radical philosophers, who did so much for political freedom half a century ago, but whilst John Stuart Mill, under the softening influence of Helen Taylor, moved forwards to a catholic and generous form of communism, Morley has as steadily receded to a barren and sterile individualism.'

About John Burns, Hardie speculated: 'It is round John Burns that

greatest interest centres. In his early Socialist days he fought magnifi-
cently but he has not shown himself the man to lead a forlorn hope
or to stand above in a crisis. He is a hard worker and that alone will
create a stir in his department and may lead to surprising results. It
would be very difficult for anyone to go to the Local Government
Board without doing good work of some kind.'

He dismissed Asquith and Haldane as 'cold-blooded reactionaries
of the most dangerous type. With professions of Liberalism on their
lips, they are despots at heart, and as they are the strong men of the
Cabinet and are great upholders of the Roseberian interpretation of
Liberalism, they can be reckoned upon to see that their view is well
upheld in the inner councils of the Cabinet.'

After referring to other members of the Government, Hardie concluded: 'Labour folks will withhold their judgment in suspense while
the Cabinet has justified itself by its works. They will note without
any great enthusiasm that there are seventeen landowning peers and
sixteen place-hunting lawyers in the new Government and, apart from
John Burns, will scan the list in vain for any name which has been
actively identified with the cause of social reform . . . .

'The fact we have to face is that this combination of Tories, Whigs,
Unionists and Radicals contains a number of astute, able men and that
their ability will be used to divert the attention of the people away
from Socialism and the Labour Party. How far they will be successful
in this depends not upon them but upon the Labour Party itself. A
straight, bold course, free from trimmings, scheming or temporising, is
a line of action for which the politician has no checkmate. *Verb sap.*'

These were shrewd political comments which the subsequent history
of the Liberal Government justified.

At the General Election there were fifty-two Labour Party candidates, ten of whom were I.L.P. nominees. Hardie threw himself into
the election campaign with great vigour and enthusiasm.

He warned Labour candidates that they had nothing to gain by
timidity upon the election platform:

'Why should a Labour candidate be timid on the hustings? The Labour
man enters the contest with the advanced men behind his back, and feels
that his business is to win over the cautious and timid electors to his side.
Within limits, this is quite allowable, but it is none the less a very
dangerous game to play. Once a man begins to play fast and loose with
his principles, he gets on a slippery slope, at the bottom of which is the

125

slough of time-serving expediency. . . . What shall it profit a man though he gain a seat in Parliament and lose his own self-respect?'

After outlining the difficulties with which Labour candidates were faced, he continued:

'There is but one way to overcome these difficulties and drawbacks, and that is for the candidate and his supporters to give the earnest, enthusiastic, thinking portion of the electorate a good, strong, well-informed fighting lead. He must first of all win their support by being straight, and keep it by the same means. Should he ever forget that he is a pioneer and sink to the level of a mere vote-hunting, popularity-seeking candidate, then he is in a more false position than either Liberal or Conservative.'

Labour candidates were advised not to 'wobble' or temporise:

'The candidate who courageously pursues a straightforward line of action, who has knowledge of the social problem and makes intelligent use of it, is not in the least handicapped by being a Socialist; nay, is rather helped thereby. It is the man who wobbles, who seems to face all points of the compass at once, who earns the contempt of friend and foe alike. The nation needs a strong lead; the eyes of the thoughtful of all classes are fixed upon the Labour candidate to see what hope for the future lies in him. If he temporises and hesitates, when he should be firm and unbending; if he, because victory appears to be within his reach, nervously begins to unburden his candidature of principles which he thinks may offend some whose support he is anxious to secure, then he is sapping and undermining the foundation upon which alone, an enduring movement can be built.'

Hardie believed that his seat in Merthyr was safe and so he spent most of his time in other constituencies helping other candidates. He spoke at Croydon, Birmingham, Norwich, Blackburn, York, Sunderland, Stockton, Middlesbrough, Jarrow, Newcastle, Stockport, Wakefield, Dewsbury, and Huddersfield, travelling by train to most of these places, for the day of the lightning tour by fast motor car had not then arrived.

The travelling itself was a great physical strain, especially on a man who had undergone a serious operation only a short time before. In Merthyr they wondered when their candidate was going to arrive. Frank Smith, his old friend, was deputising for him but that was not enough and when Hardie finally arrived, he had to address nineteen meetings in two days.

At the last moment Ramsay MacDonald, who had just been elected M.P. for Leicester, arrived along with Mrs. Pankhurst. It was a two-Member seat. The other Liberal Member was D. A. Thomas, later to become Lord Rhondda, and the new candidate was a Cardiff shipowner by the name of Radcliffe. The local correspondent of *The Labour Leader* reported that 'the plan of the enemy was simplicity itself. Lawyers and other hangers-on were hired by the dozen to go about the place and whisper from ear to ear that Keir Hardie was an atheist and a foreigner.'

In Nonconformist Wales this was damaging. 'In England a charge of this kind would not amount to much, but in these villages among the hills, where the older people do not even speak English and where they are cut off from all connections with the movements of the outer world, and especially when the ministers, remembering doubtless that Radcliffe was a rich man who had helped to build a mission hall in the constituency and would probably be a generous subscriber to their funds, went over to him almost in a body, their charges acted like poison in a healthy body.'

But the two-day campaign before the poll stemmed the tide. 'On polling day the enthusiasm for Keir was tremendous and the men and women worked like Trojans. On Radcliffe's side were nearly all the Nonconformist ministers, the bulk of the publicans, the tariff reformers, leading Conservatives and disgruntled Liberals. But in the end honesty and hard work won. Our final word is that we expect Keir in future to remember that his first duty is to himself and his own constituency.

'Had he been here a week before the poll there would have been no contest; had he had two days longer in which to get round the constituency he would have headed the poll.'

The result in the two-Membered constituency was:

D. A. THOMAS (Liberal)	...	...	13,971
KEIR HARDIE (Labour)	...	...	10,187
RADCLIFFE (Liberal)	...	...	7,776
Majority for Hardie		...	2,411

When the last results came in it was found that 29 Labour candidates had been returned.

In future there was to be what Hardie had toiled for so long, an independent Labour Party in Parliament.

Hardie had every reason to be gratified with the result of the General Election but he thought Labour should have done better. He was rather disappointed with Scotland, where only two seats, one in Dundee and the other in the Hutchesontown Division of Glasgow, had been won. At Paisley, Robert Smillie 'waged one of the hottest fights of the campaign' but the ground had not been sufficiently prepared by organisation beforehand.

Pointing out the weaknesses in Scotland, Hardie wrote:

'With the exception of North-East Lanarkshire, which had been fought on two previous occasions, little or nothing was done either in the way of propaganda or organisation until the election was at hand. In North Ayrshire and the three Lanarkshire miners seats the cause of defeat can be attributed to that too common fault, lack of preliminary organisation.'

With all his idealism, Hardie was the hard-headed Scot when it came to election organisation. He knew that enthusiastic meetings did not mean that the candidate just went in on the day of the poll. In fact a quotation from his summing-up of the election might have been taken from the *post mortem* Labour Party report on the election of 1955: 'I think the principal lesson which the election has taught is the urgent need for some systematic method of organising constituencies which are to be fought by Labour candidates . . . .

'The nucleus exists in the Trade Union organisation but unless this is properly utilised and trained for action it falls lamentably short of what is required when the election draws near. The L.R.C. will probably tackle this matter by appointing a permanent election agent who will periodically visit all the Labour constituencies and see that the electoral machinery is kept in good working order.'

The General Election had been fought without the Labour Party even having a national agent. Hardie was 'amused to hear complaints from Labour candidates at the unfair way they have been treated by the Press.' He was accustomed to this. 'What,' he asked, 'could anyone expect?' He was also amused at what had happened in Arthur Henderson's constituency. 'In the Barnard Castle Division, Mr. Arthur Henderson's opponent issued a placard declaring that every vote given to Henderson is a vote given to Keir Hardie, but even this did not seem to frighten any of Mr. Henderson's supporters from voting for him.'

He thought that one of the lessons that should be learnt from the election was that Labour should have a daily paper of its own.

'We must, however, be prepared for even great misrepresentation in future contests and there is but one way in which we can hope for even a semblance of fair play in the Press and that is by having a daily organ of our own, even if it should only be issued at election times to begin with. Some of the older papers with a tradition of honourable journalism still strong upon them gave the Labour candidates decent reports but the

Keir Hardie and Bernard Shaw at Merthyr, 1910.

Women's Suffrage Demonstration, Trafalgar Square, 1910.

Merthyr Election Poster by Cosmo Rowe, 1910.
(The original drawing of the portrait is in the National Portrait Gallery, London.)

newer rags of the Harmsworth type sounded the depths of gutterdom all through the campaign. To me the most encouraging feature of the campaign has been the fact that the candidates who fought straightest fared on the whole best at the polls. Not only so but time will show that their triumph is a permanent kind.'

He went off for a fortnight's holiday to Ireland and returned for the opening of Parliament. The first meeting of the Parliamentary Labour Party was held in Committee Room No. 13 on Monday, February 12th, 1906.

Keir Hardie was elected Chairman of the Party for the ensuing session, D. J. Shackleton Deputy Chairman, J. Ramsay MacDonald Secretary and Arthur Henderson Whip. In the 'Parliamentary Notes' of *The Labour Leader* there appeared the news item:

'An amusing story told in connection with Mr. Keir Hardie may be recalled appropriately just now. Just before the opening day of the session a year ago he had occasion to repair to the House of Commons to consult some books, but found himself intercepted in a friendly fashion by a policeman, when the following conversation resulted. "Are you working here, mate?" "Yes." "On the roof?" which was undergoing repairs. "No, *on the floor.*" '

On February 23rd *The Labour Leader* made the brief announcement:

'The Labour Representation Committee will be known no more among us. It has discarded its unwieldly baptismal name and adopted the simple unqualified title of "THE LABOUR PARTY." '

It was a new experience for Keir Hardie to be treated as the Leader of a Party. A copy of the King's Speech was sent to him in advance and he was given the Parliamentary courtesies usually accorded to a party leader. He appointed F. W. Jowett, of Bradford, and George Roberts, of Norwich, to be his Parliamentary Private Secretaries.

The Labour Members sat below the gangway on the Opposition side and Hardie had one of the best seats in the House.

' "He had to travel over a wide variety of subjects," said the special correspondent of *The Labour Leader,* describing Hardie's first speech as Chairman of the Labour Party. He had to speak of Secular Education, the Trades Disputes Bill, the Franchise for Women, Chinese Labour and the liqueur bar in the smoking room. One might have been excused for getting tedious on such a variety of subjects, but the Liberals opposite soon drew our leader out of himself.

'Here is how it happened. In the course of his speech he spoke of "the pocket interests which led men of the middle class parties to desire workers to remain in their power".

' "No! No! No!" came from about fifty Liberal throats. "No! No!

129

No!" they repeated. They looked shocked at this blunt statement of the truth. The contradiction drew Hardie out of himself. He raised his voice beyond its usual pitch, and in his excitement he got out on the floor of the House until he reached the table which had been used for members to swear themselves in. It reminded one of Ajax defying the lightning. A man of the people had been able to tell the plain truth in the presence of principalities and powers.'

THE RED PAINT.

'Steady on with that red paint, mate, you're splashing it about a bit too thick!' (a cartoon of 1906).

The same week, the sixth Conference of the Labour Representation Committee, now the Labour Party, met in London at the Memorial Hall. There were over 350 delegates. Hardie received an ovation as he mounted the platform.

The chairman, Arthur Henderson, announced that the local membership was 900,000, an increase of 21,000 over the previous year.

Henderson said that the victory of Labour at the elections made the Conference a historic one. 'Now we have impressed the public mind with the thought that the new Labour Party is the greatest factor in the present highly interesting political situation we must demonstrate our determination to make the work of the Party comprehensive, effective and permanent.' He knew that the advanced Socialists and the Trade Union M.P.s had their differences, but they had a lot in common which they could obtain through the new Labour Party. He ended by stressing that one thing 'they should regard as sacred was the basic principle of independence which alone had secured the success of the movement.'

It was this 'principle of independence' that Hardie had stressed in all his campaigning for a Labour Party. He wanted a Labour Party with its own separate identity and its own organisation in Parliament. Once that was attained, he believed, it would inevitably develop into a Socialist Party with a Socialist programme and policy. He knew that as a Socialist he was far in advance of the big majority of the members of the new Labour Party in the House of Commons. Apart from the candidates that were definitely I.L.P. — Ramsay MacDonald, Philip Snowden, F. W. Jowett, James Parker, G. H. Roberts and Hardie himself—the rest had come in as trade union candidates. Their election expenses had been paid by their unions, although many of them were also individual members of the I.L.P.

Some of them were to play a prominent part in British politics in the years that were to follow. Ramsay Macdonald was to become Prime Minister of the first Labour Government, Snowden was to become Chancellor of the Exchequer and end up in the House of Lords, Henderson was to become a Minister in the Coalition Government and afterwards Home Secretary, and Foreign Secretary in Labour Governments, and George Barnes, John Hodge and J. R. Clynes were also to become ministers. All of them were in the first Labour Party over which Hardie presided. There were lesser-known men, some of whom shivered at the idea of being called Socialists. They were there because their unions had joined the Labour Party. Hardie, of course, knew this. He thought that the pressure of events and their experience would make them Socialists but he recognised what they were and made no attempt to coerce or dragoon them into his way of thinking.

Sufficient for the time being that they were the rank and file of a Labour Party which was independent of the Liberals and had its own line. He knew what the line should be in Parliament and would do his best to get the Labour Party to follow it.

Hardie, in his own way, was as irreconcilable and as determined and as single-minded as Parnell, but he did not wish to try to be a

131

dictator or to rule his following as ruthlessly and as fiercely as Parnell had led the Irish.

The Labour Party was different. Its members were accustomed to the democratic rules and procedure of the trade unions, and they were not revolutionaries or fanatics. Many of them were all quite new to politics, and rather subdued and awed by Parliament.

They respected Hardie and realised that he had considerable Parliamentary experience, but they did not want to go all the way with him. Hardie understood this was the human material that he had to deal with and to mould into a party that would do effective work in Parliament and command respect outside. It was only the beginning. He had been in the trade union movement a long time, himself, and knew human nature. He did not expect too much. But he would give a lead, do his best to encourage the hesitating and help the new men.

Nearly all the new Labour M.P.s had been, in their youth, manual workers and had known the hardships of unemployment, hard work and poverty. They were miners (although the Miners' Federation had not yet joined up), railwaymen, gasfitters, factory workers, labourers.

None of them had had more than an elementary school education and Hardie not even that. Only MacDonald, who had been an uncertificated schoolteacher and a clerical worker, and Snowden, the ex-civil servant and excise officer, could have been described as intellectuals. Middle-class intellectuals interested in political careers were still with the Tories and Liberals. They had not yet realised that there were prospects in the Labour Party. The Liberal benches were crowded with lawyers and middle-class politicians. There was not one lawyer on the Labour benches in the 1906 Parliament.

The passing into law of the Trades Disputes Bill was a first notable success for the new Labour Party and Hardie, in an article 'The Bill the Whole Bill, and Nothing but the Bill', told how it had been achieved. It reversed the legal decision of the Taff Vale Judgment which had laid it down that the trade unions were liable for damages if their members went on strike. Strangely enough some of the Right Wing trade union leaders did not want the Bill or only partial immunity from legal action. Hardie was strongly of the opinion that there should be complete immunity and the Labour Party took up that view and successfully appealed to the government to support a Labour Party Bill. The Liberal lawyers in the Cabinet were hesitant at first but finally agreed. It was not a Government Bill and so the

Tories, led by Mr. Balfour, strangely enough, decided to allow the Bill to go through and this helped to smooth its passage through the Lords. Hardie wrote:

'Finally, had there been no Labour Party in Parliament and the country, it is a moral and political certainty that complete immunity would have been impossible. Few people realise the value of independence as a means of raising a distinct issue and creating that psychological atmosphere, which much more than argument, influences a deliberative assembly. It is much easier, also for men to be true to their election promises when they are faced by *a party*, to vote "yea" or "nay" on a question on which they are pledged. The Labour Party is an element of strength on the side of reform which it would be difficult to over estimate, if only as a corrective to the blighting and demoralising influence of the two party system.'

When the Bill finally passed through the House of Lords, which was not anxious at this stage to fight on an industrial issue, it was hailed as a political victory for Keir Hardie!

In the first week in December 1906, Hardie introduced a Women's Suffrage Bill. It was a non-party, one-clause bill which was backed by Arthur Henderson and Philip Snowden.

This was a direct challenge to the Liberal Government, which had an overwhelming majority in the House. If it believed in Women's Suffrage why should it not support Keir Hardie's Bill? It was not, however, going to be so easy to pass as the Trades Disputes Bill. In a letter to *The Labour Leader* on December 21st, Hardie replied to correspondents who had written to him about the attitude of the Women's Social and Political Union (the organisation of Mrs. Pankhurst and the militant suffragettes) towards the Labour Party and the I.L.P.

He had been asked whether he thought the women suffragists should support the Labour Party candidates at election times in view of the fact that some members of the Labour Party were not as strong supporters of women's suffrage as he and Arthur Henderson and Snowden.

He replied:

'You ask me whether I think the women suffragists should support the Labour Party candidates at by-elections. My reply is, Yes, most emphatically, at the present time. Where, *therefore*, there is a Labour candidate in the field I am sure the women suffragists would best serve their own cause at present by sturdily backing him.

'My reason for saying this is that the Labour Party, as a party, has agreed to place a Bill for the political enfranchisement of Women in the front rank of its programme for next Session, and this completely changes the position, in which the question of women's enfranchisement has hitherto stood. There are individuals in all other parties who are prepared to support your claims but there is no other party which, as a party has taken the question up and made it a party measure.'

He went on to stress that women's suffrage was only the beginning, not the end of the struggle for women's emancipation: 'Further I should deplore the fact that any woman should leave the I.L.P. over this question. To do so would show a degree of ingratitude which is rare even in politics. From the day of its inception the Independent Labour Party has never wavered or hesitated in its allegiance to the women's cause. The political enfranchisement of women will only mark the beginning, not the end, of their struggle for emancipation. The vote is a weapon which can be used with effect in changing the conditions under which men and women alike suffer under the present system. We want, therefore, to make women Socialists as well as suffragists.'

Mrs. Pankhurst, however, who had been an old friend of Hardie's and one of the first members of the I.L.P., thought that Women's Suffrage was the political question of paramount importance and was frantically determined to wage her militant campaign against all parties and politicians. Later Hardie was to have the experience of being howled down by the suffragettes himself.

On December 12th Hardie, as Chairman of the Labour Party, was called on to state its case on the Lords amendments to the Education Bill.

The Labour Party was not enthusiastic about the Liberal Government's Education Bill. It had asked for Secular Education. Hardie said:

'The House was discussing an essentially working-class question, and one upon which working-class opinion had been clearly expressed. The Government Bill settled nothing, and it pleased no one. Had the Government been courageous and logical enough to face the secular solution nine-tenths of the time of the House of Commons which had been wasted over this question would have been saved. There would have been one big fight, and the religious difficulty would then have been got out of the way once for all.'

He was not, he said, one of those who was in a hurry to see a conflict with the House of Lords on this issue.

'A great constitutional crisis like that would absorb all the energy and attention of the people. Social reforms would go by the board, but if the issue was to be forced upon the country, and if the Constitution was to be thrown into the melting-pot, he trusted the Government would attempt to be logical in finding a solution of the difficulty which would then arise. Any attempt to compromise on the question whether the House of Commons or the House of Lords should be supreme would be fatal to the party which attempted it. In conclusion, he said the Labour Party would support the Government in the motion for the rejection of these amendments *en bloc*.'

If there was to be a fight with the Lords, Labour wanted a fight to the finish.

Hardie was still very far from being well, but he stuck to his post in the House of Commons with his characteristic dour tenacity.

The Parliamentary Correspondent of *The Labour Leader* noted on December 14th, 1906:

'Keir Hardie has been a great deal in evidence this week. His health is not of the best just now and he has evidently to struggle against physical weakness but nevertheless he has stood true and staunch at his post, and when others succumbed to the terrors of an all-night sitting, he was to be seen, at half past three in the morning, in his corner seat as eager and active as he had been at half past three in the previous afternoon.

'To him last Thursday fell the honour of having, for the first time, obtained justice for the illegitimate child and the mother of an illegitimate child in the discussion of the Workmen's Compensation Bill. Lord Robert Cecil grew dark with sectarian passion when he found that the Government were going to accept the amendment of our leader but the amendment went through all the same.'

The House did not realise why Hardie was so personally proud of the result of his fight for the illegitimate child and the mother of the illegitimate child. He had been thinking of the ordeal of the mother with the illegitimate child in the one-room cottage in a Lanarkshire village fifty years before.

Hardie had a deep distrust of the members of the Liberal Cabinet who had supported the Boer War, 'the Liberal Imperialists', as he called them, and especially for R. B. Haldane, who was Secretary of State for War.

Haldane had been studying the structure of the German Army in Germany and had returned with proposals for a 'National Army'.

Hardie thought that the Haldane proposals would 'require the most careful watching and unflinching opposition from all friends of peace'. He wrote:

'At a time when Continental nations are growing weary of conscription and are agitating for its abolition we are having it insidiously introduced to this country under the specious guise of broadening the basis of the Army.'

135

He continued:

'Haldane's mental make-up is more akin to the German militarists than to the best type of British statesman. He tells us that he thinks the day not far distant when the democracies of the world can themselves initiate the task of freeing themselves from the intolerant and crushing burden of military armaments.

'Until that time,' he says, 'we must play our part. The wise, far-seeing statesman would have found his part in heading and guiding and inspiring this movement of the democracies; Mr. Haldane conceives his part to be that of strengthening the system which he professes to hate.'

This was to be one of the first of many warnings against Haldane. Hardie loathed anything that looked like militarism. He wrote:

'Militarism and all that pertains to it is inimical to the cause of progress, the wellbeing of the people and the future of the race. The Labour Movement of every country is anti-militarist, with a strength born of deep intuitive conviction and dear-bought experience. We in Great Britain should join with the democracies abroad in battling for the dethronement and overthrow of the war god.'

When it came to the test Britain and the other democracies were not so anti-militarist as Hardie thought. One can never prophesy exactly what will happen in politics. Haldane was praised first because he had prepared the Army for war and then driven out of the Liberal Government by the jingo Press which made him the victim of an anti-German campaign and recalled his statement that Germany was his 'spiritual home'.

Hardie certainly did not dream in 1906 that, less than twenty years after, Haldane would be the Lord Chancellor in the first Labour Government!

· The National Council of the I.L.P. celebrated Hardie's jubilee with a reception in the Memorial Hall, London. Hardie, it was reported, did not arrive at the hall until nine o'clock for 'he had been addressing a meeting at Poplar on behalf of the Labour candidates'.

There was a big representative gathering of Labour M.P.s and sympathisers and messages from all parts of the country. There were 447 telegrams from I.L.P. branches, trade unions and other organisations, and many letters from prominent people ranging from Arthur Henderson to the Executive of the Social Democratic Federation which had often quarrelled with him but whose message read:

'This Executive Council of the S.D.F. congratulates comrade Keir Hardie on the attainment of his fiftieth birthday, expresses their admiration of his independent Parliamentary career, and his outspoken declaration of Socialist principles as the object of the working-class movement, and wishes him many years of life in which to carry on his work for the people.'

The Executive of the Fabian Society congratulated the Labour minority in Parliament on Keir Hardie's fiftieth birthday and hoped 'to congratulate a Labour majority on his hundredth'. It looked as if Bernard Shaw had had a hand in that.

Cunninghame-Graham wrote: 'I am very sorry I am so far from town or I should be with you. I do not wish him anything so horrible on his own account, but on account of the party I hope Keir Hardie may live a thousand years.'

They presented him with something he had always longed for, a gold watch (it was stolen from him later in a by-election), and he made a short speech.

'He spoke with considerable emotion, declaring that he had done what he had done only because he could not with peace of mind have acted otherwise. He usually found that when he obeyed his intuition, which was a higher faculty than reason, all went well, but when he yielded to political expediency, he was sure to regret it. He was above all things a Socialist, and for no temporary political gain would he ever willingly sacrifice the interests of the Socialist cause. He thanked them sincerely for their token of appreciation to himself, but he was even more grateful to them for their kind recognition of his wife, who had borne so well the toil of his home and so often his long separation from her and their children.'

He went home to spend his fiftieth birthday at Cumnock and stayed up late at night to write an article for *The Labour Leader*:

'To-night it is difficult to say whether I have been fifty years or fifty centuries on the earth. The cloudy day has given way to a starless night. Darkness has crept down from the hills and shut out from view the wood opposite. Sitting in the darkness and looking out into the blackness of the night, with no sound save the rustle and the sough of the wind in the trees and the murmur of the river as, like time, it glides ever on and on, memory is busy in restoring the past. The single room, the dark thatch showing above, and an earthen floor shining black underfoot, the kitchen dresser with the rank on which the delf gleamed in the light of the glow from the cannel coal fire. Even a candle was an occasional luxury; lamp, there was none save the pit lamp. How the figures stand out clearly limned as they and their shadows move about in the little room. Strange that nearly all the memories of those days are of evenings . . .

'The turmoil of a contested election. Howls, curses, execrations, peltings with mud and stones; one poor, solitary figure knocked and buffeted about bodily and mentally, and yet compelled to go forward by he know not what.

'Looking back over the way I have come I can honestly say I have never had reason to regret following the steep, straight path of duty, and,

I may add, I have never yielded to the temptation to try the apparently easier way without having cause to rue it.'

Then he turned to moralising on the political situation and the outlook for Socialism:

'There is much I fain would say about the present situation, but that can wait. Socialism is to me more of a certainty, also more of a necessity than ever before. As for political independence, that must be maintained even if it involves the loss, at the next election, of every Parliamentary seat we now hold. We must keep faith with the brave souls whose toils have made the situation what it is. Reforms will come in any case; it is the rebellious spirit of self-sacrifice in the people which is going to renovate the life of the nations. The agitator who has a touch of the seer in him is a far more valuable asset than the politician. Both are necessary, but if one must be sacrificed let it not be the agitator.

'A final word. I am younger in spirit at fifty than I ever remember to have been. I am of the unfortunate class who never knew what it was to be a child—in spirit I mean. Even the memories of boyhood and young manhood are gloomy, Under no circumstances, given freedom of choice, would I live that part of my life over again. Not until my life's work found me and stripped me bare of the past and absorbed me into itself did life take on any real meaning for me. Now I know its main secret He who would find his life must lose it for others. One day I may, perhaps, write a book on this. But there! I have just entered my fifty-first year. And so one more pipe and then to bed.'

In February 1907 Hardie was re-elected unanimously to the chairmanship of the Parliamentary Labour Party. In *The Labour Leader* he replied to critics who wanted to rigidly lay down the lines that the Party in Parliament should follow:

'If the Party in the House is to be successful it must be free to select its own course. If the members cannot be trusted to be loyal and faithful to their great trust, then no programme and no regulations will be of any avail.'

Among the issues that the Party intended to raise were Miners' Eight Hours, Old Age Pensions, Unemployment and Women's Suffrage.

'It will be strange indeed if we cannot do something effective for both the aged poor and the unemployed. If we don't succeed it will not be for lack of trying.'

Then there was the land problem.

'This season I hope to see the party grappling at close quarters with the root cause of all our troubles, private ownership of land. Everything else is mere skirmishing leading up to this, which must be for every democratic party, whether Socialist or Labour the main citadel to be attacked.

When it falls much else that is powerful for evil will fall also. Those who put their trust in the party will have no reason to be ashamed.'

In February he went to Cambridge to address a meeting under the auspices of the Fabian Society.

One of the students was young Hugh Dalton. In his autobiography *Call Back Yesterday,* Dalton tells how he first met Keir Hardie:

'A memorable event for me and many others was Keir Hardie's visit to Cambridge early in 1907. He had just upset conventional people by some blunt criticisms of British rule in India. He was a red rag to all Tory bulls. So when it was announced he was to speak in the Cambridge Guildhall under the auspices, the bulls got busy.'

Dalton and his friends arranged for V. H. Mottram, later to become well known as a scientist, to be disguised as Hardie, and so thwarted attempts to kidnap him.

'Meanwhile, another party of which I was one met the real Keir Hardie on a later train and took him to Kings' for a meal and then to the meeting. This was soon broken up, before he had been able to say much, by stink bombs and cat calls. An attempt was made to rush the platform and there were cries that he should be thrown into the river. So we formed a bodyguard around him and fought our way across the Market Square and King's Parade into the shelter of my own college where he held court awhile and then slept peacefully.

'In a crowded room I sat at his feet, literally and spiritually. I admired his total lack of fear or anger, his dignified bearing, his simplicity of speech and thought and faith. That night I became a quite convinced Socialist.'

Hardie was always prepared to go to Oxford and Cambridge and to face hostile receptions. He liked to be among young people and to encourage them. His own comment on the Cambridge incident was:

'A dozen years ago it seemed that Oxford was designed to have the honour of being identified with Socialism, as it has with great movements in the past. For the moment it is Cambridge that leads the way. It may be that both will now fall into line. I would like to take the opportunity of acknowledging the many letters received from gentlemen connected with Cambridge and to say that I have, from the first, carefully distinguished between the University and the few students responsible for the disturbance; I thank those who have written me.'

Hardie did not realise that among the young students was a future Socialist Chancellor of the Exchequer.

Hardie again attacked Haldane's plans for reorganising the Army:

'What we are now asked to consent to is a proposal for turning 540,000 of our male population into a machine, ready to be used in filibustering ways by political adventurers in any quarter of the globe . . . I cannot conceive of the working class favouring proposals, which whilst encouraging and developing the military spirit in all directions emphasises the fact that workers are an inferior class to be governed and officered by "the young men of the upper and middle classes" . . .

'Labour must be on guard, lest it, even by its silence, appears to sanction proposals so fraught with evil possibilities.'

At a meeting at Lancaster he was congratulated at having again been elected Chairman of the Parliamentary Labour Party. Hardie said:

'Some thought it was a matter for congratulations; he was not sure about it himself. There was a time, not long ago when he formed the Labour Party in the House of Commons. Which was the greater honour it was not for him to say. He wished to say he did not seek the position of chairman, and he should not again be a candidate for the position at the beginning of the next session. He had always felt that the chairmanship of the Labour Movement was too big to be a one man job. Whatever honour, responsibility and work attached to the position of chairman of the Labour Party should go round among the members. By that means he was certain they should preserve harmony in their ranks and each man would be appointed on his own merits and not because of some fictitious value attached to the office he occupied.'

He ended his speech by remarking:

'Socialism might be inconsistent with some orthodox forms of Christianity but they were sick unto death of having Christianity preached; they wanted it practised.'

Hardie was ill and driving himself on remorselessly, but he went to the annual conference of the I.L.P. at Derby and spoke on resolutions on unemployment, railway nationalisation, women's suffrage, and militarism. It was an encouraging conference, the largest that the party had held.

He went back to London to draft a report on Haldane's new Army Bill for the consideration of the Parliamentary Labour Party. It was a long report, examining the Bill in great detail.

It concluded:

'In view of the facts here summarised, the report recommends that the Labour Party oppose the Bill for the following among other reasons: (a) Because it introduces militarism in our public schools amongst boys at their most impressionable age and before they have reached years of discretion. (b) Because the method by which officers are to be secured bars out the working class and creates an army of workers officered by rich men. (c) Because it introduces the military element into industrial and civil relationships in a way hitherto unknown.'

And finally:

'Because we are not convinced of the need for turning Great Britain into an armed camp.'

In his opposition to the Army Bill he was strongly supported by MacDonald and Snowden and the Party accepted the report and made it the basis of its line-by-line attack.

Hardie was, however, not able to join in the Parliamentary fight. He had been working desperately hard and Nature asserted itself. He collapsed in the House of Commons and was removed to St. Thomas's Hospital for special examination. Mrs. Hardie came down from Scotland to be with him and his old friend Frank Smith took over his correspondence.

After a week's rest he was able to go home to Scotland and whiled away the time on the long journey in the train by writing a May Day message to the readers of *The Labour Leader*.

Someone had given him Liebknecht's chatty memoir on Karl Marx and there was a paragraph dealing with the way Marx had overworked:

'And gradually that iron constitution was undermined. I am convinced —and this is also the verdict of the physicians who treated his last, that Marx if he could have prevailed on himself to lead a natural life, that if a life corresponding to the requirements of his body or let us say of hygiene might be alive to this day. Not until the last year, until it was too late, did he give up night work and then he worked all the more during the day time.'

Hardie knew that this also applied to him and he added: 'I shall try to remember it after I am well again, but there is so much to do and so few to do it. I pray that the end may be sudden when it comes, a lingering illness must be dreadful.'

He arrived safely at Cumnock that night and his wife was glad when they arrived.

He spent a few weeks at home and then went for rest and treatment to a hydro at Wemyss Bay on the Clyde Coast. But recovery was slow; he was not getting into his stride again.

Robert Blatchford had written to him telling him to take a long sea voyage.

'I am seriously thinking of taking the advice first tendered by Nunquam, and since repeated from a hundred quarters, and trying a sea voyage . . . This session is now wrecked, and I could not do anything worth doing by going back at its fag-end. I think it probable, therefore, that I have seen all that I am likely to see of the House of Commons this session. I came here to try and get well, and settled down to the task as I would to the fighting of a by-election. Six and seven times every day I have dressed and undressed to undergo treatment of one kind or another. To leave the job only half-finished would, I feel, be neither fair to myseif nor to those who look to me for guidance. The sea voyage idea is not quite settled, but I give the thought as it has begun to shape itself in my mind.'

There was a final note on politics:

'Compulsory withdrawal from the hurly-burly has not been altogether without its advantages. When we are on duty we are apt to get so impressed with the importance of what we are doing that we are apt to forget the point of view of the looker-on. If politics and politicians seem as petty and peddling to others as they have seemed to me of late, then I do not wonder at the apathy and indifference of the crowd. And yet politics could be made inspiring, and made to loom large in the outlook of the people. But only by the inspiration which comes from a great cause nobly and fearlessly championed. Surely it is to give that inspiration that a Labour Party has come into being!'

His friends were relieved when he finally made up his mind that he would take a long holiday.

CHAPTER 14

FROM SERFDOM TO SOCIALISM

HARDIE had spent some of his convalescence in writing a little book in which he expounded his views on Socialism. It was a modest little book of a little more than twenty thousand words, in a series that George Allen had decided to publish, in view of the interest in Socialism that had been roused by the appearance of the Labour Party in Parliament. In a Foreword, Hardie explained that he had not 'entered into an elaborate disquisition on the historical basis of Socialism' or tried 'to embody its economic theories and principles in a learned treatise'. He thought there was a 'need of a brief, unadorned statement of the case for Socialism, easily understandable by plain folk and which incidentally some of the objections of opponents may be met and some of the difficulties in the way of the earnest seeker after truth may be removed.'

Hardie all his life was an indefatigable pamphleteer but his pamphlets were usually short, terse, and topical, dealing with some current political issue of the moment. He did not often write about Socialist theory in the abstract. In *From Serfdom to Socialism,* however, he dealt with basic principles and answered the usual arguments against Socialism that he had encountered on the political platform. He had been used to answering questions at innumerable meetings and he knew what his opponents and critics were saying.

' " Socialism," he asserted in the first sentence of the first chapter, "is much more than either a political creed or an economic dogma. It presents to the modern world a new conception of society and a new basis upon which to build up the life of the individual and the State." '

Much of Hardie's time had been taken up by replying to critics who objected to Socialism because they said it was anti-Christian. He devoted a chapter to discussing Socialism and Christianity.

'The charge that Socialism is a materialistic creed comes with a bad grace from those whose every waking hour is spent either in striving to accumulate wealth at the expense of their neighbours, or in sensuous and luxurious enjoyment of the pleasures of life.

'It would, however, be an easy task to show that Communism, the final goal of Socialism, is a form of social economy very closely akin to the principles set forth in the Sermon on the Mount . . .

'The Sermon on the Mount is full of the spirit of pure Communism. Christ's denunciations of wealth are only equalled by the fierceness of the diatribes which he levelled against the Pharisees. It was St. Paul who enunciated the doctrine that he who would not work neither should he eat, whilst Saint James in his Epistle rivals the old prophets in his treatment of those who grow rich at the expense of the poor. Contrary to the generally accepted opinion, it is now known that Communism in goods was practised by Christians for at least three hundred years after the death of Christ. Almost without exception, the early Christian fathers whose teachings have come down to us spoke out fearlessly against usury, which includes interest also, and were on the side of Communism . . . It shows how little modern churchmen knew of the history of their own religion when they charge Socialism with being anti-Christian.'

Hardie devoted a chapter to what he called 'Socialism and the Woman Question'. The Suffragettes had made Women's Rights a topical question.

'Woman is clamouring for the vote and will ere long succeed in getting it,' he wrote. 'Whether it will realise all she expects from it when it has been won is more than doubtful, but at least it will place her on terms of political equality with man.

'Now I regard all this, with all its drawbacks, as a healthy sign of the times—as an indication, in fact, of better times in store for mankind. Unrest and discontent are the heralds of coming change, and forerunners of reform. The more women agitate, the deeper they probe into their grievances, the more clearly will the real root cause of all their trouble which is their economic dependence upon man. Under Socialism when the woman, whether as wife, mother or worker, will have a claim in her own right to share in the national wealth, she will at once emerge into greater freedom . . .

'For woman, as for man, therefore, it is to Socialism we must look. No reform of the marriage laws or the franchise laws, will of themselves materially alter her condition. At best the vote is a means to an end, and the end is freedom, and freedom means the right to live and to the means of life in exchange for the performance of some duty to the community. The time will come when motherhood will be regarded as the most sacred of all duties and be rewarded accordingly.'

Hardie was the only leader of any political party who was talking and writing like this. The leaders of the Liberal and Tory Parties were afraid of the Women's Agitation. Hardie was not. His little book dealing with the political controversies of the first decade of the

CAUSE AND EFFECT.

SOCIAL LEGISLATION
1906 - 1908
TRADE DISPUTES ACT
WORKMEN'S
COMPENSATION ACT
SCHOOL-CHILDREN'S
MEALS ACT
OLD AGE PENSIONS
UNEMPLOYED GRANT
£300.000
MINERS EIGHT HOURS BILL

Keir Hardie: 'Look at that list, Mr. Bull—not one of them would have been passed if it hadn't been for our Labour Party!' (a cartoon of 1908).

twentieth century is now out of date but he was looking ahead when he wrote:

'Socialism we believe to be the next step in the evolution of that form of State which will give the individual the fullest and freest room for expansion and development. State Socialism with all its drawbacks, and these I frankly admit, will prepare the way for free Communism on which the rule, not merely the law of the State will be—from each according to his ability, to each according to his needs.'

Hardie called himself a Communist in the William Morris meaning of the word. The Russian Revolution had not yet come.

'We have seen how in our own country the boundaries of freedom have been widening with the progress of the ages. The slave of a thousand years ago, with no more right than the swine he tended, has fought his way upward from serfdom to citizenship. The modern workman is theoretically the equal in the eye of the law of every other class. His vote

145

carries equal weight in the ballot box with that of the millionaire who employs him he is as free to worship when and how he pleases as the noblest baron; his rights are in all respects the same as theirs. Combination and energy have raised him to where he now stands. But his task is not yet finished; the long drawn out struggle is not yet over. There is one more battle to be fought, one more fortress to be assaulted ere he stands within the charmed circle of perfect equality. He has yet to overcome property and win economic freedom. When he has made property his servant not his master, he will literally have put all his enemies under his feet. He will also have proved his fitness to survive as being the best fitted to live.'

Hardie ended his little book by referring to the downfall of the civilisations of the past:

'Must our modern civilisation with all its teeming wonders come to a like end? We are reproducing in every detail every cause which led to the downfall of the civilisations of other days—Imperialism taking tribute from conquered races, the accumulation of great fortunes, the development of the population which owns no property. Land has gone out of cultivation and physical deterioration is an alarming fact. And so we Socialists say the system which is producing these results must not be allowed to continue. A system which has robbed religion of its savour, destroyed handicraft, which awards the palm of success to the unscrupulous, corrupts the Press, turns pure women on to the streets, and upright men into mean-spirited time servers, cannot continue.

'In the end it is bound to work its own overthrow. Socialism with its promise of freedom, its larger hope for humanity, its triumph of peace over war, its binding of the races of the world into one embracing brotherhood must prevail. Capitalism is the creed of the dying present, Socialism throbs with the life of the days that are to be.'

At the end of the book Hardie gave a list of books 'for the guidance of those who desire to learn more about Socialism and the Modern Labour Movement'.

The list was headed by Karl Marx's *Capital* but it was not a list of Marxian text books. It included *News From Nowhere, Merrie England* by Robert Blatchford, *The Historical Basis of Socialism in England* by H. M. Hyndman, *Past and Present* by Thomas Carlyle, *Industrial Democracy* by Sydney Webb, *Poverty, a study of Town Life,* by Seebohm Rowntree, books by Edward Carpenter, John Ruskin and Peter Kropotkin, and Henry George's *Progress and Poverty.*

He not only advised his readers to study the writings of the economists and the sociologists, there were the dreamers and poets as well.

CHAPTER 15

IN INDIA AND AFRICA

IN July he announced that he had decided to extend the long sea voyage he had contemplated to a trip round the world. The funds for this had been found for him by a number of well-to-do I.L.P. members and Quakers who had been anxious about his health. Hardie liked travelling in foreign countries, meeting strange people and studying their political and economic problems. He would be fifteen weeks on the water and then would be forced to rest and be idle. 'I am at last to be able to gratify what has been the dream of my life. Like other boys, I used to indulge in daydreams of foreign travel, especially to those mysterious Eastern lands which have always been to me the realm of wonder.

'I may say that the Party in the House of Commons offered to make itself responsible for the cost of the trip, for which I can never be sufficiently grateful. It was good comradeship.'

He would go to India to study conditions there, where 'a lying Press campaign' was being waged to prejudice the people of this country against Indian aspirations. He would go as 'a warm supporter of the claims of the people of India'.

He would go to Canada and South Africa, Australia and New Zealand, where he hoped to meet old friends and to learn how 'our' movement is progressing. Japan and China would be touched in passing—that and little more . . .

'We want all the understanding possible in our great world-wide movement and even a handshake in passing may not be without its value in bringing the forces of Labour closer together . . '

He thanked all his friends for the kindness they had shown him.

'I hope,' he said, 'to repay them by renewed service next year and the years to follow. If I cannot be active I don't want to live. Work, for me, is the one thing which makes living possible, and without the capacity to work the gift of life would be too burdensome to be borne. It is in the hope, then, of coming back early in the New Year better equipped for service than ever I have been. "Au Revoir." '

He had agreed to write a series of articles for *The Labour Leader* under the title 'A Scamper Round the World'. The first deal with his voyage in the *Empress of Britain* across the Atlantic to Canada. The poet in him came out in a description of the sea:

'Those who want to understand the mystery of the sea should avoid it when the sun is glaring upon it. On Monday evening the sky overhead was black and lowering, the dark waters underneath were rolling across the ship's bows in a long, irregular swell, with a sound between a groan and a sob. Twixt sea and sky everything was rendered indistinct by the grey blur of the mist. Standing on the deck and seeing the strong ship, completely manned, sullenly ploughing her way through the waste one thought of the legends of the North and realised why it is that seafaring races have always been strong, self-reliant and of indomitable will. This that I was looking upon seemed as if man were battling with destiny and proving more than a conqueror.'

He had been down to the steerage 'and found a great improvement both in the way of accommodation and food to anything I had ever seen elsewhere'. He was invariably interested in what was happening to the underdog, even on board a ship. He had a good rest on the voyage and the steward looked after him well and 'when he thought you were likely to be sick, he had a bedside expression which would make a fortune for a doctor in fashionable society'.

He made his way leisurely across Canada, staying at Quebec, Montreal, Ottawa, Toronto, Winnipeg, Calgary, Banff, Victoria and Vancouver, avoiding meetings but receiving deputations from trades unions and Labour organisations that came to greet him. He found a great deal of unemployment and things very much less rosy than the emigration agencies had pictured in their propaganda. 'Emigration,' he noted, 'is pouring men into the country more rapidly than they can be absorbed.' Wages were high and so was the cost of living.

The two articles he wrote on Canada were commonsense and factual. He thought the trade unions were putting up 'a good fight against heavy odds to enable the workers to hold their own'.

'I admit,' he added, 'that a man has more room to breathe here than he has at home, but let no one think of coming here in the hope of finding a workers' paradise.'

The British Press left him alone during his stay in Canada but in India he was followed everywhere by reporters and he complained bitterly about the way he was treated by Reuter's Agency.

Hardly had he landed before the British Press was receiving cables of how Keir Hardie was making inflammatory speeches and stirring up sedition. He was accustomed to having his speeches misrepresented in the Press, but reports of his speeches in India were impudent inventions. To combat this he sent home a batch of Indian newspapers which deprecated the reports that were appearing in London. *The Advocate of India,* Bombay, described the suggestion for Mr. Keir Hardie's deportation as 'inconceivably absurd'. He had visited the Viceroy, Lord Minto, and the Governor of Bombay, addressed the students of Ripon College, winning their applause as he urged the necessity of free and compulsory education in India, 'which was the nearest thing approaching sedition that he had said', and had been inspecting mills, factories and markets.

Bande Mataram, the daily organ of Indian nationalism, had said: 'We have met and talked with Mr. Keir Hardie and we have found him a strong, shrewd-witted man possessed of a great deal of common-sense. He is a Labourite and a Socialist. As a Labourite he will do whatever he thinks best in the interests of Labour, and as a Socialist he is interested in the progress of internationalism. He may take Indian questions with a greater sincerity than the Cottons and the Wedderburns. But to suppose he can do anything for us is a delusion. India, like other countries, must work out her salvation for herself, and the less she trusts to foreign help, the swifter will be her deliverance.'

Hardie agreed with every word of this. But the article clearly showed how little truth there was in the British Press campaign that he was in India, stirring up hatred and spreading sedition.

On October 2nd, 1907, *The Times* published the following items of news of what Keir Hardie was doing in India in the following paragraphs which appeared on its Foreign Page:

'Mr. Keir Hardie delivered a speech at Barisal yesterday in the course of which he said that he would do his best to assist in making India a self-governing colony like Canada. What was good for Canadians, he added, must be good for the Indians.

'The Barisal Mohammedans have presented a petition to the magistrates stating that they are unable to say their prayers owing to the continual shouts of "Bande Mataram!" by the Hindus in connection with Mr. Keir Hardie's visit. *The Englishman* and the *Indian Daily News* condemn Mr. Keir Hardie's tone as very mischievous. The *Daily News* says, "To talk of Armenian horrors in connection with Eastern Bengal shows an amazing lack of a sense of proportion."

'The Bengal papers express their deepest gratitude to the Labour leader.

149

The *Amritar Bazar Patrika* says, "The people are delirious with joy at the advent of Mr. Keir Hardie" and adds "God has sent Mr. Keir Hardie, whose advent will end the gigantic conspiracy against the Hindus." '

On the basis of these reports *The Times* proceeded to denounce Hardie in a leading article headed 'Fostering Indian Sedition'. It said:

'We have never doubted the powers for mischief which persons like Mr. Keir Hardie possess, nor their readiness to exert those powers. By selecting Eastern Bengal as the theatre for the display of his qualities as a demogogue, he has given a conclusive proof that the estimate we had formed of his criminal ignorance, or his yet more criminal recklessness is but too just . . .

'He promised, we are told, "to assist in making India a self-governing colony like Canada" and he went on to declare that "what was good for Canadians must be good for the Indians". We could desire no more illuminating example of the childish generalisations which are characteristic of arrogance coupled with half-education. The fallacy of this sample of Labour logic in the affairs of Empire is transparent and contemptible.

'He has made other statements as foolish and more criminal.'

When Hardie arrived at Calcutta he promptly pointed out that what he had said had been distorted. He had not delivered a speech at any meeting but had discussed the situation with some representatives of the Indian Press.

Reuter's correspondent had not been there but he had based his report on what Hardie had said that had appeared in a Bengal paper. He had, as Sir Henry Cotton proved conclusively later by placing side by side a translation of the actual report from the Bengal paper and the report that appeared in the British Press, shamelessly misrepresented what Hardie had actually said.

Even the English papers published in India thought that *The Times* had taken the wrong line. 'The English Press, said the *Times of India*, takes a wrong view of the matter.'

There followed a spate of attacks on Hardie by prominent British Conservatives. Lord Cromer denounced him at a dinner at the Guildhall 'for culpable folly' and 'for accepting the ill-regulated enthusiasm of a portion, and by no means the wisest portion of the community in Bengal'. 'The agitators in India,' he added, 'will no doubt, should the occasion arise, be kept well in hand by the firmness and the sagacity of the Viceroy.'

Actually Hardie had visited the Viceroy, Lord Minto, and even *The Times* correspondent admitted that the meeting 'was of a cordial character and the questions of education in India and the emigration of Indians to the colonies had been discussed'. If Hardie had been engaged in 'inflaming sedition' it is hardly likely that his meeting with the Viceroy would have been cordial.

Lord Faber, at a meeting at Leeds, asked how long the Government was going to allow Mr. Keir Hardie 'to lecture on seditious subjects

Sedition!

A cartoon from 'Punch' which advocated Keir Hardie's expulsion from India.

151

in the most seditious part of India, with the sedition-mongers themselves in attendance'. He was afraid that if they did not stop Mr. Keir Hardie, what he did in India 'would be washed out with much blood and money' and he hoped the Government would ask Mr. Keir Hardie to return home and leave India alone.

The Durban correspondent of *The Times* reported letters in the newspapers there urging the application of the Immigration Restriction Law on Keir Hardie if he tried to land in Africa and failing this that the people of Durban should prevent him landing 'as it is believed his presence among the natives would stir them up to a dangerous state of agitation'.

The Statesman of India, however, said, 'It is difficult to understand the London papers. Mr. Hardie may have expressed opinions where silence would have been wise, but to read the English comments one would suppose that he had been parading the provinces inciting to a second Mutiny. The fact that Mr. Hardie was the guest of the Maharajah of Mymansingh disposes of the suggestion that he had been guilty of anything serious.'

The Times, in a paragraph 'The Mischief Maker', drew attention to a cartoon about Hardie that appeared in *Punch.*

'*Punch,*' it said, 'has not failed to put the feeling of the country towards Mr. Keir Hardie and his mischievous speech in India into pictorial form this week. The words beneath point the moral admirably: "Britannia to Keir Hardie — Here, you'd better come home. We know all about you there and you'll do less harm." On another page, too, "Dum Dum" has some timely lines on the same subject.'

The abusive doggerel that *The Times* commended was called 'Hogwash' and judging from the references to agitators and traitors and sedition had obviously been inspired by *The Times* leading article.

Henry W. Nevinson, the war correspondent, was in India at the time and wrote: 'Morley, then Secretary of State for India, compared the unrest to a crying for the moon, the demand for Dominion Home Rule to a demand for Indian fur coats in the Deccan and lamented the "tragic miscarriages of impatient idealists such as he had once been himself".' In these words he was referring to Keir Hardie who was in India at the time and whose speeches had been shamelessly distorted by reporters instructed to discredit him. As Keir Hardie himself said, 'The lie goes round the world while truth is putting on her boots.' Once

152

I spoke upon the subject of India side by side with Keir Hardie and any contact with that great-hearted man was always a delight to remember, so fearless and honourable he was.'

A study of the impressions he wrote for *The Labour Leader* shows how careful and moderate he was in studying the facts. More and more as he proceeded on his way through India, the Indians realised that Keir Hardie was a new kind of British politician and a new kind of Member of Parliament such as they had never met before.

It was shown in many ways. There was the incident when he refused to visit a jail because his Indian secretary would be left outside.

'I was about to visit a prison,' he wrote, 'and was waiting outside the gates in company with some local gentlemen, amongst whom was also Mr. J. Chowdhury, who had acted as my secretary. They were all in native dress, though each of them was a man of some standing and social position, all having received a university education, and some of them having taken degrees at Cambridge and Oxford. When the local magistrate came up to the spot I stepped out from my group of friends to meet him, and after conversing with him for a minute or so we were about to proceed towards the prison gate when he suddenly wheeled round, and speaking in an identical tone with that used by the warders to the native prisoners at the Singapore Goal, he shouted: "Get off the prison compound!" The tone and the manner of the man were so offensive that Mr. Chowdhury suggested that he should not speak in that way; whereupon he kept shouting at intervals of about twenty seconds; "Get off the prison compound; the public road is your place!"'

'Mr. Chowdhury explained to him who he was that he held a seat in the Provincial Legislative Council and so on.

'But this only seemed to make the irate magistrate more angry, and he still kept shouting, until my friends moved away. My feelings were those of shame and humiliation at the scene I had witnessed. After the native gentlemen had gone, the magistrate followed them with his eyes until they were back on the main road, he turned to me and said that we would now go inside. It took me about twenty-five seconds to express my opinion of him and his conduct, at the end of which time I left him standing where he was and joined my friends.'

He went north to Simla, about which he wrote:

'Simla is a hill station seven thousand feet above the sea. Away down in the sultry plains millions of human beings are steeped in never-ending poverty, their loved ones dying like flies, and they themselves always hungry. To the ravages of plague the horrors of famine have this year to be added. To me it appeared as though a black cloud was enveloping the lives of those people with never a gleam of sunlight athwart the gloom. But here in Simla all is changed, as though by the stroke of a magician's wand. In its splendidly appointed offices, competent, capable men compile and prepare their reports out of the material supplied to them by their officials.

'In most countries something in the nature of a gulf separates the governors from the governed; but here the gulf becomes an unbridged chasm.

'The officials in the villages are face to face with the hard, grim facts of the situation, but when their reports reach to the heights of Simla they have undergone a process of sifting and purification, during which all the grosser elements have been eliminated and only rose-tinted ether reaches this serene height. Tons of Blue Books will prove conclusively that the condition of the ryot is everything that the heart of man could desire if only wicked agitators would leave him alone.'

He went on to describe the British Government of India as 'a huge soulless bureaucracy in which every form of popular rights is supposed to be a menace to the stability of the Empire'.

'Such, then, is the Government of India, bureaucratic in form, and, as a consequence, harsh and exacting in all its relations towards the people. To the heads of departments the people of India are but so many seeds in an oil-mill, to be crushed for the oil they yield . . . Sooner or later a beginning must be made towards enfranchising the masses and opening up the way for the educated native to fill the higher and better-paid positions. A native head of department would be more in touch with the people, less easily imposed upon by the lower-paid officials, and generally make for the better government of the country.'

He described a visit to an Indian village:

'From the school we went into the centre of the village, the dominie and his staff leading. Imagine a collection of mud huts, with some of matted palm leaves, all thrown higgledy-piggledy together, with the goats and cattle moving about or being fed from earthenware troughs, and you have the village.

'At first the villagers held aloof, and I subsequently learned that they thought I was the doctor who had come to vaccinate them. But at length they were induced to come together, and finally I got their confidence. They brought me handfuls of boiled rice, which was being prepared for their one and only meal and pieces of bread, some made thick like Scotch oatmeal bannocks and others thin, like ordinary oatmeal cake. I went inside their hovels and saw how they live. One poor woman, her face averted and partially covered by a scarf, showed me her bed. It was the ragged remains of a thick cotton sheet, which at night was put on the ground, without bedding or bedclothes of any other kind. Last year there was a partial failure of the crop, and this year, owing to the drought the failure will be complete, and so they are face to face with famine. Last year they sold their jewellery and mortgaged their land to pay their rent and buy food; this year they are quite destitute of all resources. I had been cross-examining one old man, and finally said: "Last year you mortgaged your land to pay your rent and buy food; this year you have no land to mortgage, and famine is coming. What will you do this year?" Every rib could be seen through his skin, and his face was gaunt and drawn, but his faith was strong. Looking at me simply in the face, he answered: "Trust in God." '

Hardie listened patiently to the British officials' point of view, but he kept one outstanding fact always in his mind.

'It is a fact given on the authority of Lord Curzon when he was Viceroy, and is this—that the average income of the people of India is only two pounds per person per annum.'

It was the hunger and famine that he saw in India that appalled Hardie.

'In fifty years thirty millions (30,000,000) of people died of hunger in India—that, too, under the benign rule of the British Raj. What number died of diseases in the same period will never be known, but we are all agreed that the plague is now persisting and continuing in a way and manner hitherto unknown, and I find the cause to be the growing poverty of the people.

'I have no wish to minimise all that has been done by the British Raj to introduce a settled form of government in India, but we must not overlook the fact that there is another side to the picture, and that the main concern of the rulers of India is not the improvement of the condition of the people, but the increase of the sources from which profits can be drawn.

'In saying this I am not imputing evil motives to the men who rule India, but simply stating a fact which, in my mind, admits of no dispute.'

The colour bar annoyed and distressed him.

'When I entered the train at Madras there were two Indian gentlemen in the compartment. One of them rose as I entered and said, "Shall we move to another compartment, sir?" I stared at the man and asked if he had paid his fare. "Oh, yes," he replied, "but English gentlemen don't as a rule like to travel with natives." Now I knew that in parts of America, the colour line was strictly drawn, but I was not prepared for this kind of thing in India.

'There are carriages labelled "Europeans only", there are others labelled "Females". At some of the principal stations the urinals placed as they usually are at home, are labelled "European gentlemen" whilst out at the end of the platform is a corrugated iron structure labelled "Men" at one side and "Females" at another. Any scallawag in a white skin, even if travelling third class is a "European Gentleman", whilst a titled Indian with a Cambridge degree and perhaps the blood of princes in his veins is only a "man" for whom the corrugated iron structure has to suffice.'

Hardie later revised the articles that he wrote on India and published them in book form. In the preface he wrote:

'I have neither claim nor desire to pose as an authority on India and its affairs, but two months spent in the country during which every minute was occupied either in travelling or in interviewing officials or representative men of all stations in life and of all creeds, castes and classes, led me to certain conclusions.'

These conclusions he outlined in his book. At the time they were considered to be revolutionary conclusions. He wrote in 1907:

'The Congress movement in India is not seditious. It is ultra loyal. Part of it is extreme in its moderation, whilst the other part is moderate in its extremes. There are men in both sections who have grown grey in trying to win for their people some rights of citizenship, and who until the other day, found themselves as far from the realisation of their hopes as ever. What wonder that some of them have become soured, and that they and many of the younger men are now advocating a more forward policy? There is no sedition worth mentioning in India to-day. What there may be ten years hence, unless there be a great change for the better, I would not like to predict.'

The Viceroy of India had been asked by the India Office in London for a special report on Keir Hardie's activities in India.

The Viceroy replied in a telegram on October 7th, 1907:

'You desired information about Keir Hardie. As your information is described as scanty we think it worth while to give you a connected narrative of Keir Hardie's movements and utterances as reported in newspapers, English or Indian. He arrived Calcutta 24th September from Straits.

'On 25th had interview with representative of Empire newspaper, in which he said he had come to India in consequence of the unrest and because he thought Press telegrams on the subject unfair like those sent at time of South African War. He said that he would take no part in Indian politics and did not propose to attend any political meeting.

'He had come to learn and not to teach, and intended to see all classes, including officials.

'His intention was to find out extent and causes of unrest and to ascertain what the agitators sought to accomplish. The Labour Party at home were intensely anxious to see a new departure made giving educated Indians a much larger share in the Government of India. He intended to lay his experience before the Labour Party and to discuss possible action at next session of Parliament. Speaking of Swadeshi, he compared it to Sinn Fein movement, which was consequence of refusal to meet the legitimate demands of Irish people. The cause of unrest in India might be similar.

'On the same day he left Calcutta for Serajganj, where he was received by local agitators in gaily-decorated houseboat. Other boats formed a procession and at Hardie's request "Bande Mataram" was sung. A formal programme of his tour in East Bengal was published in the *Amrita Bazar Patrika*. On morning 26th, he saw Mr. Anslie, the Sub-Divisional Officer, and visited places of interest in the town.

'In the afternoon he went to visit jail with permission of Mr. Ainslie, who came to show him round. Mr. Hardie was accompanied by a number of native gentlemen, including J. Choudhury, son-in-law of Surendra Nath Banerji, and a prominent agitator, who has acted as guide throughout his tour.

'As Sub-Divisional Officer would not allow these gentlemen to enter the jail, Mr. Hardie left without seeing it and went to inquire into a recent strike by jute bailers and other popular grievances.

'On the 27th he arrived Mymensingh as guest of Maharaja Surja Kanta Acharjya. He remarked on number of police in evidence in the streets and said that it reminded him of a city in a state of siege. In an interview he said that the facts which he had learnt that day showed that the Russian methods of administration were closely parallel to those existing in Mymensingh, while some of the atrocities recently committed would, if known in England, rouse as much indignation as Turkish horrors in Armenia. He was convinced that partition was the root cause of all the mischief, that repressive policy had increased unrest, that people had lost faith in the criminal administration, and that union of judicial and executive functions was a scandal. His party was full of sympathy with the Indians and though not numerically strong, was powerful and its power was increasing daily.

'On 28th he left Mymensingh, arriving in the evening at Dacca where he saw the District Magistrate and Nawab Ali Choudhury and inquired into the relative prices of English and swadeshi cloth, expressing his opinion that the latter was the cheaper. He inquired also regarding the boycott and the general political situation and expressed the opinion that the causes of the agitation were the union of the judicial and the executive, the Comila case, the official opposition to swadeshi, the official patronage of Muhammadans, and the refusal of the Lieutenant-Governor when on tour to see the Gauripore zemindars who have supported the agitation.

'On 29th he arrived at Barisal, where he was met by Aswini Kumar Dutt, the chief agitator of Eastern Bengal, and the Editor of the *Amrita Bazar Patrika*.

'Large crowds of students lined the road and shouted "Bande Mataram".

'Here Mr. Hardie delivered a speech thanking the assembly for their kind reception and said that on his return to England he would move Parliament to remove the grievances of the Indians and would recommend the grant to India of self-government on lines similar to Canada.

'On 30th he was entertained at the house of local zemindar and agitator and made a speech to about a thousand persons, in which he said that on return to England he would try to get better justice for Indians and that his inquiries had convinced him that there was no emnity between Hindus and Muhammadans and that both were justified in shouting "Bande Mataram". The agitators in Barisal, where the Ordinance prohibiting political meetings is in force, have been much encouraged by his visit.

'On 1st October he left for Khulna. We have no information as to his doings there. On 2nd October he reached Calcutta and is reported to have announced his intention of convening a conference of Members of Parliament to decide on definite action with regard to India. It is believed that he intends to visit Benares, Delhi, Bombay, and Madras, and that his stay in India will extend to a month or perhaps longer.'

There was nothing very treasonable in this. It was not to be wondered at that Hardie had been fraternising with 'agitators'. For he was one himself.

The British Press misrepresented, maligned and ridiculed Hardie and his warnings and appeals were ignored. The history of the next forty years was to prove how right he had been about India.

BOMBA OCTOBER 13, 1907.]   HINDI PUNCH.   27

Mr. Punch: 'That's the way some Anglo-Indian scare-manufacturers welcome you, friend Keir Hardie.' Mr. Keir Hardie: 'I'm used to this treatment, and I don't mind a bit. It pleases them, and it doesn't hurt me.

Hardie went on from India and Ceylon to Australia. At Fremantle in Western Australia there was 'the inevitable reception', but it was not an official one.

The Mayor, an ex-Labour man, flatly refused to do anything in the way of a civic reception to a man who had been preaching 'sedition' in India, but 'The Labour men more than atoned for Mayor Murphy's loyalty and the reception took place in the Trades Hall, where the leader of the Labour Party in the House of Representatives had come down to assist.' They took him to see the Kalgoorlie goldfields where the Labour Party 'was strong in the industrial places and gaining ground among the farmers'. He was encouraged by his first glimpse of the progress that Labour was making in Australia. At Adelaide he found the Labour Party of South Australia led by a Welshman who had been a stonemason on the building where he was now Prime Minister.

In the Broken Hill mining area he had a warm welcome and at Adelaide he was conscripted to play cricket for Parliament versus the Press and made eight runs. A twenty-year-old friend, H. H. Champion, was there to welcome him at Melbourne and so were Tom Mann and the Honourable Andrew Fisher, who was later to become the first Labour Prime Minister of Australia and who had been associated with Hardie in the very early days in Ayrshire. He had pleasant interviews with His Excellency, Lord Northcote, the Governor-General, and Mr. Deakin, the Commonwealth Prime Minister, and found the Labour Party very much like it was at home. 'There are perhaps,' he noted, 'half a dozen lawyers and doctors in the Labour Parties in the whole of the Commonwealth, all the rest being working men in true ordinary meaning of that word.'

He was welcomed by a large crowd at Sydney where he thought of Thomas Muir, of Huntershill, who had been deported there, a century before, 'sentenced to 14 years for being a Radical'.

'Radicalism in those days was "sedition" in the eyes of the authorities just as the reform movement is in India to-day.'

He was entertained by the Labour Party in the State Parliament where they were looking forward with confidence to a Labour victory at the General Election, and he found all the meetings responsive to the Socialist message.

His next stop was in New Zealand. He was delighted to find that the State coal mines sold coal three shillings cheaper than those under private ownership and 'an eight-hour day from bank to bank'.

At most of the places he visited in New Zealand there were Labour deputations to meet him and many old friends and comrades who had emigrated.

New Zealand, with its progressive spirit and Socialistic legislation which was more advanced than in any part of the British Dominions, impressed him greatly.

It had been a pleasant visit to Australia and New Zealand.

South Africa was different. The conditions of the natives in

Natal appalled him. 'Natal,' he wrote, 'has a native problem and the handling of it has been of the most unsavoury kind. For callous, cold-blooded heartlessness some of its doings during the past few years would be hard to beat, even in the bloodstained annals of the Congo.'

Capetown deeply depressed him and also the conditions of the native population.

He wrote:

'One of, in fact the greatest of, the problems to be faced is the native question. Is he to be recognised as a human being and allowed to vote and own property or is he to be treated as being part wild beast and part child . . . Closely connected with these is the further question of whether the native is to be admitted as a competitor with the white man, or whether certain territories are to be set apart for his exclusive use. These and kindred questions are all bound up in the unifying of South Africa and I found little evidence that they were even being considered. "Make South Africa a white man's country and keep the nigger in his proper place" sums up the prevailing opinion on this point. Keeping the native in his proper place I usually found to mean getting him to do the work of the whites for his mealies . . .

'There is room and to spare for both races in South Africa, but if the white workman is to retain his footing he must not connive at the exploitation of the coloured man. That way ruin lies.

'By refusing to work, and by getting the kaffir to work for him, the white man is tacitly admitting that South Africa is not a white man's country.'

Anyone with the reputation of Keir Hardie could only expect hostility in South Africa. He had been a pro-Boer in the South African war and he had expressed sympathy with the coloured people.

'I landed at Durban,' he wrote, 'and was, of course, soon being interviewed by the Press. Then, as now, the racial question was acute, and the Unions were alarmed at the manner in which the coloured people were supplanting them, even in the skilled trades. To meet this competition the Unions refused to admit the coloured races to membership, which, of course, only aggravated the evil. My suggestion was that as they would then claim the same pay as the whites, a thing they were anxious to do, their competition as cheap workers would end. It will scarcely be credited by those not on the spot, but this produced as much sensation as though I had proposed to cut the throat of every white man in South Africa. The capitalist Press simply howled with rage — there were, of course, exceptions—and at Ladysmith a mob, led by a local lawyer, wrecked the windows of the hotel in which I was staying.'

This, however, was but the beginning.

'At every station at which the train stopped on the way north to Johannesburg, there were crowds of sightseers to hoot and jeer and threaten. Many of these were Boer farmers, who had already forgotten the stand I had made on their behalf at home, and for which, also by the way, I had been stoned and hunted through the streets of towns and cities in both England and Scotland; but these, as a rule, stood looking on and grinning. At one station where the train stopped 15 minutes, and where the mob was specially menacing, I got on to the platform and succeeded in addressing the people. I explained what I had said, and then invited the working men present to say whether they disagreed. For a time no one moved, until a young sturdy blacksmith stepped forward and gripping my hand said, "Here's one that's going to stand by you; you have spoken the truth", whereat quite a big cheer went up, and one fellow, a black-guard of a journalist who had led the opposition, rushed at me with uplifted stick, but was seized by some of those about him and rushed to the outskirts of the crowd. Next morning the Johannesburg Press reported that I had been stoned out of the station.'

It was at Johannesburg where the storm burst in all its fury.

'Mr. Connolly, President of the Natal Railwaymen's Union, and a member of the Legislative Chamber, had very courageously accompanied me up from Ladysmith. An Irishman with the heart of a lion, he was in indifferent health, and for some years I have lost trace of him. When we were entering the capital of the goldfields, he was visibly alarmed. He had had some experience of Johannesburg, and knew what its cosmo-politan crowd could do. The station, the approach leading thereto, and the bridge over the railway was one black mass of seething, howling demons. As the train drew up, young Crawford, one of the deported nine, saw me, and signalled to a number of constables, who formed a cordon round the doorway, whilst a number of them surrounded me and led me by a by-path up from the station to where a cab was waiting. The crowd, which was waiting for my exit by the main doorway, was for a minute or two outwitted, but as the cab, guarded by the police, passed over the bridge, someone awoke to what was taking place, and with a shout the mob started in pursuit. Showers of stones smashed the windows, and both the driver and the policeman came in for some nasty cuts. But the horses were good, and we soon outdistanced the pursuers and reached the hotel in safety, and there was a cordon of police which kept mischief-makers at bay.

'One little incident gave a human touch to my Johannesburg experience. The street was wide and brilliantly lit, and a cordon of police kept a space round the hotel. When I appeared to go to my meeting the usual howl was set up by the crowd, but just as I reached the middle of the street a child broke loose from the footpath, and rushing towards me, clasped me round the legs and looked up and laughingly greeted me. She had been a passenger on the way up from Australia, and we had become very fast friends, thanks chiefly, perhaps, to a daily supply of chocolate. But it was sweet of her to run out and greet me.'

The meeting he addressed at Johannesburg was more like a riot

L

than a meeting. He was lucky to escape with his life. There was one
souvenir that he kept. When in later years visitors used to come to his
rooms at Neville's Court they were surprised to find a torn Union Jack
on the wall. 'Yes,' he used to explain, 'that was captured at
Johannesburg.'

Hardie was not sorry when the time came for him to depart from
South Africa and sail for home.

CHAPTER 16

THE LABOUR ALLIANCE

THE Socialist Movement was glad to see Keir Hardie home again. He had an enthusiastic welcome at a crowded meeting at the City Hall, Glasgow, and was given a complimentary dinner at the House of Commons by the Parliamentary Labour Party. But the biggest meeting of all was that organised by the I.L.P. at the Albert Hall in London on April 5th, 1908. Ramsay MacDonald presided. The great hall was crowded and there were many Indians present.

It was the first time that Socialists had held a demonstration at the Albert Hall and had filled it.

Hardie had an enthusiastic reception. He began his speech by referring to a remark by George Barnes that it was not as a politician they welcomed him but as a Socialist leader. He had never posed as a leader, he said, he had not even tried to please the Labour Party; his whole work had been a long attempt to make peace with his own conscience. 'I am an agitator,' he said with approving cheers. 'My work has consisted of trying to stir up divine discontent with wrong.' Then he went on to give an account of what he had seen in his tour of Canada, Australia, India and South Africa. He turned to home affairs, to the controversy over the Licensing Bill, to the Right to Work Bill, to the prospects of Labour and the advance of Socialist ideas in Britain. He concluded with an earnest appeal to the undecided to join the ranks of the Party. 'By coming into the Socialist Movement they would find the true and high inspiration. They might have to suffer—there were troublous times ahead of them yet, but if they could not make riches for themselves, they would make their own lives and that of their fellows richer and happier.'

It was a meeting long remembered in London. At the I.L.P. Conference at Huddersfield in April 1908 Hardie had a warm welcome, being re-elected to the National Administrative Council with 367 votes. This was the sixteenth conference of the I.L.P. and 401 delegates attended. The party had made progress all over the country. Hardie spoke twice, moving a resolution declaring sympathy with the aims of the Indian Congress and on a resolution on the Licensing Bill. This resolution condemned the present licensing system but declared that 'no temperance reform can be accepted which does not make provision for enabling the community to undertake the municipalisation and complete control of the liquor traffic'.

Ramsay MacDonald presided and Philip Snowden presented the Parliamentary Report. Hardie could congratulate himself on the fact that the I.L.P. was now a big and growing influence in British politics.

In May, at a by-election in Dundee, Winston Churchill stood as the Liberal candidate. Churchill was the type of ambitious politician that Hardie detested.

'What is Mr. Winston Churchill's record?' he asked. 'Returned to Parliament as a Tory, he was not long in discovering that the political days of that party were numbered, and so like a rat in a sinking ship, he scuttled over to the Liberals and was at once pitchforked into office. The electors of North-West Manchester were at first taken in by his glib tongue and his fatal facility for making promises, but when they saw the true character of the man took the first opportunity of turning him adrift again. They refused to be pawns in his game of ambition . . .'

In his election campaign Churchill attacked the Labour Party's Right to Work Bill (which Hardie regarded as vitally important to the unemployed) because 'it would entitle a man to claim work no matter how bad his character, no matter how much he was given to drink, and work at trade union rates of wages at the expense of the municipality'.

Hardie described this and other similar colourful descriptions of the Bill by Churchill as 'either gross and wilful misrepresentations or the outcome of ignorance'.

'If Mr. Churchill has read the Bill, I repeat, he is wilfully trying to mislead the people and the man who would do that in a matter of this kind cannot be trusted to go straight on any other subject under the sun.'

Nothing roused Hardie to indignation more than anything which looked like injustice to the unemployed. He replied angrily to Churchill:

'This Bill, says Mr. Churchill, will ruin industry and add to the miseries of the poor. Set the idle to work, he says, and you ruin industry! Take the poor off the streets and give them useful employment, and you add to their misery! Was there ever such mockery? Mr. Churchill knows that this Bill sounds the death-knell of sweating, and that it means more wages, fewer hours, and happier homes for the worker. Little wonder the sweater and oppressor of labour fears it, though it says little for Mr. Churchill that he stoops to play their dirty game. Remembering, however, what the Marlborough record has been, how from the beginning it has been a great parasite sponging on the State in one form or another, it is, perhaps too much to expect clean politics from such a contaminated source. It is as difficult as ever to "mak' a silk purse o' a soo' lug".'

Hardie thought that his Right to Work Bill had a chance if Churchill was defeated at Dundee and the Labour Party could win the seat. He made a personal appeal to the people of Dundee to keep Churchill out:

'Since the day, twenty years ago, when I first began seriously to look at the causes of poverty, I have regarded unemployment as the root cause. When I entered the House of Commons in 1892 I begged the then Liberal Government to hold a special session to deal with the problem, and from then till now have never ceased to press it on Parliament and the country as the greatest and most pressing problem of the age. Now the question is within the arena of practical politics. The Right to Work Bill received 118 votes this session with 269 against. We are on the point of winning this Magna Charta for Labour.

'The return of Mr. Churchill for Dundee, as an opponent of the Bill, will give the movement a decided rebuff; the return of Mr. G. H. Stuart will make its enactment next session a certainty. In the name of the starved and broken millions of hungry men, women, and children due to unemployment, I ask the workers of Dundee to keep Churchill out by voting for Stuart.'

Churchill won the Dundee by-election and Hardie lost the Right to Work Bill, which he described as 'the greatest humane measure ever brought before Parliament, which would remove from our midst the greatest social and industrial evil of our times'.

Hardie went to Dundee for the eve-of-the-poll meetings, but the Labour candidate polled only 4,014 votes against Churchill's 7,079.

Hardie had long been a friend of the Russian exiles in London. The Russian Revolution of 1906 had been suppressed by the Czar's Government and following it there had been the executions and savage reprisals which had roused indignation in the Western world.

When it was announced that King Edward was to meet the Czar, Ramsay MacDonald declared in *The Labour Leader*: 'It is officially announced that our King is to meet the Czar of Russia. Will our people tolerate such an insult? The Czar is a common murderer.' Hardie protested in a speech at Bristol:

'They were shocked to read that King Edward was about to visit the Czar of Russia. They knew what Russia was at the present time, with its prisons full to overflowing with men and women who dared to claim a constitutional form of government. They knew, too, how strikers had been shot down in the streets which ran with the blood of martyrs. The announcement that the King of Great Britain was to lend the weight of his presence to a Government which was bankrupt in finance and in moral standing was a matter which a good many would regret. When the late King of Serbia was murdered the British Government broke off diplomatic relations. Were we to apply one law to the murder of Kings and another to the murder of a King's subjects?'

When the matter came up for debate in the House of Commons, Hardie declared that the action of the King in going to Russia on an official visit was to condone the atrocities for which the Czar's Government and the Czar personally must be held responsible.

The Chairman of Committees, Mr. Emmott, ruled that the word 'atrocities' was not in order and called upon Mr. Hardie to withdraw. Hardie replied: 'My difficulty is, sir, that I know no other in the English tongue to express my meaning.' There were loud Labour cheers and there followed a long argument with the Chair. Hardie repeatedly refused to withdraw until the Chairman threatened to name him and suspend the sitting. He wanted to finish his speech and the Party wanted the Division. So at last he withdrew the word 'atrocities' and was allowed to continue his indictment of the Czar's Government:

'The number of official hangings and shootings showed no diminution in the policy of repression was being pursued as rigorously as at any time during the past two years. The Czar was not to be trusted in diplomatic matters. There was a danger and a menace to this country to have alliances with a Government over which he was autocratically responsible. Whilst the Government had pressed His Majesty into going to Russia the big financiers of the City had pressed the Government into pressing His Majesty. What would follow the visit would be a fresh Russian loan, which would put millions into the pockets of those gentlemen whose power to-day was greater than that of either Kings, Czars or Emperors . . . It would be better to offend the Czar than to give offence to conscience of Britain. He hoped the result of the Division would put an end to the proposed visit and preserve our reputation for assisting nations struggling to be free.'

When King Edward read the report of the debate he immediately ordered that the names of Keir Hardie, Victor Grayson and Arthur Ponsonby should be deleted from the list of M.P.s invited to Royal functions.

This did not worry Hardie because he had never been to Buckingham Palace, but other M.P.s took the view that the King had no right to do anything which might be regarded as interference with the rights of Members of Parliament.

The Parliamentary Labour Party met and unanimously passed a resolution which said:

'That the action of Mr. Hardie regarding the King's visit to the Czar, which incurred the displeasure of His Majesty and led to Mr. Hardie's name being removed from the list of Members of Parliament recently invited to Windsor, having been taken by instructions of the Party, the Party desires to associate itself with Mr. Hardie, who in its opinion, exercised his constitutional right on the occasion of the Foreign Office debate and it therefore requests that until his name is restored to such official lists, the names of all its members shall be removed from therein.'

The resolution was sent to the Lord Chamberlain. King Edward had not expected this and later Hardie's name was restored.

At a meeting in his constituency Hardie said that personally he had no desire to attend the Garden Party, never had attended and probably never would do so. It had been suggested that he was not invited because he had not attended in the past. He did not mind that but he would not accept or allow any interference from the Crown with his duties as a Member of Parliament. Since the days of Charles I the King had stood outside politics and if the present King was foolish enough to interfere with the politics of Members of Parliament it would be a bad day for him.

On August 14th, 1908, Hardie contributed a long full-page article to *The Labour Leader* entitled 'Socialists and War. The Anti-German Scare in reply to Blatchford, Hyndman and the Jingo Press.'

It was a closely-reasoned attack on the big armament vested interests. He expected war propaganda from them and from the *Daily Mail*, but Socialists had every reason for protesting when Blatchford and H. M. Hyndman, the Socialists, supported it. The kind of anti-German propaganda that they had joined in was 'a discredit to the Socialist who writes it or a Socialist paper that prints it'. 'Hyndman has ransacked the columns of the gutter Press for innuendo and insults levelled against the Germans and dishes these up with all the assurance with which he is accustomed to predict the date of the coming Social Revolution.'

He concluded:

'Let us assume the danger of a German invasion to be real. What is our duty as Socialists and Labour men? When there was trouble threatened between France and Germany over the Morocco affair, what did Jaures and Bebel do? Hyndman knows; he was present at the International

Bureau at the special meeting held to consider the matter. They saved their countries from getting the fatal feeling that war was "inevitable". So long as that feeling can be warded off the danger of war is not great. But Blatchford and Hyndman seem to have set themselves the task of producing that very feeling of inevitableness. Is that work worthy of the traditions of Socialism?'

Hardie was perturbed that Socialists should line themselves up with the jingoes.

'I tell Blatchford frankly that in all that pertains to war he is suspect in the British Socialist Movement. We have not forgotten his attitude over the Boer War. If it is true, as he says, that there are Fabians who are also believers in the German invasion, then they are probably the same as those who agreed with Blatchford about the Boer War. He and they were wrong then. They are wrong now. Their attitude at present is an injustice to the British and Socialist and Labour Movement.'

This was one of the long series of warnings that Keir Hardie was to give about the dangers of European war. He could see these dangers in 1908, inherent in the alliance with the Czar's Government and the Press propaganda for bigger armies and armaments that had begun.

He took the opportunity during the Parliamentary Recess to pay another visit to Canada and the United States. He was glad to note the growth of the trade union movement in the U.S.A., urged the trade unions to enter politics and become Socialists. 'America,' he wrote, 'is the land of big things and a big Labour movement which would impress the imagination with its size and the judgment with its sanity would proudly result in the United States having the first Socialist Government in the modern world. The thing seems worth an effort.' He was over-optimistic about the prospects of Socialism in America.

He was back in Britain for the opening of Parliament and attended a meeting in London at which Karl Kautsky and Ledebour, the German Socialists, spoke. *The Labour Leader* gave a short report of his speech:

'Mr. Keir Hardie in supporting the resolution emphasising the solidarity of Labour and pledging the working class to wage unceasing war against militarism said that armies of all kinds, whether capitalist or otherwise, were a menace and a danger to the workers, the whole world over. In telling and prophetic language he warned his hearers against the danger of placing reliance on armies, whether citizen or by whatever name they might be called. He instanced the experience of the English workers in connection with industrial disputes, how the police, in all essentials a citizen force, had time and time again been used against the workers whenever they came to close grips with the forces of capitalism. In a fine and telling speech he denounced war, and the preparation for war, under whatever disguise it might be put forward.'

Later he entertained the German Socialist leaders to dinner in the House of Commons.

The controversy with Hyndman and Blatchford was renewed in *The Labour Leader* of October 23rd. He was sorry if he had been too personal. 'If there was anything in the article which gave offence to either of the Comrades I ask them to remember that whom the Lord loveth he chasteneth.' But he was perturbed at the way a possible split in the Socialist Movement might be developing.

Victor Grayson, a young Socialist who had been returned at a by-election in Colne Valley, was taking an independent line in Parliament with the encouragement of Blatchford and Hyndman. Hardie wrote about Grayson:

'I can quite understand his restiveness at the forms and procedure of Parliament. I have been through it all under circumstances widely different from those of to-day. If, however, we are to remain a political party we must do our duties seriously and what was pardonable in a party of one is quite unpardonable with a party of 31 with much drudgery work to be done in committees, not only of the House, but committee of the Party: and as every member of the Party knows, not only hours, but days, require to be given up to this kind of work every week if anything real is to be accomplished. By standing aloof from the Party, Grayson has never had any share in this work, nor in consequence has he any real knowledge of what the Labour Party in the House of Commons is doing.'

He went on to point out how busy the Labour Party had been in framing plans to deal with the unemployment situation. Grayson had taken no part in these but had simply come down to the House and made a scene and been suspended without telling anybody that he intended doing it. He could 'understand comrades feeling impatient with apparent slowness of our progress'.

'I share that feeling. I am as full of unrest as the youngest recruit but I cannot allow this feeling to over-ride my own judgment. The Labour Party by its work in Parliament has more than justified its existence. The way in which its principles and policy have commended themselves to the Trade Union movement would of itself be a justification for its existence if such were needed.'

Bernard Shaw was quite wrong, he said, in comparing Victor Grayson with Plimsoll, who had made scenes until he had obtained the raising of the safety line on ships. Circumstances were entirely different. He pleaded with the Social Democratic Federation to come inside the Labour Party: 'There is room inside the Labour Party for every section and phase of Socialist thought and activity; and working from within it would be a stimulating and binding force, whereas without it tends to become merely disruptive. Workers of the World Unite is the slogan to which all that is best in the Socialist and Trade Union ranks will most enthusiastically respond. We are out to capture power not to create sects and a heavy responsibility rests with those who from either want of thought or mistaken zeal play into the hands of our enemies by creating discords in our ranks.'

In October he moved an amendment on behalf of the Labour Party to a motion welcoming the Government's unemployment proposals. It was tantamount to a vote of censure and the Labour Party succeeded in getting 68 votes against the Government's 236.

At the November municipal elections that year the Labour Party at Merthyr won four seats and the Town Council elected a Labour Mayor.

Hardie was delighted at this. He wrote an article to *The Labour Leader* entitled 'Electing the Mayor at Merthyr' in which he took the opportunity of giving more advice to his critics who were urging Socialists to leave the Labour Party.

'I have earnestly and honestly tried to gauge the trend of opinion in our movement—nothing else counts with me—and I find no alternative to the Labour Party.

'Behind the Labour Party stands in solid array the intellect and will, and the sense of every section of Socialist and Labour thought and feeling. The men and women of our movement are not fretful children. That which they laboured so long and hard to create they will amend and improve, but not destroy. I am not to be taken as saying that the Labour Party is faultless; no human institution is. Its shortcomings are many and manifold. There are tendencies to be guarded against, lest they become dangerously strong. Experience, backed and stimulated by frank and open criticism, will do all in this respect that is needed. Where our critics destroy their own usefulness is that their criticisms are so carping and so petty that when the opportunity for genuine criticism arises what they have to say is discounted in advance. Mankind in the mass is not ungenerous, and is very discriminating. I think the Parliamentary pace might be quickened with advantage. Probably many people think the same. But a great chasm yawns between saying that and the disruption of the movement. It may be that we have slipped into the habit of making the path of the Government too smooth. I like not that save when the pathway makes for our goal. The imagination of the people requires to be appealed to, as well as their reason. Where there is no vision the people perish.

All this I know, and freely admit. But I would rather have Andrew Wilson, a plain working collier, Labour Mayor of Merthyr with twelve trustworthy Labour colleagues under him, than have every ward in the borough strewn with the remains of the slaughtered Socialist candidates, however valiantly they had waved the red flag and shouted out their class war dogmas.'

Speaking at Cardiff, he referred to the suspension of Victor Grayson:

'Referring to the question of unemployment,' he said, 'there was no sacrifice he was not prepared to make to bring relief to the millions of homes in the country where there was now destitution and misery. If he could advance the cause more rapidly by making scenes in Parliament, he would make scenes galore, but he held that better work could be accomplished by steady solid plodding, and the Labour Members best served the interests of the people by remaining in their places than by leaving the House or being carried out. What the Capitalist class feared was not neurotic shouting, but steady plodding, undermining work which would bring the whole structure about their heads.'

Feeling within the Socialist Movement was now running high, and Hyndman, Blatchford and Grayson refused to speak at the Holborn Hall if Hardie appeared on the same platform, and the meeting was held without him.

On December 18th, 1908, he wrote on the passing of the Miners' Eight Hours Bill: 'Twenty-two years ago I sat under the gallery in the House of Commons listening to a discussion on a legal eight-hour day for miners, and on Monday last I voted in the majority for the third reading of the Bill.'

The Bill would not have gone through the House of Commons 'even now but for the presence of the Labour Party'.

He drew the moral:

'Had even the present party, small in numbers though it be, been in the House of Commons in 1886 the miners would then have got their Bill and there would have been twenty years of solid and substantial progress behind us. Twenty years hence this country will be a very desirable place to live in provided our movement continues to make headway along the lines of the past few years. The progress of those years has not been slow, and it has been solid. We are building for the future as well as for the present, and what has already been done is but earnest of what shall yet be done provided we keep pressing steadily forward.'

Early in January 1909, Hardie paid another visit to America. He told the Civic Forum in New York:

'Experience has shown us that working men who were formerly Liberal or Conservative are prepared to come out from their old political associations and join their forces on a Labour platform common to both. They do so in the Trade Union Movement, there is no reason why they should not do so in the field of politics. I am convinced however that any movement for a Labour Party is bound to fail unless it draws inspiration from the Socialist ideal.'

Wishing his *Labour Leader* readers the 'Compliments of the Season', he expressed gratification at the progress of the I.L.P.:

'For good or ill, to the I.L.P. belongs the credit of bringing the Labour Party into being. The influence of the Party is felt on every trade union lodge and Trades Council in Britain as an inspiring and binding force. Its long line of branches extending from Cape Wrath to Penzance are so many encampments of trained warriors, stimulating, urging, exciting to constant warfare with the capitalist system.

'There is consolation in the thought that, as the result of the work of the past few years, thousands of school children are being fed and tens of thousands cared for medically and otherwise, that on the first day of the New Year close upon a million of aged people will have a gleam of brightness cast upon the desolateness of their lives with a pension; that when July is filling the land with beauty half a million of those who toil underground will be given from one to two hours each day in which to exchange the death dealing gloom of the mine for the life giving sunshine of field and forest. These things, small in themselves are more than isolated reforms they are indications of the new spirit which is abroad.'

The year 1909 was to be a busy one for Hardie. He had benefited in health greatly from his world tour and he was again to be found nearly every week-end addressing big meetings in different parts of the country. The Labour Party Conference held at Portsmouth was the largest that had yet been held. There were over 400 delegates, 'of whom six were women', and 24 Labour M.P.s attended. For the first time Bernard Shaw appeared at the Labour Party Conference as the delegate of the Fabian Society. Shaw and the Fabians had now come completely over to the Labour Party and had given up trying to 'permeate' the Liberals. Shaw supported the proposal that Labour M.P.s who were being paid £200 a year from the Party should be paid an additional £20.

Hardie was elected to be Chairman for the next year.

In the King's Speech there had been a definite promise to deal in a big way with the problem of unemployment. Instead of this there was a promise of a Bill to set up Labour Exchanges. Anything that looked like unjust treatment of the unemployed always roused Hardie. He wrote:

'If men behaved like this in private life they would be drummed out of decent society. The code of social honour—and there is said to be honour even among thieves—could not be violated with impunity. And is the word of a Prime Minister to the poor to be any less sacred that it would be if given in a drawing room to his friends? Do not the interests of public morality demand that pledges publicly given in Parliament on the honour of the King and his leading Ministers should be honourably kept?'

There had been a big demonstration of unemployed at the opening of Parliament.

'Monday saw thousands of workers now marching through the streets of London. Tuesday saw thousands of the wives of these, many of them with children in their arms, together with hundreds of working women of all ages, from the girl in her teens to the widow of sixty also on the streets. Chivied about by the police, some fainting by the way, hungry, weary and footsore, they trudged along making mute appeal to the conscience of the nation—little emaciated, paling babies, pinched and wan mothers—the most heartbreaking sight it has even been my lot to look upon.

'And the reply of the Government to it is to mock their misery by a proposal for Labour Exchanges.'

Not that he was against the establishment of Labour Exchanges.

'Labour Exchanges do not create work; they make it easier for the employers to select "hands" when they need them. Every member of a distress committee knows that it is more work that is needed not more regimentation. Labour Exchanges plus a really generous scheme (for enlarging the area of employment, such as is well in the power of the Government to provide, would have been welcomed; Labour Exchanges themselves are but an attempt to fool the nation.'

In March he went to Oxford and had a stormy meeting. The meeting was arranged by the Fabian Society and there was a good deal of interruption, organised disturbance and some fighting. Hardie treated it all with good humour:

'I have seen a good deal of fighting in my time but never anything quite like what I saw that evening. There seemed to be no bad temper or ill-feeling about it. Young men seemed to punch each other for the satisfaction it seemed to give them. And the moment the struggle was over everyone settled down as though nothing had occurred. Some of the gentlemen had brought oranges and apples, small potatoes and pieces of sugar with them and these they shied at the platform, despite the fact that a number of ladies were there. It is thus they set an example of that "gentle courtesy" which is supposed to characterise the conduct of the cultured classes towards "women".

'After the chairs had been piled up the audience gathered close up to the platform standing and I was able to get a good look at those who were leading the noise. They were for the most part objects of pity. Someone afterwards expressed admiration for the way in which I kept my temper but seeing the type who were indulging in the noise the uppermost feeling I had was not anger or contempt, but pity.'

Lord Robert Cecil had introduced a Bill to prevent disturbance at public meetings but Hardie was not too enthusiastic about it. 'It might lead to policemen being given power to disband a meeting when they thought that "sedition" was being uttered.'

But he thought an Act under which persons whom the Press incited to break up meetings would be prosecuted would be justified. One of the daily papers circulating in Oxford had published an article advising the students to imitate Cambridge, where his meeting had been broken up. The anti-Socialist Press thought that Keir Hardie was fair game and delighted to publish reports of his being howled down.

But Oxford and Cambridge were the exceptions. When he was billed to speak in any of Britain's big cities and towns he was now sure of a big crowd, mostly of working-class people, but others came to listen as well. The very virulence of the Press attacks upon him made people come to listen.

There was a new interest in politics. The social reform programme of the Liberals was being keenly discussed. Lloyd George and Winston Churchill were making radical speeches and denouncing the House of Lords and the privileged rich. But they repudiated Socialism. They were attacked by the millionaire Press too. But its most unscrupulous and venomous attacks were reserved for Keir Hardie. Whenever anything remotely approving of him appeared in the Press, which was not often, he would shrug his shoulders and ask, 'What have I done wrong now?'

Hardie had attacked Haldane over his plans for the Army. In April he denounced what he called the 'Navy Scare'. New Zealand had offered Britain the gift of a battleship and the demand for some battleships was growing. War propaganda was increasing. Hardie wrote:

'The scare has served its purpose. It has given a fresh fillip to militarism and familiarised the public mind with the idea of spending many extra millions upon things naval and military. I see with genuine apprehension how the mind of the nation is being debauched, not only by the daily Press but by the weekly pictorials, the boys' magazines and papers. War pictures, war tales, the glorification of everything savage and brutal, almost hourly, for the public reading of youth and age, the Press, the stage, the pulpit are all being used to the same end.'

The I.L.P. Conference was held that year in Edinburgh. It was a strange conference. Hardie, Snowden, MacDonald and Glasier for about the first time found themselves attacked from the floor by the delegates who had been impressed by Victor Grayson. Grayson, who was at the height of his brief popularity, attacked the leaders of the I.L.P. because they had not been extreme enough in Parliament. The Labour Party was not a Socialist party and the trade union M.P.s were not Socialists. The I.L.P., he argued, should take its own line. Hardie made a vigorous reply, going into details about Grayson's attitude in the House and his refusal to consult or co-operate with other members of the I.L.P. and the Labour Party, and the platform won the resolution which stated that 'no salary be paid out of Party funds to M.P.s who did not sign the constitution of the Labour Party' by 332 votes to 98.

Grayson, however, succeeded in carrying the reference back of a paragraph in the National Council's Report which stated that 'it was useless to try to arrange meetings for him through the Head Office of the I.L.P. because he had refused to appear at a meeting along with Hardie and because of the casual way he dealt with his engagements.'

The reference back was carried by 217 votes to 194. There was an acrimonious discussion and shortly afterwards Hardie, MacDonald, Snowden and Glasier announced their decision to resign from the National Council. They had been elected by overwhelming majorities, Hardie practically unanimously, and their action caused consternation in the conference. But they refused to withdraw their resignations. Hardie, replying to the discussion, said:

'A big effort was being made to sever the alliance with the Labour Party and to disrupt the I.L.P. Grayson was being used by others who were more unscrupulous than he was. The trouble with Grayson was that success had come to him too easily and that he was surrounded by malign influences which would ruin his career. Grayson, Hyndman, and Blatchford had refused to appear with him and it had gone abroad that he had lost the confidence of the movement. Self-respect demanded that a stand should be made. They must fight that down and if need be fight it out. With his colleagues he was going to test the question whether the I.L.P. was to stand for the consolidation of the working class movement, or whether departing from the lines of sanity they should follow some chimera called Socialism and Unity, spoken of by men who did not understand Socialism, and were alien to its very spirit.'

The four members refused to reconsider their resignation and issued a lengthy statement in defence of their action. They were leaving the National Council but they were remaining in the Party.

They concluded:

'We shall in no way slacken our efforts to make the I.L.P. strong and respected in the future as it has been in the past. But our work for the I.L.P. will be on the lines which have been followed since its formation the wisdom of which has been proved by the achievements of the Party. The Labour Party in all its strength and fullness, its weakness and mistakes, is not only a time reflex of working-class thought and life but also the only means by which Socialism can be realised. It is because we believe this that we have taken our present course of action, and because we feel how vital it is that there should not only be nominal adhesion to the policy of the Labour Party but a rejection of all methods and tactics alien to that policy, or tending to its subversion.'

Hardie's name headed the list of signatures and the statement seems to have been mostly written by him.

Grayson lost his seat at the General Election and little more was heard of him. His complete disappearance is one of the mysteries of our time. Hyndman, in his reminiscences, explains how Grayson let him down, too. He was a gifted orator but quite unstable and unreliable.

Out of office in the I.L.P., Hardie continued to write articles for *The Labour Leader* and also found time to write a vigorous political pamphlet in reply to the Socialists who were trying to get the I.L.P. out of the Labour Party and carrying on a campaign against the Labour Party in Parliament. He called it *My Confession of Faith in the Labour Alliance,* and in it replied in detail to the attacks of Blatchford, Hyndman and Grayson.

Indeed it was a very vigorous counter-attack and carried the war into the enemy camp.

Hardie did not often quote Marx but this time he surprised the leaders of the S.D.F. by claiming that 'the Labour Party is the only expression of orthodox Marxian Socialism in Great Britain'. He wrote:

'I wish it to be understood that I am not apologising for the I.L.P. alliance with the Labour Party. I am carrying the war into the camp of the enemy . . . I know that many of our young comrades are having it dinned into their ears day after day by members of the S.D.P., and by the newspapers which represent the disruptive and dissentient element, that the Social Democratic Party alone embodies the Socialist tradition of Karl Marx and the great founders of modern Socialism.

'Doubtless some of those who repeat those statements believe them. They have read and heard them so often that they have accepted them as

Left to right: W. C. Anderson, Jean Jaurès (France), Hermann Molkenbuhr (Germany), Keir Hardie, 1910.

Keir Hardie at work.

Granville Bantock and Keir Hardie, 1914.

A Spy cartoon from 'Vanity Fair'.

being true. They have neither the time nor the opportunity for reading and understanding the evolution of Socialist policy as laid down by Marx, Engels, Liebknecht, and the other classical founders of modern scientific Socialism.

'They have been led away by the veriest claptrap, by the mouthing of mere phrases. The Social Democratic Party, and those who are now trying to form a Socialist Representation Committee, are not only not representing the Marxian tradition; they are outraging every principle of Marxian Socialist tactics.'

Hardie recalled that Friedrich Engels had written to a friend in America a criticism of the S.D.F. Engels had written:

'The Social Democratic Federation here shares with your German American Socialists the distinction of being the only parties to accomplish the bringing down of the Marxian theory of development to a rigid orthodoxy. According to them the working man is not to attain to this complete development ("class consciousness") through an evolution set in operation by this class feeling; but he has to swallow it down immediately as an article of faith and without development. Therefore both remain only sects, and come, as Hegel says, from nothing, through nothing, to nothing.'

Hardie went on:

'That is a biting criticism of the S.D.F. attitude in standing outside the Labour Party, and makes mincemeat of those superior persons who want to form a Socialist Representation Committee. The old International Workingmen's Association was not a Socialist organisation. It was, as its name implies, an association for uniting the working classes of all countries. It was founded in 1864, and in 1871, the year before it perished in the carnage of the ill-fated Commune of Paris, Marx made this fact clear in one of his letters.'

Hardie quoted from Marx:

'The International was founded,' he wrote, ' to establish a real organisation of the working class in place of Socialist and half-Socialist sects . . . The growth of Socialist sectism and of the real Labour movement are always in inverse proportions. As long as the existence of sects is historically justified, the working class is not yet ripe for an independent historical movement. As soon as Labour reaches maturity all sects become retrograde.'

He concluded:

'Thus it is proved that the founders of the I.L.P., and, even more so, of the Labour Party were, if I may use the expression, in the direct line of apostolic succession from Marx and the other great master minds of Socialist theory and policy. They never conceived Socialism as a narrow pettifoging dogmatic sectarianism, but as a wide all-embracing working-class movement toilsomely learning by failure and experience the lesson of working-class solidarity, and proclaiming the conquest of political

177

power as the method by which the workers would achieve their economic emancipation.'

He went on to reply to Blatchford, whom he said had rendered great service to Socialism by his *Merrie England* and *Britain for the British*.

But Blatchford knew nothing about political organisation or political action. He lived, as he had admitted, 'in practical seclusion, engrossed in his books'.

Hardie claimed that the work of the I.L.P. in helping to bring the Labour Party into existence had been justified by results:

'To have taken working-class organisations representing 1,500,000 of the pick of the workers, and weaned them away from Liberalism and Conservatism and organised them in a party financed and controlled by themselves is a fact which in itself is in the nature of a revolution. To have over thirty Members in the House of Commons organised as a separate party, independent of both Liberal and Conservative standing out as a distinct entity, is a standing testimony which cannot be gainsaid to the success which has crowned our efforts. Critics may disagree with the policy of the I.L.P. but they cannot deny its success. Be it noted that all this has been accomplished without any leadership from the so-called intellectual classes. Not a single member of the Labour Party in the House of Commons ever had any educational advantage beyond what the Parish School could give, and some of them not even that. They have been drawn from the mine, the mill, the furnace, the gas works, the workshop bench, the railway siding, and from behind the counter; yet, despite their educational disadvantages and their lack of social standing, friend and foe alike admit that they have shown more than average capacity in the parliamentary arena. The fact alone has destroyed for ever the theory of a ruling class. The Labour Party has shown conclusively that the common people can rule themselves.'

Blatchford had written that 'the comparative failure of the Labour M.P.s in the House of Commons is due to the fact that they are working men. It arises from no other fact whatever. It is not lack of intellect, nor lack of courage, nor lack of knowledge which palsies the Labour Group. With one or two natural aristocrats to lead them, all would be well.'

Hardie retorted:

'Is it the opinion of the I.L.P. that the Socialist movement in Parliament could be more safely entrusted to the leadership and guidance of aristo-crats, "natural" or other, than it can to those working-class leaders who have been thrown up from the ranks of labour? That the leadership of the party might be more brilliant, I who was for two years its chairman, heartily concede. With an aristocrat to lead us we might even say and do things which have neither been said nor done yet: I can even believe that we might provide more sensationalism and consequently more

178

picturesqueness in connection with our work at St. Stephen's, and all these things would have a distinct value: but the price we should have to pay would be fatal. It would no longer be a working-class movement; Labour would again have sunk to its old traditional position of a drudge carrying out the will of an imperious master. The outstanding value of the Labour Party is that it is what its name implies, an uprising of the working class, overseered and guided by men of that class painfully, and slowly working out its own emancipation. It is a favourite saying of Mr. H. M. Hyndman that "no slave class ever emancipated itself". This is the orthodox view of the ordinary middle-class philistine, who, with all his professions of sympathy still regards Labour as a badge of inferiority. To that doctrine I can give no assent.'

Hardie did not accept the idea of aristocrat leaders but he made it clear that he was not against middle-class people coming into the Labour Party. There were in the ranks of the I.L.P. 'thousands of what without offence I may describe as the lower middle class and a fair sprinkling of the middle class itself. Most of these are good comrades and their services to the Party are invaluable. They often bring into the movement a higher ideal of Socialism and a much-needed sense of business methods.'

The pamphlet was an all-out defence of the political tactics of the I.L.P. Blatchford had written: 'I do not approve of the I.L.P. alliance with the Labour Party. I think a Labour Party is a good thing, but the I.L.P. was a Socialist Party. In joining the Labour Party it ceased to be a Socialist Party.'

Hardie strenuously denied this. He pointed out how bitterly the anti-Socialist Union was attacking the I.L.P. 'The men at the head of the anti-Socialist Union are no fools. Dukes, and others of that kidney, earls, Members of Parliament and businessmen (especially if they happen to be Scotch, as some of them are), would not spend their money fighting a party unless they believed it to be a menace to their vested interests.'

He pointed out that the I.L.P. had grown steadily in membership, since the foundation of the Labour Party, and had now nearly a thousand branches in all parts of the country. It was 'what it had been from the beginning, a definitely Socialist organisation carrying on its Socialist propaganda with a success scarce equalled in any country in the world'.

He stressed the fact that 'a broad tolerant catholicity had always been a leading characteristic of the I.L.P.

'It has never had a hard and dry creed of membership. It has always recognised that only by encouraging freedom of thought and activity could growth and expansion be expected. The I.L.P. has never expelled anybody, never had occasion to do so. In its early days battles fierce and keen were waged yearly over questions of policy, of internal organisation, but the commonsense of the Party always came to the rescue and kept it free of swaddling bonds.'

Hardie made no claims that the Labour Party was perfect or should be above criticism.

'I say quite candidly that the action of the Labour Party in the House of Commons might be, and probably even should be, much more strenuous than it has been; but I say with even more emphasis that no movement which is going to live to be a permanent force in the life of the nation can subsist upon scenes and emotional excitements. Only in so far as a party, whether Socialist or Iabour, can impress its thought and its power on the mind and will of the nation by acts of constructive statesmanship is it going to be of service in the long run.'

My Confession of Faith was a clear and challenging statement of what Hardie believed to be the way to achieve Socialism in Britain.

CHAPTER 17

'NOT A POLITICIAN'

WHILE Hardie was carrying on his polemical campaign against Blatchford and Hyndman and the doctrinaires who wanted Socialists to break away from the Labour Party, his critics in the Liberal Party and in the Liberal Press were contrasting his attitude in the House of Commons with that of Ramsay MacDonald and the other Labour M.P.s who were not so strongly opposed to the Liberal Government.

To A. G. Gardiner, the editor of the *Daily News,* Hardie was 'a rebel ridden by a theory'.

'He is not a politician or a statesman. He is a fanatic. The politician must temporise and compromise. He yields as little as he can, and takes as much as he can. He studies the weather, and is governed by the seasons. He equivocates and waits upon circumstance. The fanatic knows nothing of this opportunism. The thunder is always on his brow, the lightning always in his eye, the fire at his heart always smouldering into flame. He is a man obsessed with an idea. It gives him no rest and he gives you no rest. Hence Mr. Keir Hardie's failure as a Parliamentarian. He has none of the plasticity necessary for the man of affairs. He is stiff and irreconcilable. He is indifferent to detail. He has no gratitude for small mercies. His eye is on the far-off vision. He is the only man who could have created the Labour Party, for concentration and intensity are the creative impulses. But he is almost the only man in the party who is not fitted to lead it.

'It is plain, commonsense men like Mr. Shackleton and Mr. Henderson, and astute politicians like Mr. Ramsay MacDonald who have made it a political instrument. His party is not as himself. He is as isolated in it as when he stood alone in the House. For no party can exist on anathema and prophecy. A cause comes into being at the breath of the prophet, and then leaves him in the desert.'

Hardie was familiar with this line of criticism. He had heard it in two Parliaments, usually from the Liberal Press. In the past they had contrasted his uncompromising attitude towards the Liberals with the reasonableness and moderation of John Burns, who was prepared to tone down or drop his Socialism to suit them. Hardie had never pretended to be the conventional party politician. As his controversies with Blatchford and Hyndman showed, he was far from being the revolutionary doctrinaire. But he had come to the conclusion that while the Liberals were prepared to give small concessions in the way of social reform they had no intention of changing the capitalist system. The Liberal coalowners and shipowners, the Liberal railway directors, manufacturers, bankers, insurance magnates and lawyers were in politics to protect their own vested interests.

They wanted no Socialist legislation.

If the Tories represented the landed aristocracy, the old Army and Navy traditions and interests, the Liberals represented the industrialists and the plutocracy who in the last resort dictated Parliamentary policy, and paid the piper and called the tune.

That was the reality of British politics as Keir Hardie saw it.

This was the idea with which Gardiner thought Hardie was obsessed and made him a failure 'as a Parliamentarian'. He was not interested in the day-to-day clashes in the 1906-1910 Parliament because he felt they had little to do with the realities, with the big issues. The last thing he was concerned about was to make a reputation as a great Parliamentarian in the conventional House of Commons meaning of the word. He had no ambitions to become the Mr. Gladstone of the Labour Party. 'Hardie had not the accommodating spirit which is essential in a successful Parliamentary leader,' wrote Philip Snowden in his autobiography. 'The humdrum everyday work of the House of Commons was never to Hardie's taste. During his chairmanship of the Party he left the arrangement of business, which must necessarily be carried through by conversations with the Government Whip, largely to Mr. Henderson.'

It was not that Hardie was incapable of doing hum-drum detail work. In his life he had done an enormous amount of it and he was meticulous and methodical in what he thought were the important things that mattered. The way he had pushed the question of unemployment to the front of politics during the two previous Parliaments when he had been alone was sufficient testimony to his ability to use every political opportunity that the House of Commons offered to anybody who was prepared to use every device of Parliamentary procedure to advance a cause. The Parliamentarian that Hardie most admired had been Parnell. But the conventional Parliamentary fighting, especially when it was about matters largely irrelevant to the interests of the working class outside, definitely did not interest Hardie. He was far more concerned that the Labour Party, now that it had arrived in Parliament, should by its stand on important issues stir public imagination outside and show that a new inspiring force was at work in British politics. He wrote to Snowden at the end of 1907 explaining his reasons for not wishing to continue in the chairmanship of the Parliamentary Labour Party.

'My strongest reason for desiring to get out of the Chair is that I may be free to speak out occasionally. In the last session the Party has practically dropped out of public notice. The comic papers and the cartoonists are ignoring us. A fatal sign! The tendency is evidently to work in close and cordial harmony with the Government, and if this policy is persisted in we shall lose our identity and be wiped out along with Liberals, and we should richly deserve our fate. By another session those of us in the Party who are Socialists and who believe in fighting will have to go occasionally on our own account, and if we cannot drag the Party with us, we will "gang oor ain gait".'

In his *Life of Ramsay MacDonald*, Lord Elton, referring to Hardie, writes : 'Temperamentally, like many idealists, he was an individualist, accustomed to follow his own intuitions and apt, in Parliament, to take his own line independent of his colleagues. Unwaveringly clear as to the end, he was often indifferent to the indispensable means. To MacDonald, constantly preoccupied with both means and end, a Parliamentarian to his finger tips, and inevitably bearing a disproportionate share of responsibility for the tactics of the group, Hardie's combination of idealism and individualism was often profoundly exasperating . . . In Parliament at least they were not fitted to work together without friction. In Parliament Hardie could only be a free lance, and MacDonald was not fond of free lances.'

Hardie was of course a very strong personality who preferred to follow his own line rather than MacDonald's opportunism, but he was not just a free lance. He could never have built up the I.L.P. or pioneered the Labour Party if he had been just the free lance in politics. His defence of the Labour Alliance against Blatchford, Grayson and Hyndman showed that he realised the need of working in the Party. It was because he was so anxious for the future of the Labour Party that he was not satisfied with the policy 'of working in cordial harmony with the Government'.

He recognised that MacDonald had done an enormous amount of hard work as Secretary of the Labour Party and frequently paid tributes to the service that MacDonald had rendered. Both men had something in common, both were Scots the one Highland, the other Lowland, often an important temperamental difference. Hardie, however, remained fundamentally, defiantly, proudly, independently working class. 'It is the fierce antipathies of the theorist that the world sees,' wrote Gardiner, 'but deep down in his heart these antipathies are seen to have their roots in a sympathy as fierce—the sympathy with the class from which he sprang, and which he has never deserted. He hates the palace because he remembers the pit.'

MacDonald was, however, already nearer to the palace than he had ever been to the pit. He moved in different circles, he thoroughly enjoyed the day-to-day intrigue of the House of Commons, was, in Lord Elton's words, 'the Parliamentarian to the finger tips'. He had been a Liberal M.P.'s secretary and had mixed socially a great deal with the Liberals, and he was extremely ambitious and decidedly vain. Hardie, who had frequently observed and remarked on the facility with which politicians like John Burns and Lloyd George adapted themselves to the environment of Westminster, watched MacDonald's activities in Parliament with a great deal of misgiving. Hardie intensely disliked vague and obscure language; he always spoke out bluntly and directly himself and agreed with Carlyle that words were too often used to disguise and obscure thought. MacDonald was given to woolly rhetoric even in his books. He had written a book called *Socialism and Society,* passages of which bordered on the metaphysical. Hardie had a habit of writing marginal comments on the books he read. He was obviously irritated with *Socialism and Society.* 'Don't agree,' 'Reads like an apology for Liberalism' were some of the comments he wrote. 'What does this mean?' was another. This question was to be asked a lot about MacDonald's utterances and writings by many other people in the years that followed.

To Gardiner, Hardie was a grim, dour personality, a typical Scot; the most typical Scot in the House, in appearance and outlook.

'He is "the Knight of the Rueful Countenance". His face is cast in a tragic mould, and his temperament had the gloom of Calvinism and the severity of the Shorter Catechism. When your eye passes from the cheerful Irishmen behind him to his sad and foreboding figure, you recall a passage in one of Scott's letters: "While a Scotchman is thinking about the term day, or, if easy on that subject, about hell in the next world—

while an Englishman is making a little hell in the present because his muffin is not well toasted—Pat's mind is always turned to fun and ridicule." There is no fun and ridicule about Keir Hardie, and the perfectability of his muffin leaves him uncheered. He has a soul too sorrowful to be moved by muffins. His figure brings up the vision of the Covenanters and that grey Galloway land, "where about the graves of martyrs the whaups are crying". One seems to see him out-rivalling Habakkuk Mucklewraith in the dark frenzy of his declamation, and rushing to the attack at Bothwell Brig with damnatory psalms upon his lips.'

This was the impression that Hardie made on his not altogether unsympathetic critics. Had this been the whole truth about Hardie he would hardly have gathered round him so many devoted friends and followers. The Lowland Scot is often accused of having no sense of humour because his is the dry, pawky variety.

G. K. Chesterton put it more penetratingly in his study of Dickens:

'The English democracy is the most humorous democracy in the world. The Scotch democracy is the most dignified, while the whole abandon and satiric genius of the English populace comes from its being quite undignified in every way. A comparison of the two types might be found, for instance, by putting a Scotch Labour Leader like Mr. Keir Hardie alongside an English Labour Leader like Mr. Will Crooks. Both are good men, honest and responsible and compassionate; but we can feel that the Scotchman carries himself seriously and universally, the Englishman personally and with an obstinate humour. Mr. Keir Hardie wishes to hold up his head as Man. Mr. Crooks wishes to follow his nose as Crooks. Mr. Keir Hardie is very like a poor man in Walter Scott, Mr. Crooks is very like a poor man in Dickens.'

Lloyd George's Budget was the great political event of 1909 and Hardie welcomed it because he believed in the taxation of land values.

He said he was glad the Budget was called Socialism—because it was robbing the word 'Socialism' of much of its terrors — it was popularising the word. The Labour Party would support the resolution, hoping and expecting it would be the forerunner of many similar resolutions in the future.

Hardie was taking more and more interest in foreign affairs. In an article in *The Labour Leader* on May 21st, 1909, he deal with Turkey and Persia and Egypt. He welcomed the movement of the young Turks which opened out new hope for Turkey and the fact that the Shah had been forced to accept a new constitution. Dealing with Egypt, he pointed out that after twenty-five years British troops still occupied that country and that we had bought off the French by giving them a free hand in Morocco. The constitutional movement in Egypt was being hinted as 'seditious'.

'Editors of Nationalist newspapers and other reformers are being cast into prison and our resident British agent is indulging in stale platitudes about reforms which are to be granted some day when the people become fit. It is the old game of hypocrisy and bluff once more being worked off on the British nation in the interests of the moneylenders, who for close on half a century have been "spoiling the Egyptians" without mercy.'

Then there was India.

'For over a hundred years we have made ourselves responsible for the conditions of the government and the welfare of that great Empire. There can be no question here concerning the responsibility for the condition of the people. Nor can it be alleged that they are unfit for self-government . . . A great educated class exists in India which manages universities and higher grade schools, supplies the country with lawyers, professors, newspaper editors and the heads of great business concerns. Wherever these men have had an opportunity they prove that whether as administrators of legislators, they have a capacity of a very high order. For over a quarter of a century they have been conducting a great reform movement, not for separation from the British Empire, but for self-government within its borders.

'But in India as in Egypt this claim has been treated as seditious . . . I can only say that unless a change of policy comes developments may be expected in both countries referred to which will compel the Government to concede reforms in hot panic stricken haste which they now refuse to give in cool reason. It may then be too late.'

He was used to giving warnings which went unheeded.

When he spoke in Arthur Henderson's constituency in Barnard Castle in June he said that the time was when he would not have appeared with Mr. Henderson because he was not a Socialist and Mr. Henderson would not have appeared with him because he was not a respectable Liberal. Mr. Henderson did not call himself a Socialist, but he would not like to examine too closely into that.

'He represented trades unionism and he was a trade unionist representing Socialism. And trades unionists and Socialists were uniting together for the uplifting of our class. Surely then the new time was better than the old. If anything great was to be achieved, unity in the ranks of the common people was the first indispensable step.'

Hardie went on to denounce the visit of the Czar of Russia to Cowes:

'The Czar of Russia would not dare to set foot on British soil because he would be hissed in the streets if he dared to appear. Surely it was unworthy that any Government, should hold out the hand of friendship, to a man who was loathed and detested by the great masses of the people of this country.'

In July the Labour Party protested against the Czar's visit to Britain and Hardie again spoke in the debate. He replied to the Government's argument that it had nothing to do with the internal affairs of other countries by quoting what Gladstone had said about the atrocities in Armenia:

'Twice the Duma had been dissolved because the members elected by the people were not lickspittles, almost every popular leader elected to the Duma was rotting in prison. He agreed that the people of England wished to be on friendly terms with the people of Russia but the man who was coming here to meet King Edward did not represent the people of Russia and King Edward did not represent the people of Russia and King Edward would not represent the people of Great Britain in this visit. The Czar represented an official despotism that had few parallels in history.'

On this occasion the Labour motion was defeated by 79 votes to 187, Irish M.P.s and a few Radical M.P.s voting against the Government.

In September, Hardie attended the Trades Union Congress, his old battle-ground, as fraternal delegate from the Labour Party. *The Labour Leader* reported:

'Hardie's reception, after years of absence, was a rousing one. His rising was the signal for a storm of cheering that seemed as if it would never end. The gallery joined with the floor in doing honour to him on his return and even the Press men, usually so stolid, seemed tempted to break the traditions of years and join the tempest of applause.'

His speech was mainly an appeal for developing the political side of the movement and was in great contrast to the speech of Samuel Gompers, the fraternal delegate from America.

Some of the veterans recalled the years that Hardie had fought, almost alone, at the T.U.C. as a delegate from the Ayrshire miners, against the old leaders who had been opposed to the very idea of a Labour Party. 'Hardie ought to be the proudest man in Britain to-day,' said one of them. It was a great personal triumph.

Twenty-two years had passed since Charles Fenwick, M.P., referring to Hardie, had said, 'there are some men and some movements who are like Jonah's gourd in this that they spring up in a night and wither in a night'. 'Some things,' wrote Hardie, 'sting a man and stick like burns in his memory. Many a memory of these days has been effaced, but the incident remains fresh and vivid though I cannot tell why.'

Later in the year he wrote an article in *The Labour Leader* which he headed 'Jonah's Gourd'. It was on the occasion when the Northumberland miners voted that Burt and Fenwick should join the Labour Party.

'Now times have changed. The green shoot which was then making its appearance above ground has turned out not to be a Jonah's gourd but a sturdy British oak. It is Mr. Fenwick who is now fighting for his political existence, not as a pioneer of a new movement but as the last defender of a dying cause.'

In September he went to Geneva as the fraternal delegate from the Labour Party to the Second Annual Congress of the Young Egyptian Party which was demanding constitutional government for Egypt.

He gave a lengthy review of the situation since the British occupation of Egypt. He gave some interesting advice to the young Nationalist Movement. He told them: 'A constitution is not an end in itself, it is a means to an end.

'It has often happened with national movements that the support of the working class has been enlisted until the object aimed at has been won, after which they have been cast aside and their claims ignored. We of the Labour Party are hoping for better things from the Egyptian's movement. If under a constitutional government, the poor continue to toil and starve and die in their misery, what have they gained? Even now in the midst of your agitation for representative constitutional government you might formulate proposals which would secure to the poorest peasant the use of sufficient land to enable him and his dependents by the exercise of ordinary industry to enjoy a fair measure of comfort and independence. This would be some guarantee that you were thinking of the nation as a whole, and not merely of the interests of the educated and the well-to-do.

'The education of the young, the emancipation of women, and the purification of the current of national life of your country are aims worthy of your highest endeavour.'

He assured the Egyptians that they would have the support and goodwill of the British Labour Party.

'We are divided from you,' he said, 'in language, in religion, in outlook upon life. East and West may be friends, each lending the other of her gifts; but this relationship can only exist between peoples, who being mutually free, respect and trust each other. You are bound to hate the British occupation, since it puts upon you the badge of inferiority. We who love freedom are bound to show you that hate should be directed against a system which oppresses the weak of all lands, and not against the British people. And so by strengthening the ties of fellowship between East and West we shall be binding up the world in the bonds of a lasting peace and weaning mankind from the madness of the love of gold and the power of the sword.'

It was a wise and eloquent speech, interesting to read in retrospect and again showing that Keir Hardie was at least a generation ahead of the politicians and statesmen of his day.

CHAPTER 18

ANOTHER LIBERAL
GOVERNMENT

THE Liberal Government appealed to the country in January 1910 and, in the General Election, Keir Hardie again found himself opposed by Pritchard Morgan, the Liberal company promoter whom he had defeated in 1900, and by a Tory candidate, Fox Davies. Hardie increased his vote to 13,841. It was still a two-Member seat. The result was:

EDGAR JONES (Liberal)	...	...	15,448
KEIR HARDIE (Labour)	...	...	13,841
FOX DAVIES (Conservative)	...	...	4,736
PRITCHARD MORGAN (Ind. Liberal)	...		3,639
Labour majority over Conservative			9,105

Bernard Shaw went to Merthyr for the campaign. So did Rev. R. J. Campbell, Bruce Glasier, Rev. Geoffrey Ramsay, Vicar of Radstock, and many others. Hardie's opponents did their best to discredit him by bitter personal attacks and declaring that he stood for atheism and free love.

To counteract this the local Labour Party issued a special *Election Bulletin* in which Hardie replied to his critics and wrote on the issues of the election.

In his election address he put his case for the Labour Party and Socialism. He was in favour of the Lloyd George Budget, old age pensions, the taxation of land values, all that the Liberals advocated plus a lot more. 'Socialism,' he declared, 'is the one system which offers us a clue whereby man may escape from the dreary labyrinth of poverty, vice, beggarliness of life in which we are now aimlessly wandering.'

THE OX AND THE FROG.

The Frog: 'I shall soon be bigger than you!' The Ox: 'All right, I don't mind. There's plenty of room for both of us—but mind you don't burst!'

Bernard Shaw prophesied that the time would come when the Socialists would win the General Election and when the King of the day would ask both the Mr. Balfour and the Mr. Asquith of the day to form a Ministry and they would have to advise him to send for the Keir Hardie of the day, and Shaw concluded, 'Would to God it were the Keir Hardie of to-day.'

The Merthyr Socialists reported to *The Labour Leader*: 'The pettifogging political issues never got hold of the people of Merthyr—it was the battle for Socialism—the right of the people, who produce all, to enjoy all and govern all that moved the electorate. The old warrior was in magnificent form—morning, noon and night and often far into the night he kept at it with infectious enthusiasm. It was not so much of an election campaign as a crusade.'

He had gathered round him in his Welsh constituency a band of workers who had become deeply devoted to him.

Hardie was Chairman of the Labour Party Conference when it met at Newport in February.

He opened his address by pointing out that, ten years before, the affiliated membership of the Labour Party was 375,931—now it was 1,418,868. 'At the General Election ten years ago we had 16 candidates who polled 70,009 votes. This time we had 78 candidates who polled 505,696 votes. Ten years ago we only returned two members to the House of Commons, now we send 40. Surely we have in this bald summary of facts sufficient evidence of progress to inspire hope in the breast of the most confirmed pessimist.'

He went on to review other political developments to prove the progress the Labour Party was making and added a personal note:

'I have a peculiar pleasure in welcoming to our Conference for the first time the representatives of the Miners' Federation of Great Britain. As one of the founders of the Federation and as a full financial member, it seems in accordance with the fitness of things that it should fall to my lot to welcome its representatives into our bond of fellowship. Their coming completes the first circle of our task and brings every section of the working-class movement under the banner of the Labour Party.'

It had taken a long time to win over the miners from their Liberal-Labour leaders, but it had come at last! He surveyed the political scene and referred to the General Election and the controversy over the House of Lords. The Labour Party had passed a resolution inviting the House of Commons to send the House of Lords into oblivion.

'As Mr. Winston Churchill had told the electors of Dundee, it is the growth of the Labour Party and all that that implies that has led the Lords to advance their pretensions which we all thought were disposed of generations ago. They see clearly what our coming means to their insolent pride and pampered luxury.'

He concluded with an appeal for Socialism:

'The Labour Party is not avowedly a Socialist Party in its political professions, but the feeling grows that so long as land and industrial capital are privately owned and controlled, the mass of the people are bound to be in bondage. Whether we like it or not, in any contest we wage in the future, our opponents will see to it that Socialism is kept well to the front. The last election has furnished some examples of what that will mean. Our candidates will do well to equip themselves against this line of attack. Socialism has no terrors for honest people. The caricatures and misrepresentations of Socialism will fail utterly in their effect when the case for Socialism is put lucidly before the people. We don't want to see any beating of the air, as is too often done in the case of Socialism, but it is imperative that every man who is put forward as a candidate under Labour auspices should be able to defend and expound Socialism when it is attacked by the enemies of Labour.

'Like every living organism we must adapt ourselves to a changing environment or perish. I look forward in confidence to the future. Nothing

Hardie's mother in later years.

Mrs. Keir Hardie at fifty.

The Hardie children, 1900.
James, Duncan and Nan.

Hardie's daughter, Nan.
(Provost of Cumnock.)

King Haakon and the Crown Prince, 1944

from without can hurt us if we are united from within. Sacrifice has always been and in the nature of things must be the keynote of progress.

'We want our typical representative to be like the man that Browning wrote of in his "Epilogue to Asolando":

'*One who never turned his back but marched breast forward,*
Never doubted clouds would break,
Never dreamed though right were worsted, wrong would triumph,
Held we fall to rise, are baffled to fight better, sleep to wake.'

It was an inspiring address and an impressive conference. 'This was for the first time in the record of Labour Party chairmen's addresses,' wrote Bruce Glasier, 'that the Socialist proclamation was fearlessly and proudly given.' The vote of thanks to Hardie was moved by Enoch Edwards, M.P., on behalf of the miners. He had not always endorsed Hardie's political views but his earnestness and courage he had always respected. The miners, after many years, were now in the Labour Party and in general agreement with the principles that Hardie had stated.

When Parliament met Hardie spoke in the Debate on the Address.

'He expressed this fears that on the Navy the Government were going to yield to the manufactured clamour of the Yellow Press. The cost of the Navy had been more than doubled during the last thirty years and apparently we were further off from security now than before the increases began to be made.

'He joined in the protest that had been made against any attempt to reconstruct the House of Lords . . . It was not to reconstitute the House of Lords that the Government had been returned; it was to destroy it. Let the crises come and continue until the Peers were brought to reason and democracy thoroughly established.'

In July he wrote about the naval scare:

'Britain's refusal at the Hague Conference to agree to the freedom of the seas appeared to Germans to be a deep-laid design to cripple Germany by destroying all her merchant ships in the event of war breaking out. That feeling produced the German naval programme and that in turn has led to the increase here, and apparently the end is not yet. Of course on both sides everything that has been done has been promoted by "pure patriotism and love of country". It cannot be forgotten, however, that there is an enormous profit for someone on each Dreadnought that is built; and that after the great ships have been built they require to be officered and manned and this provides quite a number of snug billets for the sons of the rich and well-to-do.'

He advocated an international conference to decide ways and means to ensure peace. It was for the working classes of both countries to find means for combining their forces so as to make war impossible.

King Edward died and the Government proposed a new Civil List

N

for King George V and the Royal Family. Hardie had opposed the Civil List before, but this time he had the support of the Labour Party which moved several amendments to the various items.

Hardie moved the amendment to delete the provision for giving each of the King's sons £10,000 a year on reaching the age of 21, £25,000 a year when each son married and £70,000 a year for Queen Mary in the event of her surviving the King.

They were paying too much for Royalty, he said. 'It was proposed that they should provide for members of the Royal Family an income that would enable them to lead lives of luxury, ease and idleness.'

Twenty voted for the amendment.

In August, Hardie devoted three long articles to a review of John Spargo's new *Life of Karl Marx*. He described the Communist Manifesto as 'the most fateful document ever written in the whole history of the working-class movement.' It was the birth certificate of the modern Socialist movement.

Hardie discussed at length the interpretation and application of Marx's theories to the situation in Britain.

'Socialism is revolutionary,' he concluded, 'it not only revolutionises the thoughts and actions of its adherents, but also of the whole of society and the fabric of the State. Socialism is without exception, the greatest revolutionary idea which has ever fired the imagination, or enthused the heart of mankind. But, in the biting rebuke which Marx addressed to some of his professed followers who would "substitute revolutionary phrases for revolutionary evolution" we must be careful not to confine the end with the means by which we are to get there. Marx knew of only one way; 'the organisation of a working-class movement which would in process of time end the landlord class, the capitalist class and the working class. That is revolution; that the working class will by its action, one day abolish class distinctions.

'And it was the inspired vision of Karl Marx which first formulated as a cold scientific fact, the inevitable coming of that glorious time. Little wonder that his memory is a consecrated treasure enshrined in the hearts of millions of the best men and women of all lands.'

Hardie visited Germany in the autumn and was impressed by the way German Socialists had organised their own Press. If Germany could do it, why not Britain?

He had received an offer from an 'unknown comrade' of £1,000 to start a fund for a British Socialist daily.

He wanted to know what support would be given to this project. It would be an I.L.P. paper, published by the National Labour Press at

Manchester and giving independent support to the Labour Party. 'Its object will be,' he wrote, 'to make the Labour movement a Socialist movement. It rests with the active spirits in our movement to say whether a Socialist daily is to see the light of day on Monday, May 18th, 1911. If it doesn't the fault won't be mine.'

In September, Hardie attended the 47th Annual Congress of the Social Democratic Party of Germany at Magdeburg, and described the proceedings in two long articles in *The Labour Leader*. It was the seriousness, the length, and the theoretical nature of the speeches that interested him.

'In our own country anything like serious discussion has almost disappeared from our Labour and Socialist Congress and probably not a little of the unrest and disaffection, which from time to time is manifested in our ranks is due to this cause . . .

'The discussion on Tuesday was opened by Herr August Bebel. On the previous day he had been chaffing me about being a mere boy of 54, compared with his seventy winters and yet he looks the younger man. As is well known he has been suffering from an internal complaint for a long time and it was doubtful whether he would be able to take part in the Congress at all. But the old man is still very alert and active. He mounted the rostrum, carrying with him a glass of lemonade and spoke for one hour and fifty minutes.'

Herr Franck replied to Bebel in a speech which lasted an hour and thirty-five minutes.

'These two speakers had thus occupied the whole of the morning sitting and the Congress adjourned from one o'clock to three. From three to seven, speaker succeeded speaker, the time limit for each being twenty minutes.'

Hardie concluded that the following morning the vote would be taken, but the debate went on until that evening.

'It was now eight o'clock and as the atmosphere had become almost unbreathable, it was decided to adjourn for half an hour and to take a vote.

'I have described the form of the debate at this length in order that our own comrades may see the thorough and exhaustive way in which our German comrades do their work. There is nothing slip-shod about their methods, nothing is left to chance, every phase and aspect of the subject under discussion is thrashed out to exhaustion and no one is left with any feeling of soreness because his point of view has not been put.'

Bebel had contrasted the political situation and Socialist tactics in Germany with that in Britain and had said:

'The English know us. Our dear friend Keir Hardie will not be offended when I say they cannot be taken as a criterion for all things.

195

Circumstances have changed in England, and the Socialist Party there is not very strong. Marx could not any longer consider the Trade Unions as the protagonists of the European proletariat. Since 1870 the German proletariat is at the head of the world's proletariat and we shall remain so if we are reasonable. The Trade Unions have obtained good results but can now hardly serve as a model to our syndicates. I hope that things will change and that the mass of the English proletariat will go forward hand in hand with the German proletariat.'

Hardie thought that 'the point in Bebel's mind was that because of the different conditions in the two parties therefore the tactics had to be different'. He went on:

'In England the working-class movement has hitherto been essentially Trade Unionist whereas in Germany it has been Socialist. Now, however, and I think our comrade Bebel sees this, the Trade Union movement in Germany is modifying the character of the Socialist tactics, whereas in England the Socialist movement is changing the outlook for Trades Unionism. One does not care to be hypocritical in matters of this kind, but I think it could be shown that the Labour Party of Great Britain is an even more genuine proletarian movement than is the Socialist Party of Germany.

'Be this as it may, however, our rivalry with our German comrades is simply to see who will first the goal which both have in common and which is the economic emancipation of the working class, and the overthrow of the capitalist system and the building up of the Socialist state.'

Hardie was obviously deeply impressed with the German Socialist Congress at Magdeburg. He concluded his article:

'Looking down the long rows of tables, at which, by the way were a fair sprinkling of women delegates, one could not help feeling that the square-jawed, heavy-footed men one saw would move on irresistible as fate to their destined end. Revisionism and Radicalism are matters of little moment. The thing that matters is that these men know what they want and know that, be the difficulties what they may, nothing can stay them in their onward march towards its attainment.'

It was not, however, to be as simple as all that in the years that were to follow. The Germans, like the British, were to be divided when war came. The majority found their patriotism a stronger emotion than their international socialism and only the minorities on both sides remaining loyal to what Bebel and Hardie had stood for at Magdeburg in September 1910.

Hardie attached immense importance to the interchange of British and Continental Socialists.

At the Conference of the Socialist International at Copenhagen, his proposal for a General Strike to prevent war had been opposed by

Ledebour, on behalf of the German Social Democrats, who had described it as 'right in theory but quite impracticable'.

He replied to Ledebour, who had criticised the attitude of the British Labour Party towards the Budget, and offered to withdraw his own amendment definitely advocating the General Strike policy if the Congress would agree 'to recommend the affiliated parties to consider the advisability and feasibility of the General Strike, especially in industries that supply war material, as one of the methods of preventing war, and that action be taken on preventing war and that action be taken on the subject at the next Congress'.

After a long debate in which at first the Germans and the Austrians had opposed the amendment, it was decided to refer it for consideration to the International Bureau.

Vandervelde, from Belgium, stated that the Belgian Party would abstain from voting but they wished it to be known that they absolutely approved of the General Strike.

'The speech of Hardie had greatly added to their admiration for him as a representative of the British Socialist and Labour Movement. He approved not only of a General Strike but a general rebellion against war. The Socialist and Labour Movement in Britain had bravely resisted the Boer War. So also had the Russian Revolutionists resisted the war against Japan, and the Spanish Socialists the war against Morocco.'

When war came Vandervelde was to change his mind too. But this was the year 1910, not the year 1914.

And Hardie was too optimistic in his belief that the International Socialist Movement could stop the war.

Later in the year French, German and Belgian Socialists were invited to address big united anti-war demonstrations in Britain. The I.L.P. organised a national campaign against militarism and war to counteract the propaganda of Lord Roberts and Robert Blatchford. It concluded with a great demonstration at the Albert Hall on December 10th. Hardie and Ramsay MacDonald spoke at a large number of other meetings. A meeting at Reading was addressed by an unknown young London Socialist, Clement R. Attlee.

The demonstration at the Albert Hall was addressed by Jean Jaures, from France, Vandervelde from Belgium, Molkenbuhr from Germany, W. T. Mills from America, and MacDonald, Lansbury and W. C. Anderson from Britain. Hardie presided.

The gathering, he said, was 'a proclamation of the gospel of international solidarity, and our distinguished visitors have come to tell us in the name of those for whom they are entitled to speak that there are to be no more wars'.

Hardie went on to argue that the old fallacies by which war had been justified were now dispelled. 'An epoch-making book, *Great Illusion* by Norman Angell, proved that nations could not even win material gain by conquest. Trade did not follow the flag, the great navy and the great army neither protected interest nor created trade. Rather was it the small nations like Switzerland, without army or navy, who were able to give the people happiness and prosperity. Science was obliterating physical barriers— between peoples and science, literature and art were welding the peoples together by giving them a common sympathy. But no influence for peace was greater than that of the International Socialist Movement which at recent elections had polled no less than ten million votes, every one of them an influence for peace.'

Hardie reminded the meeting of the proposals adopted at the Copenhagen Conference:

(1) That all treaties should be made public, and ratified by the respective Parliaments before being signed.
(2) That instruction in the principles of international solidarity should be given in all public schools.
(3) That pressure should be exercised on all the Governments of Europe to bring about first reduction and then abolition of armaments.
(4) That the organised working classes of different countries shall consider whether a General Strike should not be proclaimed if necessary— in order to prevent the crime of war.

The Chairman of the I.L.P., W. C. Anderson, moved a resolution declaring that 'there is and cannot be any cause of War between the democracies of Europe, "protesting" emphatically against the increase in armaments and the attempts that are made to foster strife among the nations and repudiating Militarism in all its forms as being inimical to the progress of the race'. It finally called upon the workers of all lands to unite under the Socialist flag and thus establish industrial peace and international goodwill.

When Keir Hardie put the resolution at the end of the speeches it was carried with a tremendous shout and the demonstration ended with the singing of 'The Internationale'.

They were brave speeches but the forces that were making for war in Europe were also already on the move, and moving irresistibly on.

CHAPTER 19

CAMPAIGNING IN WALES

HARDIE became more and more critical of the Liberal Government. He protested strongly against its policy during the miners' and railwaymen's strikes, and its readiness to send troops into the industrial areas. Behind their façade of social reform legislation, Mr. Asquith and the Liberal Cabinet were really protecting the interests of the big capitalists, the bankers, the railway companies, the shipowners and coalowners. The half-hearted insurance schemes and other social reform legislation were sops to the working class by men who were really the political instruments of Big Business, High Finance and the Stock Exchange.

In the House of Commons, at Question Time and in the debates, he was more and more in conflict with Asquith, Lloyd George, Churchill, Haldane and Sir Edward Grey. He declared that the Liberal Government had betrayed the women over the Suffrage question and, even though he did not agree with all the tactics of Mrs. Pankhurst and her friends, he championed their cause against the Home Secretary and frequently questioned him about the suffragettes in jail or on hunger strike.

In the discussions over the Lloyd George Insurance Bill, he supported Snowden who had taken the line that the scheme should be non-contributory and voted against the Bill on this ground. He was always pressing the case of the unemployed. He became increasingly critical of Haldane's military plans and the foreign policy of Sir Edward Grey.

He dealt fully with the Liberal Reform legislation in a speech to his constituents at Merthyr. First he examined the Mines Bill:

'You know about the terrible death roll in the mines and how the best mining engineers tell us that a coal mine could be as safe as a field if proper steps were taken to make it safe.

199

'If our Royal Families had to live in mines there would never be an accident. And what would be the case with them ought to be the case for you. Are you aware of this—that last time a general Mines Bill was passed was in the year 1887? I was not in Parliament then, but I was a miners' agent. I attended conferences with the employers to find how much we could get them to accept, and with the exception of the clauses dealing with electricity (which had not then been introduced into the mines), practically every amendment that is to be found in the present Bill was then pressed upon the Government. Twenty-four years have come and gone since then. During that time 30,000 colliers have been brought home dead from the pits, and there have been over 2,000,000 cases of more or less serious injury. If the statements now being made about the present Bill are true, then had our amendments been accepted by the Government in 1887, one-third of these accidents might have been prevented. Safety legislation is always a quarter of a century in arrears.'

He went on to examine in detail the provisions of the Insurance Bill:

'The Insurance Bill, we are told, is for the benefit of the poverty-stricken, disease-laden working class. Yes; but why is the "working" class so poverty-stricken and disease-laden as to require a measure of this kind? This Bill does not touch, even remotely, the real causes of poverty. We ask, for example, we of the Labour Party, that there shall be a thirty shillings minimum fixed for the lowest paid labour in the country, and an eight shillings a day minimum for all who work underground or at dangerous or unhealthy occupations. No, say the Liberals, we will give you an Insurance Bill, we shall not uproot the cause of poverty, but we will give you a porous plaster to cover the disease that poverty causes.'

He was getting more and more support in Merthyr and the influence of the I.L.P. was growing all over South Wales. He persuaded the local Socialists to start a weekly paper, *The Merthyr Pioneer,* to which he began to write regularly. The Liberals, now very much on the defensive, fell back on sentimental appeals to Welsh Nationalism and Welsh Nonconformity, and attacked him because he came from Scotland. He replied in a speech at Dowlais:

'They were hearing about Welsh Nationalism. Being a Scotsman, he believed in nationality. But they should beware that nationalism was the genuine article, and not some spurious imitation. They talked of Welsh Nationalism when they wanted votes, but when it came to doing anything for the workers they were not nationalists, they were not even Welshmen, they were simply party politicians intent upon keeping the workers in their rightful place.

'Men and women of Dowlais,' declared Hardie, 'we are going to have a Welsh Nationalist Party, and if Sir Alfred Mond can lead the "Nationalist Party" in Wales at present it is quite possible that Keir Hardie will lead the real party. The Nationalist Party I have in mind is this: the people of

Wales fighting to recover possession of the land in Wales—the working class of Wales acquiring possession of the mines, of the furnaces, and the railways, of the great public works generally, and working these as comrades, not for the benefit of shareholders, but for the good of every man, woman and child within your borders. That is the kind of Nationalism that will be emblazoned on the red flag of Socialism, the international emblem of the working-class movement of the world.'

In November, Hardie delivered an outspoken speech in the House of Commons critical of the foreign policy of Sir Edward Grey and of the incidents in Morocco.

He wrote in *The Labour Leader*:

'The rumours and revelations of the past few days must have set quite a number of people thinking. The story is that twice during the autumn we were on the very brink of war, and all because of Morocco, where France and Germany were quarrelling over the looting of territory from Moors and Africans.

'France agreed not to challenge England's sole right to exploit Egypt on condition that France was given a similar free hand in Morocco. England, it now appears, had bound herself to back France by force of arms if her right to exploit Morocco was challenged and as Germany was the only power likely to challenge the right of France, the agreement was tantamount to an open flouting of the German Empire. That is why the Admiralty and the War Office had a bad fit of the jumps. "Tis conscience makes cowards of us all." '

Hardie asked why Britain should be involved:

'Now, why all this embroiling of ourselves in troubled waters? Solely in the interest of the trader and the usurer. We have a Liberal Government in Office, and whilst Mr. Lloyd George keeps the nation in commotion over Budgets and Insurance Bills, the Cabinet of which he is a member is doing the will of the big financial houses. The Barings, the Schusters, the Cassels, and the Rothschilds, these are the real masters of the nation. We are a democratic people, believing ourselves to be popularly governed, and we allow the Government to work like moles in the dark in all that pertains to foreign relations.

'But the most interesting of the rumours is that which shows the part which the railway strike played in the crisis. Sir Guy Granet has told us that the Government told him that the action in yielding in the railway strike had been the fear that the soldiers would be required abroad.

'As *The Times* pointed out on Monday last, practically the entire Army had been called out to aid the Civil arm in protecting the railways. It is alleged that when Germany found the British Army tied up, they increased the pressure upon France, and thus made the crisis again acute. Now, this may or may not be true, but it casts a powerful light on one question in which I take a special interest. I hold the opinion that the organised Labour movement has it in its power to prevent war by simply threatening to strike.'

This led Hardie once again to advocate the idea of a General Strike to stop war:

'Suppose we had an agreement on the part of the workers in all civilised countries to make war upon war by means of a strike, the knowledge that such would take place would make war impossible. Whether it were Germany and France, or Britain and Germany to threaten to come to blows, the workers, properly organised, could drive all thought of war away, not only by stopping the supplies of war, but by making it imperative that armies be kept at home to safeguard property—and, of course, ensure the poor of their food supplies.'

Hardie could not get any support either in Britain or Germany for his idea that a General Strike policy could prevent war.

The coalowners announced a rise in the price of coal by half a crown a ton a few weeks before a threatened strike in South Wales.

At the same time a conference of religious organisations was held at Cardiff and called for a 'change of heart'.

'One good man said at the conference that what was most needed was "a change of heart". Whose heart is it that needs changing? The Cory Brothers operate on both the London and Cardiff Exchanges, and are engaged in the coal trade. The central fact is this: that the respectable, church-going men who are, without cause, raising the price of coal in the depth of winter, and raising it most against the poor, are worse than common cheats and robbers. They are robbing the poor; not merely robbing them of money, but robbing them of comfort, of health, and, in some cases, of life. They may attend church or chapel regularly; they may give to charities and Christian mission; they may be respected members of society, patriots, and loyalists, but they are robbers all the same.'

He was asked by the Dowlais Adult School to deliver a lecture and he based his address on the text, 'What think ye of Christ?'

'The trouble about modern life and modern Christianity,' Hardie said, 'was that people were attempting to live their lives in separate watertight compartments. Men went to Church on Sundays, listened to sermons, repeated prayers, and sang hymns, and on Monday they began operations as though Christ had never existed.

'Much had been said in these days about the failure of the working class to attend the Church, but there was no mystery about that. The working class was not interested to know what Christ thought of the Scribes and the Pharisees of 1,900 years ago; men and women wanted to know what Christ thought about the Scribes and Pharisees of the beginning of the 20th century. Christianity required to be restored to its pristine strength and purity as a thing affecting the lives of men and women of to-day, and not simply an abstract doctrine concerning things that were to come after this life was over.

'The speaker proceeded to apply the test of Christianity to modern life and modern institutions. Let them take, for example, the question of war. Surely if there was one matter upon which the teaching of Christ was more clear than another, it was that there was one universal Father over all, and that all men brethren. They all professed to be Christians. Europe had been Christianised for at least 1,500 years, and yet they were all piling up the instruments of war, training men and providing the implements whereby we slaughtered each other under the blessing of God proclaimed by the priests. Why did not they get together to abolish war?

'Our Cabinet Ministers, except perhaps Lord Morley, would say they believed in Christ. He (Mr. Hardie) would tell them of sins which the audience knew, and which the Cabinet ought to know, concerning the lives of the common people. He could take them to districts in London and elsewhere, where mothers were sitting over children who were crying for food. In the public schools they would see the little toddling things in ragged clothing, boots full of holes, bellies without food, and with drawn, pinched faces, and wide-open staring eyes. The statesmen who had the power to cure that kind of thing, and did not, were insulting the very name of Christ by professing to be His followers. It was time there was an Adult School or something else to rescue Christ from the hands of those who did not understand Him and restore Him to the common people.

'In so far as society was based upon self-interest, it was anti-Christian, and it was up to every man and every woman who desired to see God's kingdom established on earth to do everything he or she possibly could to overthrow an order of society based upon injustice and introduce a new order based upon fraternity and justice to all alike.'

When he was invited to lecture at an Adult School at Brotherhood meetings he made very much the same speech.

At a Brotherhood meeting at Browning Hall, London, he outlined his definition of Christianity:

'If I were called upon to define Christianity in a single sentence, I would say that Christianity represents sacrifice having its origin in love. And the Christian who professes the Christian faith is thereby under obligation to make whatever sacrifice may be necessary in order to remove sin, suffering, and injustice from the lives of those around him. It is not enough to pray to God—it is a mere mockery to sing hymns—unless our lives are consecrated to the service of God through humanity. Make no mistake about this. The only way you can serve God is by serving mankind. There is no other way. It is taught in the Old Testament; it is taught in the New Testament. Christ's heart of love went out to all mankind. He was hated. He was persecuted. He was stoned, and finally crucified, because He loved the poor so much that He refused to be a part of the hypocrisy of the age and say, Peace, peace, when there was no peace.

'And the only Christian to-day worthy of the name is the man and the woman, whether in the Church or out of it; who is sacrificing life and leisure for the uplifting and the ennobling of the race.'

He frequently wrote in the *Pioneer* some biographical notes disposing of the rumours that his anti-Socialist opponents were spreading about him.

One was that he had made a 'huge fortune' out of the Labour Movement. He replied:

'During the election campaign in January a year ago, a lady, a minister's wife, waited upon me to solicit a subscription for some local cause, and was greatly surprised and mortified when I declined to give a donation. In her zeal for her cause she reproached me for not showing a true Christian spirit, as being a "very wealthy man". I should feel it my duty to support every good cause. I explained the facts of the case to the lady, but she was only half convinced. Someone had told her that I had sold *The Labour Leader* to the Labour Party for £20,000, and that, in addition, I owned a "great estate", from which I derived a large income. Since then I have made enquiries and found out that this particular chestnut was one of the "arguments" which the canvassers for the "unofficial" Liberal candidate had circulated in 1906. Quite possibly the fake may still be doing service.'

Hardie then proceeded to dispose of the myth that he was a wealthy man who had made a fortune out of Socialism:

'I handed *The Labour Leader* over to the Party on condition that they discharged the liabilities which I had incurred in keeping it going single-handed for eight years. That was all; not a copper for myself.

'I own no estate or property of any kind. The house in which we have lived since 1891 will, all being well, be free of the loan by which it was built, in one year from now and I shall then become its "owner". My present income of £210 a year is the largest I have ever enjoyed in my life. Out of this I pay £120 a year for rent of my rooms in London, postage and clerical assistance. I never work less than 15—more often 17 —hours out of the 24 whilst Parliament is sitting and spend week-ends in travelling long distances to speak for Socialism. That is to say, my net income as a Member of Parliament is £90 a year, out of which my wife and daughter have to maintain themselves and I have to find food and raiment. Were it not for an occasional magazine article the thing would be impossible. During the first three years I was in Parliament I had no salary of any kind, having to earn every penny I got. During the whole of that time Mrs. Hardie kept the home going and brought up our three children on a wage of 25s. a week. I earned much more, but save the pittance named, every penny went in keeping *The Labour Leader* going and helping the cause.

'That is my reply to those who say I make a "good thing" out of the movement. There is no compulsion on me to work these long hours for such scant reward. I go on working because I love doing it. There are thousands of comrades doing the same, working men and women, who are devoting their lives to the cause without any hope or thought of reward of any kind. And this is the movement which so many of you call "materialistic", and would fain kill if you could!'

Socialism was making great headway in Merthyr. It was now becoming one of the strongholds of Socialism in Britain.

Hardie had great hopes for the Labour Party and the Socialist Movement in Wales. He wrote a pamphlet especially for Wales which was translated into Welsh. He addressed meetings of the students at Aberystwyth and Bangor Universities. He was confident that Wales could be won over.

Towards the end of 1910 there were a series of strikes in the mining valleys of South Wales which spread to the Aberdare Valley, which was then in Hardie's constituency. The trouble had begun in the Rhondda Valley, where the men had come out as a result of the refusal of the Cambrian Combine to meet their wage demands.

Eleven thousand men were on strike in the Rhondda Valley and as a result of the picketing there were conflicts with the police. Other police were sent into the area and the Chief Constable of Glamorgan appealed to the Home Secretary, Winston Churchill, to send soldiers. Hardie went down to South Wales. He wrote in *The Labour Leader* of November 18th, 1910:

'The Rhondda and Aberdare Valleys are thronged with police, mounted and on foot; detachments of soldiers are billeted at farm houses in the neighbourhood of collieries or quartered at Pontypridd. The entire district looks like a beseiged area in war-time. Men, women, and children have been mauled by police batons and the Press of the country has been practically unanimous in describing the people as riotous, rowdies of the hooligan type.'

But there was the miners' point of view of the strike.

They had come out as a result of a dispute over tonnage rates in one pit, the owners locked out another 800 working on other seams in the pit and then the whole of the workers employed by the Cambrian Combine had come out. In the Aberdare Valley the immediate cause of the strike had been the stopping of an old custom—the taking home by the miners of useless ends of pit props as firewood.

The local people in both valleys testified that there had been no serious disorders until the imported police had interfered with peaceful pickets and broken up the crowds, injuring with their batons not only men but women and children as well.

205

Hardie went down to South Wales and collected a great deal of evidence, not only from the strikers and their relatives, but from shopkeepers and ministers of religion who were indignant at the conduct of the police. Innocent spectators had been beaten up as the police had panicked and some of them had been thrown into a canal. Hardie raised the question in the House of Commons and strongly criticised the action of Winston Churchill, the Home Secretary and Haldane, the Minister for War, who had been responsible for sending down the Metropolitan Police and the soldiers at the request of the coalowners.

He demanded an inquiry and this was supported by the Liberal M.P. for Merthyr, Edgar Jones, and by William Abraham, M.P. for the Rhondda Valley.

Churchill refused any inquiry.

Hardie strongly attacked him for sending down the soldiers who, he argued, were not needed:

'The Welsh collier was not given to disorder. These men were almost all quiet, reasonable, law-abiding citizens and the police force brought into the district was amply sufficient to deal with the ones who were not orderly. The presence of troops was regarded as an insult; it was a source of irritation and in itself might cause disorder. On no single occasion had there been the slightest necessity for calling in the military and their continued presence in South Wales was an affront to the inhabitants and gave the impression that the Government were taking sides with the employers. There was no truth at all in the suggestion that the dispute was political. The fact that 12,000 men out of 15,000 earned 20s. or less a week was a proof that industrial conditions were not satisfactory.'

Churchill was adamant and refused any inquiry.

Hardie pursued the matter in *The Labour Leader*. He proved that the local magistrates were never consulted about the importation of the soldiers and the local police authorities had been opposed not only to the introduction of the soldiers but to the sending of the Metropolitan Police. They were sent because the coalowners had asked for them and the Chief Constable of Glamorgan had acquiesced.

This was another count in Hardie's indictment of Churchill. He said he had never known a Cabinet Minister handle a dispute so badly for 'we have never had a Churchill for Home Secretary until now'.

He wrote:

'Had he not done so what would have been the result. Would the mines have been flooded? Not a bit. The mines are very valuable. Millions are made out of them every year by their owners and when these gentlemen saw the goose being drowned which layed their golden eggs for them, they would have settled with their men. But Churchill at the bidding of the coalowners, poured in the policemen, armed with stout truncheons, and soldiers armed with steel bayonets and twenty rounds each of leaden bullets to save the masters from defeat.

'And this is what he hypocritically calls "Keeping the Ring" and allowing the combatants to fight out their quarrels without outside interference ... I hope the Trade Unionists of the country are taking note of what is happening in connection with this strike. If they, by their silence, acquiesce in, or appear to give sanction to, the flooding of a strike area with soldiers and police, they will discover some fine morning, that the precedent set has hardened into a custom and that on every occasion when there is a dispute the military and police will be on the job as a matter of course. That would indeed be a serious matter, and now is the time to stop it ere it goes too far.'

The dispute dragged on but was soon overshadowed by another General Election, the second in the year. Hardie again won Merthyr but it was not an exciting election. His election agent wrote:

'The fight in the Merthyr Boroughs this time had no reality in it. We had hoped to see two official Liberals in full war-paint but they thought discretion the better part of valour and gave the coal war as an excuse. The Conservative Association ran a man who called himself a Liberal Unionist and declared he stood as the result of an understanding between the Liberal and Conservative Associations. To judge from one or two filthy speeches and the scurrilous literature distributed, the man was in close touch with the Anti-Socialist Union.

'Hardie attacked the Liberal Government mercilessly and exposed the hollowness of the Liberal professions of solicitude for the workers, especially those of political hypocrites of the Churchill type.'

The result of the election was:

EDGAR JONES (Liberal)	...	...	12,258
KEIR HARDIE (Labour)	...	...	11,507
J. H. WATTS (Liberal Unionist)	...		5,277

Hardie had tried to get a local miner to stand as the Labour candidate for the second seat. He thought the other seat could have been won. Some of the local Socialists were not so sure. The Liberal, Edgar Jones, was strongly backed by the Nonconformist ministers and a few days before the poll the idea of running another candidate was abandoned. Hardie always argued that the other seat should be fought. During the election campaign he vigorously attacked the Liberal Government, disregarding the advice of those who urged him to tone down his criticisms so as not to lose the Liberal vote.

CHAPTER 20

THE LAW AND THE
LABOUR PARTY

THE Labour Party had more than held its own at the election. It went back with 42 Members, the newcomers being two great friends of Hardie's, George Lansbury and Tom Richardson (Whitehaven). He was especially pleased to welcome George Lansbury, who like himself had been one of the champions of the unemployed in the East End.

The Labour Party, however, had encountered an unexpected snag. This was the Osborne Judgment.

A railway signalman by the name of Osborne had raised an action against the Amalgamated Society of Railway Servants, the railwaymen's union, to prevent it from paying the shilling a member political levy paid to the Labour Party.

Mr. Justice Neville decided in favour of the union but Osborne won his case in the House of Lords. This placed the union and similar unions affiliated to the Labour Party in great difficulties.

Hardie explained the complicated legal problem in a clear, lucid way in a pamphlet called *The Party Pledge and the Osborne Judgment,* examining in detail the reasons the Lords had given for their decision.

He described the Constitution of the Labour Party and how it worked. Passages from the pamphlet are interesting in view of later controversies.

He wrote about the Parliamentary Labour Party:

'In the House of Commons, the members of the Party decide their own policy without interference from the Executive or any outside authority. This is the right which the Parliamentary Party has always claimed, and which has never been seriously challenged. Where a member has a conscientious or other valid objection to supporting a finding of the Party, the almost invariable rule has been to allow him freedom of action, both of speech and vote, and this freedom has been frequently claimed and exercised. From this it will be seen that all the talk about the coercion exercised by the Party on its well-dragooned, pledge-bound adherents is either due to misunderstanding, as in the case of Lord James or is the outcome of ignorant, implacable hostility, to the Party itself. The so-called "Pledge" refers more, much more to action of candidates taken outside Parliament than it does to the action of members within, as an ordinary careful reading of the Constitution will show.'

From this it is clear that Keir Hardie held that the Labour Party in Parliament should scrupulously respect conscientious opinions and not impose a cast iron discipline on its members.

He replied at length to the opinions of the various Judges and then dealt with the broad political issue:

'Why is the Labour Party illegal? Because it represents the working class, because its members are paid by the working class, to go to represent them. Mr. Balfour and others have been pointing out the terrible tyranny of compelling a Trade Unionist who does not believe in the Labour Party to pay for a candidate with whom he does not agree. This is a difficulty which is always bound to exist in every civilised country. They are now offering us payment of members. We shall get payment of members and of official election expenses either this year or, at furthest, next year. When we get payment of members what is going to happen? That the Tory working man and the Liberal working man, and the Tory capitalist and the Liberal capitalist, and the Tory landlord and the Liberal landlord will have to pay taxes to pay the salaries of Socialists like myself. Therefore, they are not getting rid of the dilemma by offering us payment of members; that much is certain. But what about the Party being illegal, because we are pledged to stand by the class to which we belong?'

He went on to ask:

'Is the Labour Party the only party that stands by its own class? When the Budget was being discussed a year ago, what did you see then in the House of Commons? Captain Pretyman, a young able landlord, who is receiving a big income from unearned increment in the value of his land, fought the land clauses of the Budget step by step, inch by inch. What were he and his fellow-landlords fighting for when opposing the Budget? Was it for the good of their country? Or was it for the good of their own pockets? But then, Captain Pretyman is a patriot when he opposes the Budget; it is only when a working man fights for old-age pensions for his own class, fights for an eight-hour day for miners, fights for a proper Workmen's Compensation Act, fights for the feeding of hungry school children—it is only when working men do that that they become rebels. When landlords are fighting for their class, when brewers are fighting for their class, when colliery owners are fighting for their class—and we see these things in the House of Commons every session—that is all right and proper; but when a Labour Party goes there to fight for the rights of the poor, they become rebels.'

Sir Rufus Isaacs, The Liberal Attorney-General, said that the

o

Osborne Judgment could never be completely reversed. Hardie replied:

'Neither Sir Rufus Isaacs nor Mr. James Balfour have the settlement of this question. The last word rests with the Trade Unionists at the ballot-box on the day of the poll. In 1906, Sir Rufus Isaacs' predecessor, Sir John Lawson Walton, speaking for the Government, said: "The Taff Vale decision can never be completely reversed," and he spoke for one hour and thirty minutes in the House of Commons, proving to the country that the Taff Vale decision could never be completely overturned. But there were 29 of us sitting there as a Labour Party who had drafted our own Bill, and within a fortnight of Sir John Lawson Walton making that speech he got up in his place and accepted our Bill which completely reversed the Taff Vale judgment.

'And what was done for Taff Vale has got to be done for Osborne. Who are these men that attempt to dictate to us the conditions on which we shall be allowed to have a Labour Party? I do not know how others feel about these things, but when I read the speeches of men like Mr. Balfour, Sir Rufus Isaacs, and others of less account, like some of the young whipper-snappers of both parties, some of whom are themselves paid from their party funds, saying: "Of course we want to see working men in Parliament; the working class should have some members there to speak for it," my blood begins to boil. We are not there on the sufferance of either Liberal or Tory, we are not there because landlords and employers of labour or Law Lords love us; we are there because they can't keep us out. We are not there as the representatives of some outcast class which required to have a few men from its own ranks that it may not be altogether overlooked; we are there to represent the nation, for the working class is the nation.'

The last pages of the pamphlet consisted of a speech he had made in his constituency on the subject in which he had stated the case for political action:

'They see the working class rising, they see it emerging, they see it beginning to fill the places which they have hitherto held as a monopoly. Why, every man you send to the House of Commons fills a seat which otherwise would have been filled by one of your masters or one of the idle class who live at your expense, and the more Labour men you send there the less room there is for them. And so they think to stop this movement in time before you have crushed them out, because they know, my friends—many of you do not know it, but they know perfectly well— that just as the working class increases its representation in the House of Commons, so will the laws passed there become more and more in favour of the working class.

'They would like to confine you to industrial action through your Trade Union, they would like to say to you, "the Trade Unions have no right to take part in politics;" they would like to have you where once every five or six years they could starve you into submission to their will. When the strike or the lock-out takes place it is you and your children, remember, who have got to starve and suffer and get into debt.

'The employer may have to go without a part of his dividend for three months, but he knows perfectly well that after the trouble is over he will be able to recoup himself. And whilst the strike lasts he will never miss a meal, he won't require to smoke one cigar less, he won't require to economise even in the matter of his wine bill. His life will go on in all its luxury during the lock-out as it went on before.

'It is you and those who are near and dear to you who will have to do the suffering. They would like you to confine yourselves to Trade Union action. They know perfectly well that where you can meet them on terms of perfect equality is the floor of the House of Commons. They cannot starve you there. And, what is more, at the ballot-box you are more than their masters, the reason being that you are many and they are few.'

He concluded:

'To change the policy or tactics of the Party now would be fatal. It would be like lowering the flag in the face of the enemy. We have been assailed. Let us fight to keep the ground we have won. If we don't, we shall weaken the morale in our own ranks and encourage the enemy to press us for still further concessions. A few years fighting round this issue will strengthen the *esprit de corp* of the Party, bring all sections closer together, and bring a much-needed consolidation to the movement. Therefore, so far as I am concerned, my watchword is No Surrender. The Party, Pledge and all, independent, militant, and defiant, must be legalised if it is to continue to be of service to the cause of Democracy.'

Hardie had stated the case for political action for the trade unions taking part in politics but he was in favour of industrial action, too, and during the railway dispute he took a prominent part in the railwaymen's strike for recognition of their union. It was the first time the British railwaymen had organised a national strike and Hardie put his services at their disposal to plead their cause. He went to Merthyr and spoke at a meeting organised by the railwaymen in the Public Park. He began by recalling his opposition to the use of soldiers in the Rhondda strike:

'There are men and women probably in this great crowd who thought I was very foolish when I made my strongest protest against the military being sent into the Rhondda Valley when the strike took place there. I am getting not only an old man but an old politician; I can read the signs of the times. I said then publicly, if these soldiers are allowed to remain in South Wales it means this, that every time there is a strike of any size, the soldiers are going to be sent down to intimidate and to shoot the strikers. I am sorry to think, my friends, that these words of prophecy should have had such an early and such terrible realisation. In this dispute

211

soldiers are being sent everywhere. Fifty thousand soldiers have been called up. To-night in Liverpool, to-night in Llanelly, there are weeping, mourning hearts for good men who have been shot down because they were fighting for better conditions of life.

'Ah, you say to me, the Government is bound to maintain law and order. I do not deny it. I do not dispute it. But let us begin at the beginning. When the railwaymen said we want our unions recognised; when the railway directors told the Government that they were not going to recognise the men's unions; what was then the duty of the Government? Not to promise soldiers to back up the directors, but to say to the directors: "We believe the men to be right, and not one single soldier, not one single constable, shall be moved to your assistance until you have met the men's union." '

Hardie wrote a 24-page pamphlet on the railway strike and the shootings at Liverpool and Llanelly, and called it *Killing No Murder*. It told the story of the strike in simple, concise language, telling how it had come, the issues involved and how the Liberal Government had tried to bluff the men's leaders, threatened them, placed the military at the disposal of the railway companies and then, finally forced by the strike, had yielded. In the House of Commons, Lloyd George had attacked Hardie for statements he had made at meetings during the strike. But the Railwaymen's Executive supported Hardie and unanimously passed the following resolution:

'THIS JOINT EXECUTIVE BODY REPUDIATES THE UNWARRANTABLE ATTACK BY THE CHANCELLOR OF THE EXCHEQUER (MR. LLOYD GEORGE) UPON MR. KEIR HARDIE FOR USING ARGUMENTS WHICH EACH OF THE FORTY REPRESENTATIVES PRESENT AT THE BOARD OF TRADE FEEL WERE QUITE JUSTIFIABLE AFTER THE LANGUAGE AND ATTITUDE OF THE PRIME MINISTER. WE FURTHER TENDER THE BEST THANKS OF THE JOINT EXECUTIVES, REPRESENTING ALL RAILWAY WORKERS, TO MR. KEIR HARDIE AND THE LABOUR PARTY FOR THE SPLENDID SERVICE IN HELPING BOTH TO BRING OUR MEN OUT AND TO GET THEM BACK AGAIN WHEN THE TRUCE WAS CALLED.'

He replied to Lloyd George:

'When Mr. Lloyd George, by his attack, set all his jackals in the Press howling out abuse against Keir Hardie, he doubtless imagined he had done a good thing for his party. No doubt he meant well. The actual effect has been to lead people everywhere, and especially Trade Unionists with Liberal leanings, to examine their moorings. The Government hoped to add to its laurels by claiming credit for having "settled the strike". I destroyed that little game. So long as it is a question of Insurance Bills that are being discussed, the Government is sweetness itself towards

Labour and many are deceived. The moment Capital and Labour came into conflict, and the scene of action cannot be concealed behind the curtain of make-believe, then the true affinity of the Liberal Government is revealed. It was because I drew aside the curtain and revealed a little of what had been going on in the dark that Mr. Lloyd George and his friends were so wrathful.'

He drew the conclusion:

'There is but one solution for these recurring Labour troubles, the State must own the railways. There is no other way. The gradgrinds who now mismanage them are burdening industry with oppressive rates, and sweating and grinding the faces of the employees. The railwaymen have again brought this question into the forefront of politics, and if the Government carry out their promise to the directors to give them power to levy higher rates and fares, that will give the movement for nationalisation a fresh impetus. But it will do more than that, it will add to the price which the nation will have to pay over for the railways when the time comes for taking them over.'

A new King was on the throne and there was another Coronation. It meant a repetition of the sickening adulation of Royalty which Hardie had protested against so many times and which he loathed.

He wrote in *The Pioneer*:

'The most desperate efforts are being made to popularise the coming Coronation. Public authorities have been given power to spend the rate-payers' money illegally on decorations and festivities. Poor little half-starved children are to be presented with Coronation mugs or medals to commemorate the event. The workers are to be shut out from their employment for two whole days to show how heartily their loyal hearts rejoice over the Coronation of the King. Two holidays on full pay would not be amiss, but an empty pocket is not an incentive to loyalty.

'Thus, despite all the efforts of the astute stage managers, royalty is being found out. It is a huge imposture. The atmosphere of a court is surcharged with hypocrisy, insincerity, flattery and immorality.

'The Coronation, with its pomp and show, its make-believe, its glorification of militarism, and its mockery of the solemnities of religion, is an affront to all that is true and self-respecting in our national life.'

It was not only the Coronation that Hardie criticised. There were the Royal tours in Wales, Ireland and India as well:

'Wales is to have an "Investiture" as a reminder that an English King and his robber barons strove for ages to destroy the Welsh people, and finally succeeded in robbing them of their lands, driving them into the mountain fastnesses of their native land like hunted beasts, and then had the insolence to have his son "invested" in their midst. The King is to make a Coronation tour in Ireland to view the miles of lonely waste from which the persecution of his royal forebears has driven the Irish people into exile in other lands. And, crowning infamy, one million

213

pounds is to be spent on a Coronation Durbar at Delhi, in the district round which 20,000 *people are dying every week* of plague and hunger.'

Why was there this need to boost and glorify Royalty? asked Hardie.

'The *Daily Chronicle* explains why the patient, long-suffering people of India are thus to be mocked in their misery. Here is what it says: "One can safely say that, following the visit of the King we shall see a boom in India, particularly on the commercial side. To those who are looking to our Dominions to provide either an outlet for capital of a future for their sons, India should receive the consideration to which it is entitled."

'There we have "Loyalty" of the monied ruling classes in all its shameless nakedness. The King is to be used to provide an "outlet for the capital" of the rich or more soft jobs for their sons.

'Half a century ago Republicanism was the creed of Radicalism and Nonconformity. But the corrupting influences of wealth and a debased newspaper Press have eaten the soul out of the manhood of the nation.

'If we cannot set our heel upon the thing, we can at least show our contempt for it and preserve our own self-respect by refusing to participate in any of the foolery connected with this Coronation.'

Shortly afterwards the King and Queen paid an official visit to Wales and it was arranged that during their tour they should spend a day at Merthyr. Hardie was not there but he had addressed a long, open letter to the King on conditions in the big iron and steel works of Guest, Keen & Nettlefolds where the moulders had been on strike.

It had been arranged that the King and Queen should lunch there.

Hardie's 'Open Letter' consisted of a long indictment of the company which had made huge profits out of 'Dismal Dowlais' and paid miserable wages to its workers. The moulders had been on strike.

'No thought, care or consideration for the comfort, safety or convenience of the workers was ever given by the firm.'

His 'Open Letter to the King' continued:

'You will be driven through the main street from Merthyr station, up through Penydarren, to the Dowlais works. There will be gay bunting, and great crowds to watch you pass. Look at them closely, especially from the upper end of Penydarren to the Dowlais works. I have no doubt they will do their best to make themselves look respectable, but even then you will find evidence of deep poverty to which you will not be able to close your eyes.

'Were it possible for you to leave your carriage and walk round the slums, the horrible hovels in which hundreds of the workers of Messrs. Guest, Keen and Nettlefolds are herded together, and for which they pay extortionate rent, Your Majesty would be shocked. And these disgraceful conditions are the direct outcome of the low wages—reduced still further by broken time—paid by the firm. The Municipal Council is battling bravely with the housing question, and already has made a marked improvement in this respect; but there is evidence enough left to show you the mass of unrelieved squalor which was produced by the miserable conditions imposed upon their workpeople by the great firm which you are to honour with your presence, whilst building up great fortunes for themselves.

'I respectfully ask Your Majesty, therefore, before consenting to visit Dowlais works or to be entertained there, to make enquiries concerning facts: and if you find—as you must if you enquire that they are both true in substance and in fact, to refuse to be a party to the arrangement of either visiting the works or being entertained there to lunch.

'From a people so kindly as the Welsh you are bound, in any case, as the head of the State, to receive a warm welcome, but that warmth will be turned to enthusiasm if you boldly take your stand on the side of the workers and refuse to lend the countenance of your presence to a firm whose whole record is bad. The working classes can place but one interpretation upon a visit to Guest, Keen and Nettlefolds at this stage, and that will be that you, too, are against them, and on the side of their oppressors.

'Go to Dowlais by all means. See the people and their homes, but shun the works as you would a plague spot.'

Needless to say, the King did not take Hardie's advice and refuse to visit the works of Guest, Keen & Nettlefolds. Nor did the King and Queen visit the slums of 'Dismal Dowlais'. But in one respect Hardie's 'Open Letter' was successful. Before the Royal visit the company yielded and reinstated the moulders who had been on strike.

CHAPTER 21

HARDIE, SNOWDEN AND MACDONALD

IN 1912 Hardie again went to the United States to help Eugene Debs, the Socialist candidate for the Presidency. It was of course a forlorn hope and Hardie knew that it was simply propaganda for Socialism. He was well received and well reported in the American Press, for he had become an international personality and he had big crowds at his meetings and especially enthusiastic ones at Chicago, Pittsburg and Indianapolis. They listened to him with respect and admired his honesty and earnestness. He did not claim to be the spell-binder and dramatic orator of the American electioneering platform. At Chicago he told them:

'Those who know me best are aware that I am never much of an orator. If I have any reputation at all it is not that of a talker, but it is rather this: that during the thirty-odd years that I have been out in the open for the class to which I belong, whether in Parliament or out of it, I have stood by that class through good report on all.'

He was very modest in his claims. It was true he had not a flambuoyant platform style but he knew how to get his message across. He never underestimated the intelligence of his audience, especially if it was working class, and although he scorned rhetoric and the usual platform tricks he could keep the attention of large audiences.

The same year saw the calling of the emergency International Congress at Basle, the very last before the outbreak of war in 1914. There were 555 delegates from twenty-three countries. There was a tense situation in the Balkans and it was thought that Austria would be involved and that this might mean general war.

Bebel from Germany, Jaures from France, Adler from Austria, Keir Hardie from Britain, all well-known international figures, were there and they all made impressive appeals to the nations to keep out of war.

'The situation is critical,' wrote Hardie, 'and European war will almost certainly lead to European revolution the end of which no man can foresee.' He still hoped that war could be averted. 'It was a great gathering and full of significance for the future. For those gathered there represented not only so many nationalities but the disinherited of all lands. These have now no country; they are the mob, the proletariat, the oppressed. These are the ties that bind them.

'The International has united them in a fight against bondage.'

Hardie had returned to attend the National Council of the I.L.P. and at its Manchester Conference in March 1913 was elected to be the Chairman of the I.L.P. for its coming-of-age year, which was to be held at its birthplace, Bradford.

The Suffragettes had now become hostile even to the I.L.P. and there were disturbances at the Manchester Conference. Even Hardie and Snowden, who had been their staunchest friends in Parliament, were treated as opponents and attempts made to break up their meetings.

In April, Sir Edward Grey disclosed that war had again almost broken out as a result of conflict between Montenegro and Albania. No opportunity was given for discussion.

Hardie remarked sardonically—'I suppose we shall be allowed to say a word or two before war begins.'

In June he travelled to Budapest as a guest of the International Women's Suffrage Alliance and visited Vienna and Brussels on his way home. In August, Bebel, the veteran German Socialist leader, died and Hardie attended the funeral at Zürich.

In September he was in Ireland supporting James Larkin and meeting his old friend, Jim Connolly. The week following he went once again to attend the German Social Democratic Party Conference at Jena as fraternal delegate from the British Labour Party.

The German Social Democrats did not approve of his idea of a General Strike to stop war and nothing had been done by the International Bureau.

But in Britain, Hardie was doing his best. There was a national campaign against conscription ending up with another big international demonstration in London with Jaures, Vandervelde, Adler and Hardie all on the same platform and warning Europe against war.

The twenty-first Annual Conference of the I.L.P. was held at Bradford at Easter 1914 and Hardie presided, as he had done twenty-one years before. There were 339 delegates, representing 244 branches, and

217

the National Council was able to produce a lengthy annual report of organisational and propaganda work carried out in the country.

Arthur Henderson, speaking as fraternal delegate from the Labour Party, said that it was his privilege to bring to the Conference greetings of appreciation, gratitude and goodwill.

'The majority present would agree with him that Keir Hardie was entitled to a much fuller expression of their gratitude than any words could express. Twenty-one years ago there was only a strong faith, a clear vision and a noble conception. To-day there was a great fighting force, highly organised, enthusiastic and a record of work accomplished that was creditable to all concerned. Keir Hardie and his co-pioneers who had shared in the early sacrifices could testify, both by contrast and experience, that magnificent progress had been made. He would like to testify to the amount of pioneer work that had been done and the progress that had been made. Progress of a splendid kind had followed as a result of their efforts. Direct and independent Labour representation was no longer a dream but a living reality. Not only had they strengthened Labour representation in their own ranks, but they had done more than any other separate organisation to create and strengthen the Labour Party.'

In returning thanks from the Chair, Hardie was in reminiscent mood. Recalling the work he had done, he said:

'If I had, twenty-one years ago, stopped to think about what the future would bring, I would not have dared to accept the responsibility of entering the House of Commons. During those first three years my wife kept my house going, kept my children decently and respectably clothed and fed on an income which did not ever exceed 25s. a week.'

Mrs. Hardie was on the platform and the Conference cheered her.

'Comrades, you do well to honour her. Never, even in those days, did she offer one word of reproof. Many a bitter tear she shed, but one of the proud boasts of my life is to be able to say that if she has suffered much in health and in spirit, never has she reproached me for what I have done for the cause I love.

'I leave the chair, then, as I did at the end of the first Conference, to be a pioneer. I said the other day that those of us who are more advanced in years may easily become cumberers of the ground. I am not going to die if I can help it, but there is a dead spirit which blocks the path of the young. I am not going to stand in their way. I shall die, as I have lived, a member of the I.L.P. but I want the Party to have freedom to grow, and I don't want young men and women to say: "We might have done this or that if it had not been for old Keir." I will accept no position which will give me standing over you. I will fight for what I think the right thing, but I will trust your judgment. While I have anything to give, it shall be given ungrudgingly to the child of my life—the I.L.P.'

There was a big public demonstration in St. George's Hall, Bradford, at which Hardie also spoke. Fenner Brockway, in his book *Inside the Left*, describes how at one point Hardie turned round to address the children of the Socialist Sunday Schools who were sitting behind him:

'I was sitting near the children and saw his face; never during all the times I had heard him speak had I seen it like this—the glow of its earnestness was almost unearthly. Never had I heard his voice like this—it rang with a timbre which went to the centre of one's being. He stood there, his arms outstretched, speaking to those children as though he had never had anything so important to say.

'He appealed to them to love flowers, to love animals, to love their fellows, to hate injustice and cruelty, never to be mean or treacherous to their fellows, always to be generous in service. He pictured the loveliness of the unspoiled world and the loveliness of the world as it could become. He told them how unnecessary were poverty and war and how he had tried to pass on to them a world where happiness and peace would be theirs. He and those who had worked with him had failed, but they—they, the children—could succeed. "If these were my last words I would say them to you, lads and lasses. Live for that better day." There must have been many who heard that utterance who remember it; many of those children, now grown men and women, will remember it. We did not know then, but we were within four months of the world war, the war which killed Hardie. His words were, in fact, the last which most of those in the St. George's Hall were ever to hear from him.'

Hardie was in the chair and so did not take any part in the discussions of the Conference, the chief of which centred round a report that there was likely to be some kind of electoral arrangement with the Liberals in the event of a General Election. Ramsay MacDonald had mentioned this possibility at a meeting of the Executive of the Labour Party. Brockway was editor of *The Labour Leader*. Hardie, he wrote, met him in the House of Commons after the meeting greatly disturbed. 'Something has just happened,' he said, 'which I never could have believed. MacDonald has suggested that we make an alliance with the Liberal Party at the General Election. Laddie, we must kill this plan at the I.L.P. Conference. Do what you can.'

There had been sharp differences of opinion between Snowden and MacDonald on Parliamentary policy and Hardie agreed with Snowden. MacDonald's suggestions had not been minuted but they took opposing views at the Conference. Smillie, Hardie's great personal friend, had strongly opposed any alliance. After the debate the matter was ended as far as the I.L.P. was concerned.

Personal relations between Hardie and Ramsay MacDonald had

not been cordial for two years. 'When Arthur Henderson vacated the Chairmanship in 1909,' says Snowden in his autobiography, 'Keir Hardie was strongly opposed to Ramsay MacDonald becoming chairman of the Parliamentary Labour Party. Hardie favoured George Barnes, of Glasgow, with whom he had been very friendly since the engineers' lock-out.'

'Hardie,' says Snowden, 'wrote to me to this effect. From conversations I had with him I think his reason was this: he was at the time much dissatisfied with the absence of a more militant policy by the Parliamentary Labour Party and he regarded MacDonald as being largely responsible for this. Hardie wrote to MacDonald saying he ought not to stand for the chair. MacDonald replied to him in a letter which gave Hardie great offence. I doubt if their relations were ever quite so friendly after this incident.'

Snowden was not an enthusiastic admirer of MacDonald either and they frequently clashed, especially during the passage of the Lloyd George Insurance Bill through the House, which Snowden strongly opposed. In this controversy Hardie was on the side of Snowden although they did not always agree, especially on the question of strikes, of which Snowden did not approve whereas almost inevitably Hardie championed the strikers, especially if they were miners.

'Compromise was not in the man's nature,' Snowden wrote of Hardie. 'He never captured the House of Commons, it was not his place. He was not the politician, he was the prophet and seer. He was the unsparing iconoclast who sought to break the illusions and conventions of his generation. He had set before himself an ideal which he pursued regardless of the hostility and opposition of enemies and often with scant regard for the criticism and advice of friends. But withal he was the greatest product of the democracy of our times. I had the great privilege of being intimately associated with him for over twenty years and that acquaintance is one of my most cherished memories. I am proud to believe that I enjoyed his confidence to an unusual degree. He wrote to me once (in the 1906-1910 Parliament) when I had been away from the House of Commons for two or three days: "What has become of you? You are the only man whose presence I miss." He usually wrote to me when he was on a speaking tour, telling me of his experiences and how he found the movement. The moving impulse of Keir Hardie's work was a profound belief in the common people. He believed in their capacity and he burned with indignation at their sufferings. He was no theoretic dogmatist. He never argued on the platform the economic theories of Socialism. His Socialism was a great human conception of the equal rights of all men and women to the wealth of the world and to the enjoyment of the fullness of life. Though he repudiated the dogma of the "class war", his appeal was invariable to the workers as a class. The facts of the class war he admitted, but he did not believe that its ruthless prosecution was the way to establish Socialism. He appealed to the working classes to realise their duty to act their part as citizens; and this he believed they could best be taught by organising themselves in a Labour Party . . . Few men have had so great an influence on the political life of the country. On the day when the common people enter into the Promised Land, no name deserves to be more affectionately and gratefully remembered than Keir Hardie.'

This was written in old age when he had become Viscount Snowden and was no longer a member of the Labour Party nor inclined to write very benevolently about his old associates.

But it indicates the friendship between Hardie and Snowden that prevailed in these years.

The letter to which Snowden referred which gave Hardie great offence has not been preserved but Lord Elton, in his biography of MacDonald, quotes a letter written by MacDonald to Bruce Glasier late in 1910 in which he refers to 'a beastly letter I had from Hardie on the subject of the chairmanship of the Labour Party'. There had evidently been an exchange of angry letters between them. MacDonald wrote to Glasier: 'My chairmanship would only make him more individualistic than he is and make him pitch his tent in the woods further away from us than ever.'

Certainly Hardie did not approve of MacDonald's policy of greater co-operation with the Liberals and did not approve of him becoming the chairman of the Parliamentary Labour Party.

MacDonald, later in an introduction to Stewart's biography of Hardie, wrote of him:

'The inconsistencies which are essential attributes of human greatness are the cause of much trouble to the ordinary man but these inconsistencies do not belong to the same order of things as the unreliabilities of the charlatan or the time server. Hardie's apparent waywardness often gave his colleagues concern. A great man has so many sides to which the various voices of the day make appeal. He is not only one man but several—not only man, but woman, too. But greatness is inconsistent only in the things that do not matter very much, and in the grand conflict of great issues he stood up as reliable as a mightly boulder in a torrent . . . Always willing to listen, he was never ready to yield; loyal like a man, he was, nevertheless, persistent in his own way, sometimes to a fault; humble in the councils of friends, he was proud in the world. Looking back at him now, the memory of his waywardness only adds to affection and admiration. One sees how necessary it was for his work.'

In this same preface MacDonald also wrote of Hardie:

'When he became famous his world widened and he mixed with people in different circumstances. But he met them as the self-respecting workman, all unconscious of difference and with neither an attempt nor a desire to imitate them. The drawing rooms of the rich never allured him into a sycophantic servitude, a chair at a workman's fireside hard to sit upon, never robbed that fireside of its cheery warmth. The true gentleman is he who acts like a gentleman unconsciously. Therefore this quality eludes him who would write of it, for an explanation of it suggests consciousness of it.'

This was written in 1922 before Ramsay MacDonald had become Prime Minister. It is curious in view of what people wrote of MacDonald later that he should have written in this way and stressed the fact that 'the drawing rooms of the rich never allured Hardie into a sycophantic attitude'. They certainly, as Mrs. Sidney Webb noted, had their attractions for MacDonald.

MacDonald was always an enigma of a man. It is little wonder that in these years there were intervals when Hardie profoundly distrusted him. 'MacDonald will betray the movement,' he said to his secretary, Mrs. Travers Symons. They found themselves together again when war came in 1914. But temperamentally they found difficulty in working together in Parliament.

MacDonald had been in Australia and had told Hardie's old Ayrshire friend, Andrew Fisher, who had become Prime Minister of Australia, that Hardie was difficult to work with and that when he visited England he should avoid him.

Fisher was not impressed with MacDonald and when he met Hardie told him of this. Fisher went to Merthyr and spoke of it to Hardie's Socialist friends there too, and they remembered it.

All these differences were, however, to fade into insignificance before the march of events.

There was trouble in Northern Ireland and King George was invited to preside over a conference. Hardie disliked this. He wrote in *The Labour Leader* in July:

'Meanwhile the King has been invited, or has invited himself to intervene in the Home Rule embroglio. The most serious constitutional crisis since the days of the Stuarts has thus been precipitated. The House of Commons has three times passed the Home Rule Bill by substantial majorities. Thrice the Lords have rejected it. Meanwhile, the Ulster "Loyalists" have been arming to resist the measure becoming law. That is to say they are in armed rebellion against the State and the King's

Authority. And now the King casts in his lot with the reactionary peers and the rebellious Ulsterites. He joins his influence with the forces which are working against and seeking to destroy the House of Commons and our constitutional forms of Parliamentary government.'

He had no confidence in King George and thought his intervention in the controversy undesirable.

'Needless to say, he and his servile upholders, Liberal and Unionist, in the Press and Parliament, will seek to conceal this naked truth from the public gaze. But the point is not open to dispute. The Liberal Party did not ask for his interference, whatever the Cabinet may have done. The Irish Party had no need for his services, and Mr. Redmond and Mr. Dillon only consented to attend the conference because the King "commanded' their presence. The Labour Party resents this interference. These three sections of the Parliament have stood loyally together in getting Home Rule through; the Tories alone objected, and therefore the King in interfering can have no other object than to assist his friends the Tories.

'The hypocritical assurance which is being spread abroad that the House of Commons will have the last word is a mere blind. If an agreement be reached it will come to us with the combined weight and authority of the King, and Tory Party, the House of Lords, and the Liberal Cabinet behind it. Under such circumstances the House of Commons will be paralysed.'

Nor did he believe that King George V was a statesman:

'I have never for a moment doubted that part of any settlement come to will be an immediate dissolution, and we begin to see why the Royal Family have been visiting Merthyr and many other industrial centres during the past two or three years. They desire to popularise themselves with the mob so that they might rivet the chains of their iron rule more firmly upon them. King George is not a statesman. He is not the pleasure-loving scapegrace which his father was before him, but like his father, he is destitute of even ordinary ability. Born in the ranks of the working class, his most likely fate would have been that of a street corner loafer. And this is the man who is being made the tool of by the reactionary classes to break the power of Democracy and weaken and finally destroy the power of Parliament.

'But Democracy will accept the challenge. The rights our fathers won by sacrifice shall be maintained. Once more the Republican slogan will be heard in the land, and a sloppy Liberalism as well as a reactionary Toryism will be swept before the indignant wrath of an angry and enlightened people.'

But Hardie was mistaken. There was to be no General Election over Ireland. For a month later Britain was at war.

CHAPTER 22

THE WORLD WAR

WHEN the Archduke of Austria was murdered at Sarajevo the International Socialist Bureau was hurriedly called to Brussels to consider Austria's declaration of war on Serbia, but few people even then realised that we were all so near the brink of the First World War.

Bruce Glasier, who was present along with Keir Hardie and Dan Irving from Britain, wrote:

'Although the dread peril of a general eruption of war in Europe was the main subject of the deliberations, no one, not even the German representatives, seemed apprehensive of an actual rupture between the great Powers taking place until at least the full resources of diplomacy had been exhausted.'

So little did the delegates anticipate events that they decided to proceed with the holding of the International Congress, only changing the place of meeting to Paris and altering the date to August 23rd.

Feeling in Belgium was at the date of the meeting strongly anti-war. Vandervelde, the Belgian Socialist leader, presided over a great anti-war demonstration in the Brussels Cirque at which Jaures from France, Haase from Germany and Keir Hardie from Britain all delivered speeches denouncing policies and diplomacies likely to end in war. Hardie had met Jaures in Paris before going to Brussels and had dined with him in the café where, forty-eight hours after his return from Belgium, Jaures was shot by an assassin. They had marched in the same procession and denounced war together on the same platform for the last time. The fears and war passions were growing daily, the armies were being mobilised and the soldiers ready for attack.

Keir Hardie and Arthur Henderson signed a manifesto issued by the British Section of the International Socialist Bureau headed *An Appeal to the Working Class* which read:

'The long-threatened European war is now upon us. For more than a hundred years no such danger has confronted civilisation. It is for you

Keir Hardie in 1914.

Anti-war Meeting Trafalgar Square August 1914

to take full account of the desperate situation and to act promptly and vigorously in the interests of peace. You have never been consulted about the war. Whatever may be the rights and wrongs of the sudden crushing attack made by the Militarist Empire of Austria upon Serbia, it is certain that the workers of all countries, likely to be drawn into the conflict, must strain every nerve to prevent their Government from committing them to war.

'Everywhere Socialists and the organised forces of Labour are taking this course. Everywhere vehement protests are made against the greed and intrigues of militarists and armament mongers.'

The manifesto went on to call upon the workers of Britain to do the same on a more impressive scale:

'Hold vast demonstrations in London and in every industrial centre.

'Compel those of the governing class and their Press who are eager to commit you to co-operate with Russian despotism, to keep silence, respect the decision of the overwhelming majority of the people, who will have neither part nor lot in such infamy.

'The success of Russia at the present time would be a curse to the world.

'There is no time to lose. Already by secret agreements and understandings, of which the democracies of the civilised world know only by rumour, steps are being taken which may fling us all into the fray.

'Workers stand together for peace.

'Combine and conquer the militarist enemy and the self-seeking imperialist of to-day once and for all.

'Men and women of Britain, you have now an unexampled opportunity of showing your power, rendering a magnificent service to humanity and to the world.

'Proclaim that for you the days of plunder and butchery have gone by. Send messages of peace and fraternity to your fellows who have less liberty than you.

'Down with class rule! Down with the rule of brute force! Down with war! Up with the peaceful rule of the people!'

Hardie was doing everything he could to stop Britain getting into the war. On August 18th he wrote a long letter to the *Daily Citizen* in which he attacked the governments whose policies were leading Europe into war:

'The present European situation is further proof of the incompetence of the statesmen of Europe. Much is being made of the Russian menace, but it is perfectly obvious that had Britain, France, Italy and Germany combined from the outset, Russia would not have dared to move. The Russian Government knows that it can force the situation, both France and Great Britain being apparently willing to be dragged at its heels.

'Most appalling of all is the fact that the working classes have still no effective say in the control of their Governments in the matter of war.

225

P

'The Socialist and Labour movement has not yet reached the point at which it is strong enough to control Parliaments, and because of that fact it is made to sit helpless and hopeless, while the respective Governments ride roughshod over every aspiration for peace and good relationship.'

Even then he thought that there was a possibility of strike action to prevent war:

'In most of the countries affected by the war there will doubtless be demonstrations of protest, but the futility of these, as past experience has shown, is pathetic. And yet I hold the opinion strongly that organised Labour has the power, first by more effective political action, and then by international agreement, to render war practically impossible.

'The threat of an international stoppage of work, provided it was backed by proper organisation and by mutual confidence, would of itself be sufficient for this purpose.

'As *The Times* pointed out during the railway strike, the primary object of an army is to protect property and maintain order at home.

'An international strike against war would of itself be a revolutionary movement, and there is no Government in Europe that dare take the risk of sending its army abroad with the knowledge that the working classes were so organised and educated that they would rise in industrial revolt the day it was proposed to do so.

'One feels dreadfully helpless at a moment like the present, and the need for more vigorous action and a more rebellious propaganda is borne in upon one. All social reforms of the Capitalist classes are clearly designed to act as an opiate upon the workers; and only the inspiration which comes from Socialism and the international binding together of the Trade Union and Socialist movements will ever put the workers in the position of controlling governments, thus bringing war for ever to an end.'

On August 2nd he was one of the speakers at a big anti-war demonstration in Trafalgar Square. The *Daily Citizen's* report said:

'When Mr. Keir Hardie, M.P., walked to the front of the plinth from which he was to speak with Mr. Arthur Henderson, a storm of cheering swept over the great square. He had to wait for several minutes while a long procession with bands and banners poured into the already dense throng, singing the "Internationale". Enthusiasm was intense. But the first words of the veteran Socialist brought an impressive stillness. M. Jaures was in his thoughts. Jaures had been assassinated in a Paris café.

' "Our hearts to-day are sorrowful for the loss of our great comrade, Jaures," he began. "His voice is now stilled and the great white fire of his moral enthusiasm quenched for ever. His noble example may it be ours to follow, even though from afar off." '

He went on:

'We have met to protest against the crime of war and bloodshed. To-night there are millions of hearts in every country in Europe filled with sadness and foreboding.

'What is the cause of war?

226

'You have no quarrel with Germany. German workmen have no quarrel with their French comrades. The French worker has no quarrel with his Austrian comrades. If that be so, why are we on the verge of the greatest calamity Europe has ever seen?

'We are told there are international treaties which compel us to take part. Who made those treaties? The people had no voice in them.

'Are we going to allow Courts and the ruling classes to make treaties leading into war without our having a word to say?

'We should not be in this position but for our alliance with Russia.

'Friends and comrades, this very Square has rung with denunciations of Russian atrocities. Surely if there is one country under the sun which we ought to have no agreement with, it is the foul Government of anti-democratic Russia.

'I ask again, what can we do? We can say to our Government and to our King that we, the working classes of England will not have war.

'Italy is as much involved by treaty as we are, and yet Italy has decided to stand neutral. Why cannot Great Britain do the same?

'We are not defending our shores, which are not being attacked. We are not defending our liberties, which are not being menaced.

'We are here to say that in so far as we can, there shall be no shot fired, no sabre drawn, in this war of conquest.

'The only class,' he declared, 'which could prevent the Government going to war is the working class. We should not have a great Liberal anti-war campaign as we should have had if Tories had been in office. The workers, however, could organise to stop war. They could stop it by the international anti-war strike.'

Among other speakers were George Lansbury, Arthur Henderson, Cunninghame-Graham, Will Thorne, M.P., Margaret Bondfield, Mary McArthur and Mrs. Despard. It was representative of all shades of the Labour and Socialist Movement and the biggest meeting that had been held in Trafalgar Square for years.

This was, however, to make no impression on the Government or on Parliament. After Sir Edward Grey had made his statement in the House of Commons, public opinion swung round to the view that the war had come simply because of the policy of the Kaiser and because Germany had embarked on a war of aggression. The British people, never very interested in foreign affairs, were completely ignorant of the diplomatic entanglements and the events which had led to war. All the patriotic emotions were appealed to by the Press. All the blame for the war was attributed to the German Kaiser whose soldiers were marching through Belgium to establish the rule of militarism throughout Europe.

When Keir Hardie persisted in challenging and questioning Sir

Edward Grey's statements in the House of Commons, he was shouted down. Tim Healy, from the Irish benches, interrupted to ask if the German Socialists were asking questions like this and from the Liberal benches W. M. Pringle shouted 'Coward'. The House of Commons was overwhelmingly for the war. Hardie could no longer claim to speak for the Labour Party, most of whose Members were supporting the Government. MacDonald, too, denounced Sir Edward Grey's policy and declared that Britain should have remained neutral, and finding that the Parliamentary Labour Party was against him resigned from the chairmanship. Snowden was in America. Morley and Burns had resigned from the Cabinet. But apart from these and a few critical Radicals, Hardie was again alone.

In a speech in a later debate, Hardie warned the House of Commons of the economic problems that the war was likely to bring in its train.

What was to be the fate of the unemployed, he asked?

'Both Houses of Parliament have passed, with absolute unanimity, a Bill for the relief of the Stock Exchange. We Members, from these benches, offer no objection, but we now demand to be informed what is going to be done for the relief of the inevitable destitution which is bound to prevail among the poor? Will the House pass with the same promptitude as we have done the Bill for the relief of the Stock Exchange and the business interest, the Bill to compel education authorities to feed hungry school children?

'We ask for an answer.

'We are far more interested in the sufferings of the poor than we are in the inconvenience to members of the Stock Exchange. Most Members of this House have a more direct interest in the Stock Exchange than they have in the sufferings of the poor (Hon. Members: "No, no!", "Shame!", and "Name!"). The proof of that will be found if the same promptitude be shown in the other case.'

He went on to ask what action was to be taken to deal with profiteers:

'What action is to be taken, not merely to ensure a sufficient food supply, but to safeguard the public against being robbed by food speculators? Surely that issue is urgent and important. We are entitled to demand from the Government—not merely to request, but to demand—to be informed what action is to be taken to safeguard the interests of the working classes in the crisis we are now approaching.'

He concluded with a strong criticism of the Government's decision to enter the war:

'One word more. The decision of the Government has been come to without consulting the country. It remains to be seen whether the Government and the House of Commons represent the country on this

228

question. So far as some of us are concerned—here I do not speak for the Party with which I am connected, for the present moment, but for myself personally—we shall endeavour to ascertain what is the real feeling of the country, and especially of the working classes of the country, in regard to the decision of the Government.

'We belong to a party which is international. In Germany, in France, in Belgium, in Austria, the party corresponding to our own is taking all manner of risks to promote and preserve peace. (An Hon. Member: "Why do they not control the German Emperor?") I am asked why do they not control the German Emperor. For the same reason that we do not control the Liberal Cabinet—we are not strong enough. My point is that in all these countries the party corresponding to our own is working strenuously for peace, and especially throughout Germany. I confess that I heard with a feeling akin to wonder this afternoon the refusal by our Foreign Secretary on behalf of the Cabinet, even to consider the offers made on behalf of the German Government to keep this country out of the dispute. If the neutrality of Belgium can be secured after the war, if the Germans offer not to bombard the coast of France—if these can be the basis for further negotiation, then every reason of the Cabinet for going into the war will have been taken away. I say respectfully to the House that some of us will do all we can to rouse the working classes of the country in opposition to this proposal of the Government. Our honour is said to be involved in entering into the war. That is always the excuse. I suppose our honour was involved in the Boer War. How many to-day will justify it? A few years hence, and if we are led into this war, we shall look back in wonder and amazement at the flimsy reason which induced the Government to take part in it.'

Hardie went down to his constituency to address a meeting at Aberdare. This had been arranged long before war had been declared. Nearly every paper in the country was now attacking him as an enemy of his country and a pro-German. One of his strong supporters in Aberdare had been Charles Stanton, the local miners' agent, but now he refused to take the chair at Hardie's meeting.

It was a stormy meeting which ultimately had to be abandoned. The Jingo Press exulted over it the next day. Keir Hardie had been howled down, and in his own constituency.

The local weekly paper, *The Aberdare Leader*, gave a full report of what happened:

'WAR AGAINST WAR—HOSTILE RECEPTION OF MR. KEIR HARDIE. UPROARIOUS MEETING AT ABERDARE.

'A meeting under the auspices of the Labour Party was held at the Aberdare Market on Thursday last. There was a very large attendance, but the whole of the proceedings was of a most uproarious character. Councillor E. Stonelake presided, and was supported by Mr. Keir Hardie,

M.P., Mr. T. Richardson, M.P., Councillor Idwal Thomas, and others.

'Councillor E. Stonelake opened the proceedings by stating that they had met under one of the gloomiest clouds that had ever overspread Europe. War had broken out, and it was essential for them to know something about it before so freely talking about it on street corners. Under the circumstances they ought to be grateful to Mr. Keir Hardie and Mr. Richardson for coming there, for the consequences to the working classes of the war were such as no one could measure. (Cheers.)

'Mr. Keir Hardie then started to address the meeting, but was received with loud hooting, which was mingled with cheers. A large section of the audience began singing "God Save Our Gracious King", and this was again followed by cheering. Then most of the crowd got up on chairs, etc., to have a better view of the meeting, and it was impossible to proceed. A few minutes elapsed and then a section of the audience again struck up "Rule Britannia". A slight lull followed, and Mr. Keir Hardie was heard by the reporters present to say that the meeting was organised before war was declared.

'After the declaration of the war he had considered very seriously whether the meeting should be postponed.

'At this stage the singing at the back of the hall recommenced, and it was almost impossible to hear the speaker. However, Mr. Keir Hardie was understood to say he had decided to come, and that he had not a trace of the coward in his blood. (Cheers, mingled with groans.) Ten millions of men were marching from various points of the compass to shed each other's blood. (Continued uproar and singing of the National Anthem.) No one wanted the war but the Tory Press, and it was only after the statement made by Sir Edward Grey that the Liberal Party found itself committed to war. It had been committed to war without even having been consulted. He maintained that the proper attitude for this country ought to have been one of neutrality. (Loud hooting, followed by the singing of "Rule Britannia".)

'For several minutes it was quite impossible to hear Mr. Hardie, the uproar being deafening.

'He was understood by those nearest to him to say that they should endeavour to remember the origins of war. Germany had made this country an offer, and instead of accepting Germany's offer, war was declared, and they were now in the field. They were now fighting for Russia. (A voice: "Shame!" and great uproar.) Again a section of the audience sang the National Anthem, and the intensity of the opposition to Mr. Hardie increased.

'In fact, it became evident that the meeting would soon be broken up. Mr. Hardie seemed to realise this, for after stating that there were awful times in store for the working classes of this and other countries, he concluded his address by saying that the Labour Party would continue to educate public opinion so that this dishonourable war should be brought to an end. The working classes all over Europe were working with them in the same direction. Mr. Hardie then resumed his seat amidst cheers from his supporters, and the singing of "Rule Britannia" by the rest of the audience.

'Mr. T. Richardson, M.P. for Whitehaven, then tried to address the meeting, but with very little success. All that he was understood to say was that in this war history would repeat itself, and that those who now stood for peace would in the future be recognised as the true friends of the workers. They were at least entitled to a hearing. (Hooting and singing.)

'Just before the meeting was declared closed a number of shots were fired by some person at the back of the hall.

'On departing, Mr. Hardie was hustled by a number of people, and was followed through Victoria Square, Canon Street, and High Street by a large crowd, who every now and again gave vent to groans. On reaching the residence of Mr. and Mrs. Matt Lewis, in Elm Grove, with whom he was staying, Mr. Hardie was again hooted. Mr. Matt Lewis asked the crowd to disperse quietly, as he had a child in bed, but the crowd replied by singing and crying, "Turn the German out!" Eventually the crowd left, and an exciting experience for Mr. Hardie came to an end.'

After forty years the writer of this book has vivid memories of that meeting yet. When it was over we formed a bodyguard round Hardie and made our way, followed by the mob, to the home of Matt Lewis, the schoolmaster, where Hardie stayed when in Aberdare. It was no new experience for Keir Hardie to be shouted down and mobbed, but as we sat around the fire we could see that he was deeply distressed. He had not expected this in Aberdare, among the mining folk.

'I know what Gethsemane was like,' he said. It was not just the meeting, it was the fact that war had come and the horror that it meant, the misery that it would inevitably bring to working people all over Europe, and that the Labour movement, too, had agreed to support the war. It seemed that all his life-work had been in vain.

The next morning his host suggested they should go a roundabout way to the station and avoid the main street in case of another hostile demonstration. 'We will go down the main street,' said Hardie determinedly, and with head erect he went.

Fenner Brockway attended the National Council of the I.L.P. which had been called to consider the situation.

'Hardie,' he wrote, 'although only fifty-eight, seemed an old, old man, crumpled in body and broken in spirit. The lines in his forehead were deep as his head sank on his hand. "I can't fight this war like I fought the Boer War," he said, "I must leave that to the younger comrades." '

When he returned to London the streets were full of marching soldiers and excited crowds. He was easily recognisable and he was frequently insulted on his way to the House of Commons.

'When he returned from his first meeting in his constituency after the outbreak of war,' wrote MacDonald, 'he was a crushed man and, sitting on the terrace of the House of Commons where I ran across him, he seemed to be looking out on blank desolation.'

'The war struck Hardie like a physical blow and a spiritual blight. He had had such faith that the international forces of the working class would resist it—and now in every country the Socialist leaders were voting war credits and urging their followers to fight. Hardie was utterly crushed by the tragedy of it.'

Hardie had written the leading article for *The Labour Leader* that week. 'At midnight on Tuesday war against Germany began. Already the roar of a war-maddened people is filling the streets of London. The I.L.P. at least will stand firm. Keep the Red Flag flying.'

Only two members of the National Council of the I.L.P. supported the war. The rest were behind Hardie and MacDonald and supported the attitude that they had taken up in Parliament. Hardie had prepared a draft manifesto but he was tired out and it was not in his usual style. Finally, they agreed to a draft drawn up by W. C. Anderson, the chairman:

'We are told that international Socialism is dead, that all our hopes and ideals are wrecked by the fire and pestilence of European war. It is not true.

'Out of the darkness and the depth we hail our working-class comrades of every land. Across the roar of guns, we send sympathy and greeting to the German Socialists. They have laboured unceasingly to promote good relations with Britain, as we with Germany. They are no enemies of ours, but faithful friends.

'In forcing this appalling crime upon the nations, it is the rulers, the diplomats, the militarists who have sealed their doom. In tears and blood and bitterness, the greater Democracy will be born. With steadfast faith we greet the future. Our cause is holy and imperishable, and the labour of our hands has not been in vain.

'Long live Freedom and Equality! Long live International Socialism!'

The Labour Party and the T.U.C. took up a different attitude. They were prepared to support the Government and to join in the recruiting campaign that Lord Kitchener, who had become Minister for War, had already announced.

One of the reasons given by the Parliamentary Committee of the T.U.C. was that in the

'event of the voluntary system of military service failing the country in this time of need, the demand for a national system of compulsory military service will not only be made with redoubled vigour, but may prove to be so persistent and strong as to become irresistible'. The argument was that Labour M.P.s and trade union leaders should be prepared to go on the recruiting platforms along with Liberal and Tory M.P.s so that conscription should be averted. The I.L.P. declined. Throughout the war the I.L.P. was to pursue a policy of its own.

Hardie made his way back to his home in Cumnock very tired and exhausted.

He knew himself that he had not long to live.

He had fainted in the House of Commons and had been examined by Dr. Metcalfe, a Conservative M.P. They differed in politics but were personal friends.

He wrote in his notebook:

'On saying "Good-bye" to Dr. Metcalfe in the lobby to-day, he took me into his private room, took my hand in a firm grip and held it. His voice shook and finally broke whilst he was speaking and his eyes grew moist and finally overflowed.

' "I want to say a serious, very serious word of warning to you. You must give up a lot of your work and take more rest. Compared with me you are not an old man. You have a strong frame but you are nearly done for. You are not cured and never can be and I have done all I can for you. If you go on as you have been doing, you will fall on your back suddenly before long and you will never rise again. I am a Conservative and you are a Socialist but that doesn't matter. We are both up in years and my days are nearly done. But I like you and I am serious. Good-bye, Mr. Hardie and God Bless You."

'That within an hour after is what he said. For a moment my eyes grew moist and something in my heart twitched and fluttered a little. Then came peace and a quiet joy. I nearly kissed him.'

How relieved he was to get out of London, with its frenzied war atmosphere and its marching soldiers and its hysterical Press! He badly needed a complete rest but he was soon on the move again. In September, the National Council of the I.L.P. called divisional conferences to explain why war had come and to ask for support for the line it was following.

Hardie spoke at these conferences both in Scotland and South Wales, and although there were some criticisms and some defections the branches as a whole approved of the decisions and the lead that had been given.

The present writer attended the Conference at Cardiff. Hardie traced the events that had led to the war clearly and concisely. He laid stress on the fact that not only the German Government's policy was responsible for the war but that Czarist Russia and French and British Imperialism were to blame as well. It was a calm, analytical account of how Europe had drifted into catastrophe and why the I.L.P. had said that Britain should have stayed out of the war and remained neutral. He was obviously trying to take things quietly and not to overstrain himself for he had to go on to another conference at Swansea the same evening. He gave a warning that he thought conscription was coming and was inevitable. In the mood of the country he said a big anti-war campaign was impossible. It was not like the Boer War. It was hopeless to appeal to the reason of the people until war hysteria and passion had died down. 'We must not give the impression that we were supporting German militarism or doing anything to make things difficult for British soldiers at the front. But we must watch carefully for the first opportunity to press for peace negotiations which would bring an end to the war.'

A young man asked him what he should do if conscription came. 'That is for you yourself to decide,' replied Hardie. 'If my son preferred to be shot to shooting others I would gladly go and be shot by his side.'

He had determined to face his constituents again and explain his attitude.

This time the meeting was at Merthyr and Ramsay MacDonald and Bruce Glasier were there too, to share the meeting with him and to save him. They did not know whether the scenes at Aberdare were to be repeated. The large skating rink which held a big crowd was full, but although there were a few interruptions there was no disturbance. 'Because he had taken the stand he had,' said MacDonald, 'every miserable scoundrel in the country, backed up by disreputable newspapers, called him a traitor. That was the fate of a man who had fought for the people on a field far more honourable and far more strenuous. It was harder to tell the truth than to tell lies.'

Hardie did not make a long speech. He had a good reception, which encouraged him. The local Merthyr paper reported him as saying:

'He remarked that he and Mr. MacDonald were blamed for the attitude they took with regard to the war. What about Lord Morley, John Burns and other members of the Liberal Government that had resigned . . . When we had crushed German militarism what would remain? Russian militarism? England and France's combined efforts would not kill that. (Hardie had not calculated on a successful Revolution in Russia.)

'Already the Russian papers were saying they would have a say in the settlement after the war. Did that prospect please us?

'After the war was over there would be militarism in this country. Was conscription going to be introduced? Lord Roberts had said that recruiting, far from taking the place of conscription, had proved the need for it.

'Compulsory service would become the law of Britain. Did the prospect please them? Instead of German militarism we would have British militarism . . . When Cobden, Bright and Henry Richard protested against the Crimean War they were hooted but when the war was over the country turned to honour the men who had stood by their convictions.'

Hardie concluded by stating the case for better treatment for the soldiers' wives and children and by saying: 'The Government ought to see to it that when a man fell serving his country his loved ones at home should not suffer.'

It was a successful demonstration which did something to make up for the rowdyism at Aberdare. The Merthyr Socialists were greatly heartened, but it was the last time they were to hear Hardie speak at a big meeting. He addressed meetings of the party members in the constituency and came away more satisfied with the reception he had received. Hardie thanked his constituents through the *Pioneer* and noted that the Press had boycotted the speeches, in contrast with the space they had given to the disturbance at Aberdare.

'There was quite an array of reporters at the meeting. They had forgotten, or perhaps they never knew, that Merthyr always respects the rights of free speech and gives a speaker a tolerant and courteous hearing. The speech of Ramsay MacDonald will easily rank with the finest ever heard in Merthyr. The audience was very large and the reception of the speech fairly sympathetic and yet outside the reports in the *Western Mail* and the *South Wales News,* it was boycotted by all the London and provincial dailies. Even the Labour *Daily Citizen* could only spare an inch or so for reference to the speech. Libels against the Germans overcrowded its space. The British Press will report everything in favour of the present system and of those in authority, but those who are seeking to guide the working class into self-respect can expect only abuse from capitalist-owned institutions.'

He returned home from South Wales to Cumnock a little less depressed.

But his strength came and went. He went on his usual walks slowly, leaning heavily on a stick. His days of addressing big public meetings were nearly over. But he continued writing to the *Pioneer* and *The Labour Leader* topical weekly notes dealing with the war and exposing the war propaganda of the Press.

235

When Parliament resumed he preferred to ask questions mostly about the grievances of soldiers and their dependents rather than to make speeches.

In September he was attacked by H. G. Wells in a letter in *The Labour Leader* and replied vigorously :

'Mr. H. G. Wells wants to know what we are going to do now. That is like his colossal cheek. It is for him and his fellow-warmongers to say what they are going to do now. They should have thought of that in time. The nation, we say, could have been kept out of the war without loss of honour and dignity, safety or position.'

He went on to say that the I.L.P. was the one streak of sanity in the nation :

'We shall insist that the State shall adequately pay for the soldiers and sailors who do its fighting so that their dependents may not be left to the irritating, fussy, semi-private, degrading charity which they now resent so bitterly.

'We shall try to keep the lamp of freedom and free speech burning. We shall say there is a risk of Militarism becoming supreme in Britain. We shall insist on work or maintenance for everyone . . . The day will come when German militarism will be defeated and then we shall seek a peace on terms consistent with our own self-respect and that of Democratic Germany. We shall seek, if we can, to prevent memories of rankling bitterness and desire for revenge being left behind as an outcome of the peace terms.'

But if Hardie had made an enemy of H. G. Wells he had won the approval of Bernard Shaw, who went out of his way to refer to him appreciatively in his *Commonsense about the War*. Shaw's contribution to the controversies of the war had made him almost as unpopular as Hardie. He was attacked in the Labour *Daily Citizen* and Hardie wrote to him from the House of Commons on November 26th, dissociating himself from what had been said in the *Citizen*:

'As my disgust with the *Citizen's* attitude over the war is great, I have not even looked at it for some weeks. Thus it comes that I knew nothing of its attack on you until someone told me of your letter in to-day's issue. I shall see what can be done to raise the Socialist and Labour unions to make protest. The paper is rapidly making for the void.

'In Scottish ploughman phrase, "God bless ye and send ye speed." I prohibit any reply to this or even acknowledgment. It is the expression of a heart which now throbs toward you with almost a feeling of devotion. Only a Celt could have done it.'

Writing in his notes of the 27th February, 1915, he described meeting with Lord Morley in the Lobby of the House of Commons:

'Passing along the Lobby the other day, I met a familiar figure, Lord

Morley, who had resigned from the Cabinet rather than soil his conscience by the blood-shedding in which we were now engaged. He stopped and shook hands with me. "You have been ill," he said, "What was the matter? Was it the war which so weighed upon your soul and spirit that made your body sick?" I had to smile a vague assent to the question. "The war," he said, "When will it end? What shall we gain? If we lose, we shall pay an awful penalty; if we win, the penalty will be greater still." He sighed as he walked away with the weight of 80 gathering years bending his shoulders. I stood and watched the retiring figure, and thought to myself, there goes the last of England's great statesmen. To-day it is not statesmanship or principle which actuates those who hold office. They are as completely under the power of the capitalist as any ordinary member of the Stock Exchange.'

Hardie made his last speech in the House of Commons on February 25th. He opposed the proposal to relax the education by-laws to enable children under twelve to be employed in agricultural work. 'The by-laws made to protect our children,' he said, 'are being practically swept out of existence. I think it can be demonstrated that they are being swept aside, not because of any special necessity for child labour, but very largely as a means of perpetuating uneducated and sweated labour in the agricultural districts.'

He spoke slowly, with difficulty, asking for the indulgence of the House on the ground of ill-health.

It was fitting that his last words in the House of Commons should be in defence of working-class children.

The I.L.P. Conference at Easter, 1915, was held in Norwich. Hardie addressed it only once, in a short speech on a resolution protesting strongly against severe sentences passed upon fifty-three members of the Russian Seamen's Union and on the five Socialist members of the Duma. The seamen had been sentenced to imprisonment solely because they were members of a trade union.

Their Secretary had been illegally arrested by the authorities in Egypt, sent to Russia and there sentenced to Siberia. Hardie said:

'Some of us tried in the House of Commons to get Sir Edward Grey to intervene, or at least to have him tried in Egypt. Grey then said that this country could not interfere with the political affairs of another country. One of the biggest risks we run is being allied to a government whose past and present record is a disgrace to civilisation and progress. The alliance with Russia is not to help Belgium. It is to open up fresh exploitation by capitalists. We request our protest against all the infamies and bloody cruelties of Russia.'

In all his criticisms of the policy of Sir Edward Grey he had stressed the sinister results of the alliance with the Czar's government, but he was not to live to see the Russian Revolution. His last long article on the war appeared in *The Labour Leader* of March 25th, 1915. 'What had the working classes to gain from the war?' he asked.

'And the working man? Where does his interest come in, in either war or diplomacy? His toil, his low wages, his high cost of living, his rack-rented and often insanitary house, his periodic employment; his poorly educated children; his self-sacrificing wife; his narrow and cribbed life; these things abide with him, and war and diplomacy accentuate them. And yet his toil and sacrifice are the foundations upon which all the glittering show of Imperialism, with its inevitable militarism is raised. With a self-reliant working class, there could be no cunning foreign diplomacy; no arrogant militarism; no war and no stream of untold wealth pouring into the coffers of the rich from over the seas. It is the worker who takes all the risks to life and health of raising minerals from the bowels of the earth; of working in a modern form of Gehenna to smelt them into iron and steel. It is his toil and skill which transfers these into mighty warships fitted with mechanical contrivances which amaze the beholder. It is the worker who tills the soil to produce the food whereby the nations live. It is the worker who builds the mill and factory, and who sweats therein in producing raiment for all.

'And when a set of selfish and incompetent statesmen have plunged nations into shedding each other's blood, it is the worker who is called upon to line the trenches; to fill the horrid graves of war by tens of thousands; to murder his fellow worker with whom he has not, and never had, any quarrel; it is the worker who is commanded, under the penalty of being branded a traitor, to carry woe and desolation into the hearts of womenfolk and children.

'The present war is not being waged in "freedom's holy cause"; it is not meant to safeguard the "rights of small and weak nations"; it is not meant to put down oppression; it is not meant to elevate the downtrodden and the oppressed. If it had been for these objects, every Government in Europe would have opposed it to the death. The present war, like most others, has come because many great and powerful interests demanded that it should; because statesmen have been false and deceitful to the trust reposed in them, and have deceived the peoples into false beliefs.'

He went on to point out that the rich vested interests were doing well out of the war:

'That is the reward of the rich and well-to-do; the patriotic Imperialists. And the worker; what are his gains? He is just now working much over-time and piecework. He is getting in most trades a rise in wages or a bonus to tide him over the increased cost of living. And the bulk of his leaders are teaching the virtue of unquestioning subservient submission to the commands of the Government.

'But the war will end. What will then be the condition of the worker?

Wages, after a time, will inevitably tend to go back. And the Imperialists, monied-property-owning, ruling class, who to-day are so proud of the patriotism of the working man, will still be supreme. Their income from Colonial and Foreign investments will keep increasing. Their dividends on war debts will not be touched. But the rich and the small business man will once more combine their strength to keep the working man in the lowly station of life to which it has "pleased God to call him"!'

The organised workers could end this if the Labour and Socialist Parties would give them a lead.

'So soon as the workers wish it, wars will cease. Labour Parties and Socialist Parties at home and abroad have proved broken reeds. War has been declared just as though they did not exist. Nor do I accept the excuse for this that the rank-and-file were to blame.

'They never had a lead.

'The revolutionary spirit has long been dead in democracy. There are signs of its resurrection. The Clyde and other industrial centres have certainly shown the new spirit at work. If this awakening can be strengthened; if the leaders of the working class will say frankly that Liberals and Unionists are equally props of finance and the supporters of war; and therefore equally concerned in keeping the worker in subjection, then indeed a change will come. Democracy will raise itself up from its present helpless dependence and become a real power in controlling the affairs of nations.

'When the war is only a sinking memory of a bloodstained nightmare, and we are again face to face with the real things of life, surely there will be a great and mighty agitation for complete enfranchisement of democracy—men and women alike—and thus win control over both domestic and foreign policy, and break the rule of those to whom Imperialism and Militarism means wealth and power, and install all the peoples of all lands in authority, and thus bring plenty, peace, and concord to a long-suffering race.'

He made his way back to his home in Scotland, weary and worn out. He knew that his work was over and that his life was ebbing away. He lingered on through the summer, but recovery did not come again. At the end of September he went into a Glasgow nursing home. Pneumonia had set in. On Sunday, September 26th, 1915, in the presence of his wife and daughter, he died peacefully in his sleep.

In announcing the death of Keir Hardie the following day, *The Times* said:

'For over twenty years Mr. Keir Hardie was regarded as the most extreme of British politicians. The hard and narrow environment of his youth predisposed him to take a gloomy view of the state of society, and despite his obvious honesty of purpose and sympathy for humanity, he was one of those men who spend their lives in expressing the views of a minority. He certainly spent his life in advocating unpopular causes. He did not hide his republican opinions; he was one of the strongest opponents of the South African War; he made speeches in India in 1907: which, in view of the unrest prevailing at the time, could only be branded as mischievous, and he was the most pronounced of all the pacifists at the outbreak of the European War. He was probably the most abused politician of his time, though held in something like veneration by uncompromising socialists, and no speaker had more meetings broken up in more continents than he.'

Bernard Shaw wrote in the *Merthyr Pioneer* in a different vein:

'There is, I feel, a very general feeling of relief in the House of Commons and in the Labour Party now that Keir Hardie's body lies mouldering in the grave. I wish I could revive their dread of him by adding that his soul goes marching on: but I do not feel so sure about that; he seems for the moment to have taken it with him . . .

'Now that Hardie is gone the lying will be the natural House of Commons type; placid, confident, dignified, the liar breathing an atmosphere of general approval and feeling nothing but an agreeable sensation of good taste.

'I really could not see what Hardie could do but die. Could we have expected him to hang on and sit there among the poor slaves who imagined themselves Socialists until the touchstone of war found them out and exposed them for what they are? What was in common between him and the men who are so heroically determined to resist conscription that they declared that nothing short of Lord Kitchener's telling them that its necessity will induce them to embrace it.

'He was too old to wait for a new generation. Better let them kill him and be a sort of Banquo's ghost on the Labour benches until his spiritual posterity comes to its own.'

Shaw went on to reply to the taunt that Hardie was pro-German:

'Everything that honest and humane men wish to defeat, discredit and destroy in Germany, Hardie wished to defeat, discredit and destroy there; and he proved his sincerity by spending his life in trying to defeat, discredit and destroy here also. He was not the man to shout oaths and advice at foreign enemies of the people, while diligently polishing the boots of the domestic ones. When history puts all the boots on the right legs, the stupendous impudence of the cry of "unpatriotic" levelled at a man who devoted his whole life to the service of his country by people to whom patriotism was such a novelty will be apparent . . .

'Let us hear no more about Hardie's lack of patriotism; he had more patriotism in his little finger than the Government and its flatterers in all their bodies.

'And he had one consolation to end with. His Welsh miners stood to their guns, and beat those worst enemies of England who want Englishmen to be brought up on less than three and threepence per day per

Bust by Benno Schotz, R.S.A.

ardie at
radford
L.P. Conference,
914.

20 . 11 · '14 .

Dear Emrys,

Going about the Country I have the same experience, viz, that a saner spirit is beginning to obtain. There is certainly more doubt about the wisdom of our having gone into the war than there was at the end of the first month. The press is largely to blame for the unreserved way in which it boomed the coming very early triumph of the Russian Army, and its great failure even to hold its own

Faithfully, J.K.H.

One of Hardie's last letters.

family, when so many others let themselves be deluded by fools and knaves into throwing their children's bread into the man of Mars.'

Cunninghame-Graham, who had differed with Hardie over the war, joined the funeral procession as it made its way through the streets of Glasgow to the crematorium and wrote a last tribute to his old friend:

'At funerals the Scottish people is at its best, for never more than then does the deep, underlying tenderness peep through the hardness of the rind. On foot and in the tramways, but mostly on foot, converged long lines of men and women. Yet there was something in the crowd that showed it was to attend no common funeral. No one wore black, except a minister or two, who looked a little like the belated rook you sometimes see amongst a flock of seagulls, in that vast ocean of grey tweed.

'They tramped along, the whistling north-east wind pinching their features, making their eyes run. The greater portion of the crowd were townsmen, but there were miners, washed, and in their Sunday best. Their faces showed the blue marks of healed-up scars into which the coal dust or gunpowder had become tattooed, scars gained in the battle of their lives down in the pits, remembrances of falls of rock or of occasions when the mine had "fired upon them".

'Many had known Keir Hardie in his youth, had "wrocht wi him out by", at Blantyre, at Hamilton, in Ayrshire, and all of them had heard him speak a hundred times. Miners predominated, but men of every trade were there. Women tramped too, for the dead leader had been a champion of their sex.

'They all respected him, loving him with that half-contemptuous gratitude that women often show to men who make the "woman question" the object of their lives.

'Others remembered him as a boy, and others in his home at Cumnock, they all spoke of him with affection, holding him as something of their own, apart from politicians, almost apart from men. Old comrades who had been with him either at this election or at that meeting, had helped or had intended to have helped at the crises of his life, fought their old battles over, as they tramped along, all shivering in the wind.

'When all was duly done and long exordiums passed upon the man who in his life had been the target for the abuse of Press and pulpit, the coffin slid away to its appointed place. One thought one heard the roaring of flames and somehow missed the function of lowering of the body earth to earth . . . to which the circumstances of use and wont have made us all familiar, though dust to dust in this case was the more appropriate. In either case, the book is closed for ever, and the familiar face is seen no more.

'So, standing just outside the Chapel in the cold, waiting till all the usual greetings had been exchanged, I fell a-musing on the man whom I had known so well. I saw him as he was thirty years ago, outlined against a bing or standing in a quarry in some mining village and heard his once-familiar address of "Men". He used no other in those days, to the immense disgust of legislators and other worthy but unimaginative men whom he might chance to meet. About him seemed to stand a shadowy band, most of whom now are dead or lost to view, or who have gone under in the fight . . . They were all young and ardent, and as I mused on them and their fate and upon those of them who had gone down into the oblivion that waits for those who live before their time, I shivered in the wind.

'Had he, too, lived in vain, he whose scant ashes were no doubt by this time all collected in an urn, and did they really represent all that remained of him?

'Standing amongst the band of shadowy comrades I had known. I saw him, simple and yet with something of the prophet in his air, and something of the seer. Effective, and yet ineffectual, something there was about him that attracted little children to him, and, I should think, lost dogs. He made mistakes, but then, those who make no mistakes seldom make anything.

'His life was one long battle, so it seemed to me that it was fitting that at his funeral the north-east wind should howl among the trees, tossing and twisting them as he himself was twisted and storm-tossed in his temptuous passage through the world.

'As the crowd moved away, and in the hearse and mourning coaches the spavined horses limped slowly down the road, a gleam of sunshine, such as had shone too little in his life, lighted up everything.

'The swaying trees and dark grey houses of the ugly suburb of the town were all transfigured for a moment. The chapel door was closed, and from the chimney of the crematorium a faint, blue smoke was issuing, which by degrees, faded into the atmosphere, just as the soul, for all I know, may melt into the air.

'When the last stragglers had gone, and bits of paper scurried uneasily along before the wind, the world seemed empty, with nothing friendly in it, but the shoulder of Ben Lomond peeping out shyly over the Kilpatrick Hills.'

'Had he, too, lived in vain?' On that grey autumn afternoon, outside the Glasgow Crematorium, it was quite natural to ask the question. For war was raging in Europe and all that Keir Hardie had given his life to, seemed to have gone in the flames.

Yet it was not the end of the movement and the cause for which he had toiled and fought and struggled! The memories remained. He had inspired others who remembered his courage, his steadfastness, his incorruptibility. He had been the pioneer. He had created a new force in British politics. He had led the way to a world in which there will be no poverty and no war.

INDEX